OLIVER MOWAT'S ONTARIO

Oliver Mowat at the end of his premiership
Courtesy the Ontario Archives

OLIVER MOWAT'S ONTARIO

Papers presented to the
Oliver Mowat Colloquium
Queen's University,
November 25-26, 1970.

Edited by
DONALD SWAINSON

Macmillan of Canada / Toronto

ISBN   0-7705-0900-2   Cloth
       0-7705-0901-0   Paper

Library of Congress
Catalogue Card No. 72-83703

Printed in Canada for
The Macmillan Company of Canada
70 Bond Street, Toronto

CONTENTS

PART TWO

PART THREE

OLIVER
MOWAT'S
ONTARIO

Introduction

DONALD SWAINSON

Oliver Mowat is easily the most famous provincial premier of the nineteenth century, and has long been recognized as one of the architects of twentieth-century Canada. Both his career and his accomplishments justify this fame and reputation. Born in Kingston in 1820, Oliver Mowat was the eldest son of two Scottish immigrants, John Mowat and Helen Levack. He was educated in Kingston, where he attended a private school operated by the Reverend John Cruickshank. His schoolmates included both John A. Macdonald and John Hillyard Cameron.

Mowat subsequently studied law with John A. Macdonald, who was five years his senior. All students of nineteenth-century Canadian politics know that for a brief period that small Kingston law office included three young men who were to become amongst the most powerful politicians of the late nineteenth century: Alexander Campbell, John A. Macdonald and Oliver Mowat. Mowat was called to the bar of Upper Canada in 1841 and moved to Toronto, where he quickly built up a large and profitable practice.

Mowat was born and brought up a Conservative but as an adult he joined the Reform party. His first involvement in electoral politics took place in Toronto where he served for two years as a member of the Toronto City Council. He successfully contested the seat of South Ontario in the winter election of 1857-58 and remained a member of the Union House until he resigned in November 1864. During those years he was a prominent Reform leader, serving in the famous "Short Administration" of George Brown and A. A. Dorion, in the Sandfield Macdonald–Dorion government in 1863-64 and as a member of the Confederation Coalition for several months in 1864. Mowat was thus a Father of Confederation. He resigned from the Great Coalition in November 1864 in order to become vice chancellor of Ontario. He held that post until 1872 when he was persuaded by Edward Blake and George Brown to succeed the former as premier of Ontario. He became premier and attorney general in October 1872 and held those posts until July 1896.

Mowat lent his considerable strength and prestige to Wilfrid Laurier and the federal Liberals in the 1896 general election. He accepted Laurier's invitation to join his cabinet and in 1896 became both Minister of Justice and a member of the Senate. By this time, however, Mowat was long past his prime and he remained in Ottawa for only a brief period. In November 1897 he accepted the lieutenant-governorship of Ontario and remained in that post until he died in 1903. Mowat's public career thus lasted some forty-five years and was one of unparalleled success.

The years during which Oliver Mowat was active in public life represent roughly one-quarter of the time Ontario has been an identifiable and organized entity. Historians are fond of giving labels to much-studied eras. Decades, generations or centuries are often referred to as periods of growth, expansion, reaction, consolidation or transition. While somewhat trite, this sort of typification is not without its utility. Such capsularized phrases often provide convenient frameworks for the organization of material about a particular historical period. The latter part of the nineteenth century, when Mowat was at the peak of his influence, might be called the Era of the Emergence of Modern Ontario. Three particularly important processes were occurring during these years. First, Ontario became a mature and definable unit economically, socially and politically. Second, the nature of the Canadian federal state, which Ontario had been instrumental in forming, was in many ways defined. Third, Ontario's primacy within that federal state was definitively established. Mrs. Evans is correct when she comments: "Under [Mowat's] careful but forward-looking guidance, the province left behind its pioneer youth and moved steadily and prosperously toward maturity in the twentieth century, when his type of leadership with the same success, would pass over to the Conservative party of Ontario."[1]

An understanding of these interrelated processes is dependent upon research into economic and social as well as political history. The social and economic structures of the province are as crucial to the nature and position of Ontario as are the famous nineteenth century federal-provincial battles and the long period of Liberal domination after 1871. Even the most cursory survey of Ontario's development from Mowat's first election campaign in 1857-58 until his death indicates the truth of this assertion. Agriculture, for example, was modernized. The Mowat government never underestimated the importance of agriculture, even while industry was obviously becoming more and more important. Mowat's provincial government was very imaginative in educational and scientific areas related to agriculture and the agricultural industry was in a powerful position in terms of productivity and markets at the end of the century.

During the same years the province underwent tremendous urbanization and industrialization, developments that were promoted by considerable population movement and growth. This fundamental shift in the nature of Ontario society required major adjustments. New urban problems had to be handled and the trade union movement had to be accepted as a basic fact of life. Mowat's government moved farther and farther into the field of govern-

[1] A. Margaret Evans, "Oliver Mowat and Ontario, 1872-1896: A Study in Political Success," Ph.D. thesis (University of Toronto, 1967), p. 574.

mental regulation in a whole series of areas. Increasingly sophisticated forms of education were required and in this area the record
of achievement of Mowat's government was brilliant. The need
for laws to protect industrial workers was recognized and much
such legislation was passed. By the end of the Mowat period an
embryonic welfare state existed in Ontario. Statistics began to be
collected in a systematic way. Such material is of enormous use to
a government that is becoming increasingly rationalized and
bureaucratic. The judicial system was reorganized and the laws
pertaining to the province codified, reforms reflecting the growth
of statute law and the need for a more efficient system of admin-
istering justice.

The Mowat government encouraged economic growth in a
variety of ways. It was, for example, responsible for the completion
of numerous railroads in both southern and northern Ontario.
These lines helped to intensify development in more settled parts
of the province, to integrate the various parts of Ontario, and to
open for development large sections of northern Ontario. This
latter development is crucial to any explanation of Ontario's rise
to the powerful status she has enjoyed in the twentieth century.
The exploitation of the wealth of the Shield has helped to mold the
history of twentieth-century Ontario. That process was well under
way by the end of Oliver Mowat's long years of ascendancy.

The Mowat years, then, saw tremendous economic growth and
expansion. By the end of the nineteenth century the Ontario
economy and social structure as we know it was already per-
ceptible. At the same time the provincial administration was
becoming ever more modern in the sense that it was developing
into a positive state, better able than any other regime in Canada,
federal or provincial, to accommodate the tremendous and dynamic
developments of twentieth-century Canadian society.

Mowat liberalism performed an indispensable function in late
nineteenth-century Ontario history and materially assisted Ontario
in her rise to dominance. Mowat's liberalism (if that is a reasonable
appellation) was a broad, integrative and pragmatic creed. It
permitted the maintenance of a provincial consensus during a

crucial period of economic and social growth. Mowat was able to contain within his party discordant elements that in other provinces and at other levels of government were disruptive, disintegrative and dangerous to the long-term political stability that can give an efficient regime a magnificent opportunity to facilitate development and modernization.

For example, Mowat, who in his first election campaign in 1857-58 used the slogan, "Mowat and the Queen, or Morrison and the Pope," was able during his provincial premiership to incorporate into his party most types of Protestants and large numbers of Roman Catholics. His last important political act symbolizes his success in this area. In spite of his earlier identification with the anti-Catholic bigotry of the Upper Canadian Grit movement, he built so much confidence amongst Catholics all over Canada that Laurier made him Minister of Justice so that he could deal with the aggrieved Catholic minority in Manitoba. In this capacity he was able to facilitate the betrayal of that minority. During his years as premier he was also able to retain prohibitionists and representatives of the liquor interest within his party. His Liberal party was equally able to accommodate businessman and trade unionist, farmer and urbanite, eastern Ontarian and peninsular Grit, northerner and southerner, promoter and unemployed worker, old-fashioned partisan and third-party advocate and, it must be said, Liberal and Conservative. Threats against his provincial regime were for the most part disposed of with ease, and he won six successive general elections—in 1875, 1879, 1883, 1886, 1890 and 1894. The federal Liberals were not able to achieve this enviable situation and were often divided, despondent or devoted to crusades that Mowat instinctively recognized as dangerous to both party and nation.

His pragmatism and his refusal to allow Ontario liberalism to become a vociferous voice for any theme or particular reform muted dissension within the province. While the Province of Quebec, to cite a dramatic example, was being torn apart by civil war within the Conservative party and vicious warfare against liberalism, Mowat was able to focus the energies of Ontarians on the basic work of adjusting to industry and urbanization, modernizing agriculture, opening the north, building a highly resilient infrastructure, developing a positive state, absorbing the political and social energies of trade unionism and developing Ontario into the overwhelmingly dominant economic unit within the Canadian federation.

It is doubtful that Ontario society would have matured so quickly or the economy grown so dramatically without Mowat liberalism. At the same time, the most famous examples of strife during Mowat's period aided rather than harmed this process. Mowat is best known in Canadian history because of his feuds with the federal Conservative government of Sir John A. Macdonald. He is the acknowledged victor, and rightfully so. There has been some debate over the motivation of these feuds and it is probably not unreasonable to accept the interpretation of historians who argued (and still do) that Mowat was heavily influenced by partisan, patronage and expansionist considerations. Be that as it may, his victories were profoundly important in two ways. First, by gaining control over vast areas of northern territory Mowat laid the basis for what Professor Nelles calls "Empire Ontario." Modern Ontario is inconceivable without the giant resource industries of the north. Second, his victories are important because they involved the triumph of Mowat's interpretation of confederation over the quasi-federalism of Sir John A. Macdonald. The juxtaposition of the victory of a form of classical federalism and the rise of an efficiently governed, exceedingly large and overwhelmingly wealthy province defined the nature of Canadian federalism both constitutionally and politically, and explains much about the nature of Canadian society in the twentieth century. It is thus no accident that Ontario was so much more mature than other provinces at the end of the nineteenth century and it is equally no accident that Ontario has been able to exert such a dominating influence in the evolution of Canadian life in the twentieth century.

Older patterns of research tended to obscure these developments. Heavy concentration on political parties, Dominion-provincial relations, separate schools, or Catholic–Protestant feuds dimmed the complex relationships (some of them doubtless accidental) that produced the dynamic that in turn produced early twentieth-century Ontario. Many kinds of historical analyses must be employed in order to permit a full understanding of Oliver Mowat's Ontario.

For some years the province of Ontario has followed a policy of honouring major historical figures in some appropriate manner. In 1965, for example, a great banquet was held in Kingston to commemorate the 150th anniversary of the birth of Sir John A. Macdonald. Sir Oliver Mowat was also a Kingstonian and the provincial government suggested to Queen's University that the 150th anniversary of his birth might be commemorated in some suitable way. After discussing several possible alternatives the university and its history department recommended that the occasion be marked by the holding of a seminar, to be called the Sir Oliver Mowat Colloquium. The Colloquium was held at Queen's University on November 25-26, 1970. It was designed to fulfil three main objectives. The first aim was to make public some recent research concerned with the life of Oliver Mowat and with the history of the province he presided over for so long. Much of this research is of an innovative nature. A second aim of the Colloquium was to bring together from all over the country undergraduates, graduate students and scholars of nineteenth-century Ontario. Finally it was hoped that the public of Kingston could participate in the Colloquium. These main objectives were realized. The Colloquium was well attended by undergraduates, graduate students and scholars from six Canadian provinces and one American state. Every Ontario university was invited to send delegates and almost all did. The delegates participated in three formal sessions at which papers were read, commented upon and discussed. In this way several scholars were able to present the results of their research to representative groups, and the Colloquium was able to discuss these papers, after hearing a formal commentary. The public of Kingston was invited to join the delegates at a public meeting and did so in large numbers. Professor Peter Waite addressed an enthusiastic audience on the subject of "Sir Oliver Mowat's Canada."

The original conception of the Colloquium included the proposal that the papers read at the formal sessions and at the public meeting be published as a commemorative volume. Even the most diligent scholar has absorption limits and it was felt that the presentation of eight papers in two days was sufficient, to say the least! I did not, however, want to limit the volume to those eight papers, and asked Mrs. Margaret Angus, Professor Carman Miller and Mr. S. E. D. Shortt to contribute articles germane to their fields of scholarly interest. They agreed and as a result the ensuing publication includes eleven essays.

The articles included in this volume are concerned with numerous facets of Ontario history during what might loosely be called "The Mowat Era." They are also a sample of the important research now being pursued in this area. Peter Waite, Professor of History at Dalhousie University, is a leading authority on nineteenth-century Canadian history. His most recent book, *Canada 1874-1896: Arduous Destiny* (Toronto, 1971) is devoted to the period of Canadian history during which Mowat was premier of Ontario. His article, "Sir Oliver Mowat's Canada: Reflections on an Un-Victorian Society," provides an overview of Canadian society during the late nineteenth century. A. Margaret Evans is Professor of History and head of the department at Guelph University. She is concerned with Mowat himself, and with political problems. Bruce W. Hodgins, of the Department of History at Trent University, analyses the origins of Ontario provincial rights sentiment. Carman Miller of McGill University is concerned with the relationship between Mowat and the federal Liberal Party, 1887-1897. Professor Christopher Armstrong of Atkinson College, York University, is concerned with the impact of Mowat's policies in federal-provincial relations on long-term Canadian development. The three papers in Part Two are concerned with Ontario's social history. Mrs. Margaret Angus, formerly president of the Ontario Historical Society and currently president of the Kingston Historical Society, writes about the Kingston of Mowat's youth.

Professor Hereward Senior, of McGill University, is an authority on Orangeism in both Canada and the United Kingdom. His paper is an analysis of the late nineteenth-century Orange Order in Ontario. Graeme Decarie of Loyola College in Montreal has contributed an analysis of the prohibition movement. The papers in Part Three include material on political, economic and social history. Michael Bliss, of the Department of History at the University of Toronto, uses the concept of the "protective impulse" as an analytical tool for the study of nineteenth-century Ontario society. Professor H. V. Nelles of York University contributes a study of the formation of policy germane to the resource sector of Ontario's economy. S. E. D. Shortt, a graduate student at Queen's University, analyses the Patrons of Industry during the 1890s.

All editors and authors accumulate innumerable obligations during the preparation of a manuscript. Even more are created when a book is in major part the product of a colloquium. I would like to take this opportunity to thank a number of people who helped make the Oliver Mowat Colloquium a success, and who have extended generous assistance to the editor of this volume. I would like to thank the eleven scholars whose papers appear below for the kind of cooperation and patience that makes possible the production of a multi-authored work. Michael Bliss, H. V. Nelles, Bruce Hodgins, A. Margaret Evans, Christopher Armstrong, Hereward Senior and Graeme Decarie read earlier drafts of their papers at the regular sessions of the Colloquium. Those sessions made the Colloquium a success and I would like to acknowledge the contributions of all the participants. Their papers were formally commented on by Professor R. M. McInnis (Department of Economics, Queen's University), Mr. J. C. Morrison (Assistant Deputy Minister, Eastern Region, Department of Regional Economic Expansion), Roger Graham (Professor of History, Queen's University), and John Thompson (then a graduate student in the Department of History, Queen's University and now a member of the Department of History at McGill University). Their comments provoked considerable discussion and were much appreciated by the delegates. Professor Peter Waite delivered his paper at a large public meeting at Queen's University, chaired by Principal J. J. Deutsch and attended by the Hon. John P. Robarts and the Hon. William Davis. Academic papers are not always well received at public meetings but Professor Waite's was a splendid exception and contributed in a major way to the public part of the Colloquium. Mr. J. M. Courtwright, Vice-Principal (Development and Information), Queen's University, assisted in a variety of ways. In addition to students and staff from Queen's University, the Colloquium was attended by undergraduates, graduates and professors from the prairie provinces, Ontario, Quebec and the Maritimes. I would like to thank them for making possible one of the major goals of the Colloquium—the bringing together of students at various stages in their training with a number of authorities on nineteenth-century Ontario history. Much useful discussion, both formal and informal, resulted. Principal J. J. Deutsch of Queen's University was very generous with his time and advice, as were two of his aides, Miss Mary Medland and Dr. Donald Gow (now director of Queen's School of Public Administration). Ian Wilson, University Archivist at Queen's University, and Professor J. A. Leith, Chairman of the Department of History at Queen's University, were also instrumental in making the Colloquium a success. Professor George A. Rawlyk and I were co-chairmen of the Colloquium. Professor Rawlyk's knowledge of the Canadian academic community, his organizational skills and his enthusiasm were essential to the work of the Colloquium. In addition to that, Professor Rawlyk extended extremely useful advice to me in the work of editing this volume of essays. I would like to thank him for indispensable assistance. Much of the detailed work of organizing the Colloquium was done by Mrs. Karen Babcock and Mrs. May Forrester, both of whom merit hearty thanks. Mr. Angus Mowat of Prince Edward County attended the public part of the Colloquium as a representative of the Mowat family. Finally I would like to thank the Hon. John P. Robarts, the Hon. William Davis and Mr. E. E. Stewart, then deputy minister of University Affairs, for attending the Colloquium on behalf of the province of Ontario. On behalf of Queen's University and its

Department of History I would also like to acknowledge the generous financial assistance and cordial co-operation extended to the Colloquium by the Department of University Affairs and by the Government of Ontario. Without that assistance and cooperation neither the Colloquium nor the publication of this volume of essays would have been possible.

Donald Swainson,
Queen's University at Kingston,
April 1972.

Sir Oliver Mowat's Canada: Reflections on an Un-Victorian Society

P. B. WAITE

No one can describe a society. The very word, society, applied to
Canada in the late nineteenth century, jars. The sheer diversity of
Canada makes one hesitate. Nevertheless, let me say at once that
the reason for this paper is my distrust of that adjective "Victorian." Perhaps I am tilting against windmills; perhaps I am
merely reflecting, some twenty-five years late, my own sense of
revolt against the prevailing values of the generation that preceded
me. Nevertheless, it is my overwhelming impression that "Victorian," as applied to Canada (or for that matter even to England)
in the latter half of the nineteenth century, is, in terms of the
stereotype usually associated with the word, not only devoid of
significant meaning, but incorrect. The stereotype is familiar
enough. "Victorian" is held to signify a narrow, purposeful code of
morality that eschewed liquor, kept Sundays pure and undefiled
by work or by merriment and, as Professor Bliss has suggested,[1]

---

[1] Michael Bliss, "Pure Books on Avoided Subjects: Pre-Freudian Sexual Ideas in
Canada," CHA *Papers*, 1970, pp. 89-108.

carefully avoided all public reference to the great forbidden subject. All of this had as goal the well-intentioned purpose of making Canadian society a fit place for the cultivation of the good, hard-working life of proper bourgeoisie, and the incidental enforcement of a suitably straitened and disciplined life for the working class.

This stereotype is difficult to apply to Canada in the nineteenth century. Ontario comes as near to the definition of "Victorian" as any part of Canada, and even in that land of supposedly un-frivolous dedication to work and purity, much evidence is on the other side.

The argument in this paper is that these so-called "Victorian" attitudes, if they ever did come to reflect the dominant tone in Canadian society, did not really do so in the period before 1895. If they came at all, they developed afterward, and the adjective "Edwardian," however inappropriate as far as that monarch personally was concerned, may be more accurate. Part of the difference is illustrated by the differences between Macdonald's Canada and Laurier's, reflected perhaps in the personalities of the two men themselves. Laurier did not smoke or play games, and, so it is alleged, never drank. He neither liked telling risqué stories nor being told them. G. H. Ham, in *Reminiscences of a Raconteur*, has, in fact, an anecdote that I can't resist repeating, one that he called the story Laurier did not blush at. It was of the traveller in a storm, forced to put up for the night at a farm. The farmer's daughter showed the traveller to a room, saying it was the hired man's, who was away. Late at night she quietly came back and sweetly asked, "Would you like a nice bed-fellow tonight?" (At this point Laurier looked at Ham sharply, evidently much concerned.) The traveller was more than acquiescent. "Well," said the daughter, "just roll over then; the hired man's come back."[2]

Laurier's Canada was not Macdonald's. There is a difference in the feel of the 1870s and 1880s, and that of the later 1890s and 1900s. One has the impression, at least in central Canada, of having crossed a divide, one that separates a way of life that we cannot

[2] G. H. Ham, *Reminiscences of a Raconteur* (Toronto, 1921), pp. 122-23.

really quite know from one that is, more recognizably, ours. By the end of the 1890s had come many of the inventions that we are now familiar with, which Canadian society was slowly learning to accept and adjust to. W. L. Grant wrote in the *Queen's Quarterly*, July 1894:

> The progress of discovery in electricity has been so rapid during the past fifteen years that it is possible only for the specialist to keep pace with it. It is within this period that electric lighting, electric railways, and the telephone have come into common use.[3]

Marconi's transatlantic radio signal from St. John's, Newfoundland, to Ireland was just seven years away. By 1895 the new-style bicycle, with Dunlop's pneumatic tire, was a familiar sight on city streets; newspapers were made of pulp paper; typewriters were common; Daimler–Benz had produced their first car in 1886. A catalogue is not necessary. But what lay behind these changes? And what were their concomitants within society? The answers to these more fundamental questions lie, I think, in Canada's industrial revolution.

Many of the characteristic features of an industrial society had come into existence, one might almost say, at one great bound, in the decade of the 1880s. By the end of that decade some of the problems coming before Parliament were quite different from those of 1878 and 1879: factory regulation, railway rate regulation, control of monopolies, problems of the working classes. In Ontario, in 1892, Sir Oliver Mowat's government passed a succession duty. *The Week* defended this new departure; ". . . there is a growing conviction that the weight of dead men's hands has often in the past pressed too heavily upon the rights and interests of the living."[4] It was an argument that Principal Caven of Knox College was to use in 1894 to defend Manitoba's right to establish a new school system untrammelled by the past. Archibald Lampman's

[3] *Queen's Quarterly*, Vol. III, No. 1 (July 1894), p. 79.
[4] *The Week*, Toronto, May 6, 1892.

poems of the 1890s are not quite so much the marvellous nature poems of the 1880s but brooding, half-elegiac poems like "The City," or "The City at the End of Things"—the city, "where no man rests and no man is," as he put it, as if he were regretting the changes he saw about him on every side. Sara Jeanette Duncan, in that perceptive way of hers, watched the changes:

> A hollow age, a materialistic age, a vulgar age—an age of over-production in every economic quarter but the soil, an age of socialistic upheaval and dark prediction, of dyna-mite and demagogue, and the tyranny of the majority— what can we further say to blacken the reputation of this day of ours, in which, despite our maledictions, the birds sing, the sun shines, and the clear streams run, and the corn waves golden and abundant! An age, perhaps, of dis-content, of querulousness, railing, self-conscious lament![5]

Other aspects of Canada's industrial revolution, such as the question of monopolies, are too big to be dealt with here; but even the terms used in the following bit of doggerel against the National Policy suggest the changes of the 1890s. The verse is by Senator C. A. Boulton, of Shellmouth, Manitoba (a Conservative by the way), whose poem of 1892 is found in the Laurier Papers:

> . . .
> Our eldest boy's a darling, we christened him N.P.
> His constitution's undermined, or so it seems to me
> We've fed him upon luxuries to a terrible extent,
> But still it does not keep him up this 25 per cent.
>
> We swathed him up in cotton, a most tremendous coil
> We gave him steel & iron, and rubbed him with coal oil,
> He has been taking boodle drops as an emolient,
> But nothing seems to keep him, even 25 per cent.
>
> We let him play with implements and many other toys,
> Electric lights & telephones that pleases other boys
> But in spite of all that we can do he does not seem content,
> He grumbles, grumbles, for still more than 25 per cent.

[5] *The Week*, "Saunterings," Toronto, March 3, 1887.

Our other boy's "a Whopper," we called him C.P.R.
Tho' weak at first, he's stronger now and beats the other
    far,
Has a stomach like an ostrich, his health is excellent,
He's thriving like a mushroom upon 25 per cent.

It takes a lot to keep him up with coronets for tiles,
His suits they take a lot of stuff to clothe 5000 miles
He eats up all he comes across does this voracious gent
He takes a branch line for his lunch, sauce 25 per cent.

In fact he's grown so very strong we dare not say him nay,
For fear he kicks us out of doors some bitterly cold day,
He has us all upon a string, we go where we are sent,
He'll gulp the lot, he will not leave, even 25 per cent.[6]

I am not, however, concerned here with these changes as such. I
am interested in the society that preceded them and was to be
slowly changed by them. It may be that what are called Victorian
attitudes may be a by-product, an essential one, of the factory
discipline on the one hand and the city communications on the
other that are required by an industrial society. Drinking, for
example, was no doubt a social evil long before the Canadian
industrial revolution, but its seriousness began to be felt only
when it became an economic evil as well. The same with sabbatarian laws; too strenuous excitement on a Sunday produced
ineffective work on a Monday. It still does.

The origins of temperance and sabbatarian attitudes in Canada
are by no means clear. They may lie outside of Canada, in England
and the United States, where industrial changes started earlier; but
they may also have originated spontaneously from Canadian
conditions. The idea of a federation of temperance groups, which
produced the Dominion Alliance of the 1870s, was probably even
exported to the United States.[7] In Canada the temperance movement (or prohibition, to give it its true name) had very limited
success before the late 1870s, as Tilley's disastrous experiment in

[6] Public Archives of Canada, Laurier Papers, Vol. 6, C. A. Boulton to Laurier,
December 28, 1892.
[7] I am indebted to Professor Graeme Decarie for this suggestion.

New Brunswick showed in 1855.[8] The first W.C.T.U. group was formed at Owen Sound in 1874. Prohibition grew with painful slowness, and what progress there was took place mainly not in the cities but in the countryside: one thinks of the Baptists of the Annapolis Valley, or the Methodists of south-west Ontario. These rural elements of the population inherited, in religious form, the belief in the perfectibility of human nature that was the great legacy of a pre-industrial era. The eighteenth century believed in perfecting human nature by removing laws: the nineteenth century came finally to believe that human society would have to be improved by passing laws. Even Macdonald came gradually, and reluctantly, to the view that private rights were probably going to have to yield increasingly to conceptions of public right and the public weal.

One private right that was going to be compromised was a man's right to drink, when, where, and as often, if not as much, as he pleased. It is James Gray's view that we historians have "consistently ignored the most abrasive, longest-enduring gut issue of the times—the great issue that affected every community, erupted in every election between 1892 and 1916, and touched more people in their daily lives than any of the others. That issue was booze."[9] Drunkenness on the streets was so common to Gray as a boy that it was accepted as a normal manifestation of life. His mother used to say, "Oh, God, if only we could get rid of those accursed bars!"

It was not easy. Prohibition was tried in the North-West Territories, and it worked well enough until settlement started in earnest. By the end of the 1880s, with the C.P.R. in full swing, the law was a shambles. No duty was more distasteful, or more fruitless, than the N.W.M.P.'s constant attempt to catch the uncatchable. One harassed constable at Banff described the traffic from British Columbia. The bootlegger would fill

> his berth with kegs of whisky. When he got near Calgary
> the liquor would be thrown off just before the train pulled

[8] See J. K. Chapman, "The Mid-Nineteenth Century Temperance Movement in New Brunswick and Maine," *CHR* XXXV, No. 1 (March 1954), pp. 53-54.
[9] J. H. Gray, *The Boy from Winnipeg* (Toronto, 1970), pp. 20-21.

in. Another way was that a man coming down in the colonists' car would use rubber beds and pillows filled with whisky. They had it all over the train. It would be in the berths, on the top, underneath, in front, on the engine, on the tender, and where the water was kept.

The Royal Commission of 1895 added ruefully that

liquor was brought in the country by all available avenues and by every possible conceivable means. It was brought in secreted in packages of merchandise; in tins specially prepared and labelled "bibles"; as canned fruits, a single peach, perhaps, floating in alcohol valued at $5; in casks of sugar and rice . . . in carloads of hogs or lumber, and as eggs.[10]

By 1890 the North-West had had enough. In September 1891 the Dominion government gave power to the North-West Assembly to legislate, and in January 1892 the North-West Assembly adopted a licensing system for bars; the long history of prohibition in the North-West Territories was, for the time being, over.

The other attempt at control is better known: the Canada Temperance Act of 1878. It was a system of local option, based upon the parliamentary constituencies. When 10 per cent of the eligible voters petitioned for a local option election it was held, and a simple majority of the votes determined whether that constituency went dry or remained wet. The Speaker of the House in 1878, T. W. Anglin of Saint John, stepped down from the Chair when the bill was in Committee and denounced the whole arrangement. "Tyranny more gross than this it is impossible to conceive. . . ."[11] Was a man to be prevented from buying whisky because 51 per cent of his constituency disapproved of whisky?

Apparently he was. Canada Temperance Act adoptions began in 1879 with eleven constituencies, and in 1886 reached 62 of the 215

[10] Canada, *Sessional Papers*, 1895, No. 21, Report of the Royal Commission on the Liquor Traffic in Canada, Sir Joseph Hickson, Chairman (hereafter cited as Hickson Commission), p. 197.
[11] Canada, House of Commons, *Debates*, May 3, 1878, p. 2404.

in the provinces across Canada. Then, in 1887 began a retreat from this pinnacle of achievement. By 1892, the year of the appointment of the Royal Commission on the Liquor Traffic in Canada, it was down to 30, and two more fell by the wayside in 1897. The 30 were as follows:

Nova Scotia	12
New Brunswick	9
Prince Edward Island	4
Quebec	3
Ontario	0
Manitoba	2
British Columbia	0

It had been attempted and defeated in 17 constituencies. In 30 more it had been carried in a first election and defeated in a second. The weakening of the Canada Temperance Act was very likely owing to its inadequacy, rather than to a weakening of prohibition sentiment. For the act was not effective even in the constituencies where it operated. Many of the county councils in prohibition counties, "delayed, objected, or absolutely refused to contribute anything towards the expenses of enforcing the Act...." Inspectors, where there were some, had one universal complaint, "We stand alone, no one supports us in this community."[12] Whisky was not difficult to get even in Nova Scotia, despite the fact that 12 constituencies (out of 20) were under the act. Bliss Carman, in 1892, contemplating a trip across the Bay of Fundy that June, said the first important thing to do was to acquire some "moral courage." This came, not surprisingly, in bottled form, in Kentville, Kings County (under the Canada Temperance Act).[13]

In Charlottetown, E. J. Hodgson, the Master of the Rolls, said firmly that prohibition in that city was "an unmixed evil; that drinking was increased, and that perjury increased to an inordinate

[12] Hickson Commission, p. 68.
[13] King's College Library, Halifax, Bliss Carman Papers, Carman to his sister Nancy, June 20, 1892.

extent; that it produced a class of blackmailers."[14] The regime of
the Canada Temperance Act in Charlottetown was a bitter battle.
The Act was adopted in 1879. It was resubmitted to the voters in
1884 and 1887, and sustained both times. It was defeated in 1891,
reinstated in 1894, then thrown out again in 1897. In other words,
Charlottetown was dry between 1879 and 1891 and between 1894
and 1897, and when it was dry Hodgson said there were 146 places
where liquor was sold.[15] It bears out Dr. Bergin's comment in the
House of Commons in 1886. Dr. Bergin was the member for Corn-
wall and Stormont, and had originally been a supporter of the
Canada Temperance Act. But his view had changed by 1886. Instead of respectable hotel bars, for every former licensed bar, the
act had put in their place a dozen dens operating night and day,
seven days a week, retailing a form of whisky closer to poison than
rye.[16]

Drinking habits, however, had changed somewhat in the period
from 1871 to 1893. In 1871 the Canadian average was 1.2 gallons
of spirit for every man, woman and child in the country, plus
almost 2 gallons of beer. In 1893 spirit was down to 0.7 gallons per
capita, beer up to three and a half gallons. These are only, be it
said, official returns, and they varied considerably from province
to province. British Columbia doubled the national average all the
time.[17] But even Toronto had in 1873 a tavern for every one
hundred and twenty men, women and children in the city.

Even more graphic are the figures for the relationship of crime
to drunkenness. In 1893 convictions for crime in Canada ran about
7.5 per thousand population. (In British Columbia, incidentally,
the figure was 14 per thousand.) Offences against liquor laws, or
for drunkenness, were an astonishingly high proportion of all
convicted crime. The lowest ratio was in Ontario, about 35 per
cent; in New Brunswick it was a phenomenal 72 per cent, with

---

[14] Hickson Commission, p. 100.
[15] *Ibid.*
[16] Canada, House of Commons, *Debates*, June 13, 1887, p. 941.
[17] Hickson Commission, p. 16 *et seq.*

Prince Edward Island not far behind with 70 per cent.[18] The Chief of Police in Montreal was thus very close to the truth when he said that 50 per cent of the twelve thousand arrests made in Montreal in 1873 were for drunkenness, and another 15 per cent for offences arising from drunkenness. These statistics may be inaccurate. Drunkenness is not a difficult crime to detect *in flagrante delicto*; no enterprising burglar would be so obvious for so long. Nevertheless, with due allowance, the statistics are formidable. Prohibition agitation did not arise from nothing.

The best part of this extraordinary story is that the House of Commons itself embarked upon an almighty drunk just three weeks before that august body passed the Canada Temperance Act. It had started during a long debate on the Letellier affair, a debate that Alexander Mackenzie, the prime minister, wanted to end, but with a provincial election campaign on in Quebec, Conservatives wanted to prolong. The Conservatives could not be turned off. Sir John Macdonald started drinking in the evening and by 7:30 in the morning, after a final tumbler of whisky, was quietly stowed away by the Conservative whip in the rooms of the deputy Sergeant-at-Arms. Several other Conservatives had not the sense to get themselves out of the way. William McDougall, M.P. for Trois Rivières, spent two hours talking and was barely able to stand during it; Lt. Col. C. J. Campbell, J.P., M.P. for Victoria, Cape Breton, known as "Tupper's Goose," was worse, getting onto the floor in front of the Speaker, with his hat on, flourishing a stick round his head, stamping his feet on the floor, declaring his utter independence of Governments, Parliaments, and Speakers, or any one else, daring the Government, or any member of it to fight, and all at the top of his voice. He was taken away by friends before the Sergeant-at-Arms intervened. James Domville, President of the Maritime Bank, M.P. for Kings, N.B., following a colleague at 8 in the morning, rose to be greeted with shouts of ribald laughter from friends and foes. "Button up your pants," "Shame,"

---

[18] *Ibid.* pp. 30-32.

etc. Having buttoned up, Mr. Domville commenced to read. . . .[19]

It is probable that there are definite class differences in attitudes to liquor, differences that yet remain to be explored. One of my colleagues at the University of New Brunswick thoughtfully suggested that there may also be differences between Conservatives and Liberals. It is true that the great drinkers, in Parliament at least, seem to have been heavily on the Conservative side of the House. Mackenzie said that in that great parliamentary drunk not one of the Liberals touched a drop. I think it would be naïve to accept that; still, the great promoters of temperance and sabbatarian laws seem mainly to have been on the Liberal side in Parliament. George Foster was the notable exception on the Conservative side, as Leonard Tilley, also of New Brunswick, had been before Foster.

And Parliament was not the same in 1896 as it had been two decades and more before. It may be that the great scandals of 1890 to 1892, the Rykert, the McGreevy–Langevin, Caron, Mercier scandals, and others, had a sobering effect; it was as if Sir John Thompson's determination to get it all out into the daylight (as much as was consistent with party safety) had, if not destroyed much of the old wickedness, at least made the public less disposed to tolerate it. The Pacific Scandal of 1873 had made men a little more careful in dealing with railway promoters, and a great deal more careful about safeguarding their correspondence; the scandals

---

[19] Guelph *Weekly Mercury*, April 18, 1878; London *Daily Advertiser*, April 16, 1878. Other sources are the Toronto *Globe*, Montreal *Herald*, Hamilton *Evening Times* of the same date, and Conservative papers to set against them. That the Grit papers were exploiting the incident is undoubted. There were denials in various forms by some of the principals involved, including Domville. But the fact that Domville's speech must have been wholly useless is vouched for by the *Debates* (p. 1983) where his whole speech is given in twenty-four words. Moreover the *Globe*'s report was based on a full account from Mackenzie to Brown written from the House at 9 a.m. that Saturday morning. (Mackenzie Papers, Mackenzie to Brown, April 12 [should be 13], 1878, confid.). One suspects that the London *Advertiser* and the Montreal *Herald* had access to information from David Mills and Luther Holton respectively. The whole matter was aired, on motion of privilege, on April 17, 1878. See *Debates*, 1878, pp. 2057-67. I am repeating my account of this incident from *Canada 1874-96: Arduous Destiny*, p. 4; reprinted by permission of McClelland and Stewart, the Canadian Publishers.

of the early nineties had sensitized the public to a vast range of parliamentary iniquities.

In Macdonald's time punches were not pulled in Parliament. Spades, as he once said, were called spades. There are few more savage replies than Mackenzie's to Tupper in 1876. Tupper had been needling Mackenzie about the St. Peter's Canal, in Cape Breton, between the Bras d'Or Lakes and the south-west coast, objecting that Mackenzie knew nothing of what he was talking about. Such conduct as Mackenzie's, said Tupper in his rotund, denunciatory manner, "was calculated to degrade Parliament . . . to degrade the House itself." Mackenzie got up and quietly said, "I have only to reply that nothing the hon. gentleman could say would degrade any member of the House."[20] The sheer audacity of that takes one's breath away. It seemed to take away Tupper's.

Tupper illustrates the principle that if you are to have a reputation to leave for posterity, it is as well to cover your tracks. He has done this so well that it is almost impossible to discover the authenticity of the stories that circulated about him. "Oratorical and obstetrical" was young Lord Rosebery's description in 1873.[21] Nova Scotians, who knew him better, called him, half affectionately, the "ram of Cumberland County." Thompson was furious at being made a cover for Tupper's amorous adventures in Washington in 1887;

> Tupper insisted on my going to vespers with him yesterday — I suspected he had a trick in it, and sure enough he called for a young lady. I was intended for "gooseberry" [i.e. giving the appearance of propriety for a pair of lovers] but I paid him off by taking her entirely under my charge.[22]

D'Alton McCarthy in the 1896 election actually brought it out on the hustings. McCarthy said he was ashamed of being called Sir

---

[20] Canada, House of Commons, *Debates*, April 1, 1876, p. 1004.
[21] A. R. C. Grant, ed., *Lord Rosebery's North American Journal, 1873* (London, 1967), p. 71.
[22] P.A.C., Thompson Papers, Vol. 290, Thompson to Annie Thompson, November 28, 1887, from Washington.

Charles Tupper's political son; the honour was shared by so many other, ordinary, sons.[23]

The truth is, I suppose, that no society, at any time, can get too far away from the usual incidents that come from the usual frailties of human nature. In late nineteenth-century Canada these were largely open to public view and accepted. Young Hugh John Macdonald, Sir John's son, and a bit of a devil like his father, had a knack for picking up scabrous verses on periodic binges in Ottawa and Toronto. The "Maiden's prayer" shows the roguish humour never far from the surface in Victorian Canada:

> Mary mother, we believe
> That without sin you did conceive,
> Teach, we pray thee, us believing,
> How to sin without conceiving.

The lines that follow get rather worse.[24]

In other words, Canadian society in late Victorian times was still rough and ready. There was a school of hard knocks because there was a world of hard knocks. Duels had been fought within the memory of most of the members of the House of Commons. Macdonald challenged a man in 1856, when Attorney General! In this respect Parliament was only a reflection of society. In the tense session of 1878, there occurred—among many other incidents—the Cheval–Bunster row on March 29. Guillaume Cheval, M.P. for Rouville, had been playing music—a Jew's harp was a favourite instrument in the Commons—while Arthur Bunster, representing Vancouver Island, had been speaking. Bunster was a thick-set Irishman who had taken a remarkably short time to become the ass of the House. He challenged Cheval to a fight. Cheval went, of course; a gentleman could not do otherwise, and still retain his self-respect; he found Bunster with a knife—mainly for effect, apparently. There was a fight all right, in which Cheval got struck

---

[23] Toronto *Daily Mail and Empire*, May 21, 1896, reporting McCarthy's speech at Brockville of May 20.
[24] University of Western Ontario, Coyne Papers, Macdonald to Coyne, December 15, 1871.

(not, it seems, by the knife), and Bunster got a black eye. There is conflicting evidence whether Macdonald tried to stop the fight, or tried to stop it being stopped.[25]

Private quarrels had their echoes in more public ones. A largely innocent Catholic procession in Toronto, on Sunday, September 26, 1875, celebrating Jubilee year, was set upon by Protestant roughnecks and dispersed in confusion. The escapade had been planned the day before, and "freely spoken of as an event likely to relieve the monotony of Sunday."[26] The next Sunday the procession formed again, but this time protected by militia, the Queen's Own Rifles, the Markham Cavalry (one wonders what this redoubtable unit looked like), and the whole of the Toronto police force.[27] Two years later came Hackett's murder, in reverse circumstances, in a 12th of July Orange procession in Montreal.

The newspapers partook of this warfare—even their thinking ran in warlike analogies. Objectivity was a form of treason. "It is a battle in which there is no quarter; and every soldier in every little company has to reflect that he must either share the triumph of the victors or mingle in the rout of the beaten."[28] There was a general tendency to believe that an independent position in politics was the refuge of the timid, the cowardly, or the treacherous. Failure to support the party when the chips were down—that meant when some controversial issue was before the House or the country—was the one thing in politics that Macdonald found the hardest to forget or to forgive. S. J. Dawson, M.P. for Algoma, after whom the "Dawson route" was named, indulged in a romantic reminiscence about the election of 1874 from the vantage point of 1881:

> they [the Conservatives] came back from the elections a broken band, a miserable remnant, a corporal's guard. We were like the broken band that gathered round the camp

[25] Canada, House of Commons, *Debates*, April 1, 1878, p. 1536; April 17, 1878, p. 2063-7.
[26] *Canadian Monthly and National Review*, October 1875, p. 359.
[27] Toronto *Globe*, October 4, 1875.
[28] *The Nation*, Toronto, September 24, 1874, letter from Nicholas Flood Davin dated September 22, 1874.

fires of Swedish Charles after dread Pultowa day. We had
been hunted like partridges. . . . Many of our best and
bravest had fallen; but there was no murmur for the dead
whose bones lay on many a bleak hill-side and lonely valley,
the prey of jackals, wolf and carrion crows that always
follow on the track of a defeated army. Many of our men
had a hunted look as though they still felt the breath of
bloodhounds. . . .[29]

Political meetings were much the same. In Macdonald's autumn
campaign swing through Ontario in 1886, they had a political
meeting in Hamilton on a Saturday night. It was "a very rough
crowd," John Thompson wrote, "nearly all working men looking
as if they wanted to fight." It was hard even to be heard. Thomas
White could not manage them at all; they stamped their feet until
they got Macdonald, but even he had a difficult time. Thompson
admitted that to hold crowds you had to say wicked things.[30]
There was no point in trying to reason such speeches; Thompson,
at least, could only fire off shot. And the meetings were often
crowded. At Stratford, Ontario, in November 1886, the press in
the hall was so thick that Thompson's guide was stopped dead, and
Thompson, on the point of being suffocated by the pressure, was
finally, after shouting and cursing, lifted up bodily by the crowd,
hoisted over their heads, and handed forward to the platform amid
deafening cheers and laughter.[31] It couldn't have been easy;
Thompson must have weighed a good 220 pounds.

One thinks of those audiences, dead and gone now, the noise, the
whisky, the laughter, the tobacco, the smell of unwashed humanity
(redolent, doubtless, of the farmyard): political meetings were
entertainment, the translation of newspapers into life. And what
else was there to break the daily round, and take men briefly outside themselves, and the little worlds they moved in, but newspapers and politics?

[29] Canada, House of Commons, *Debates*, January 12, 1881, p. 405.
[30] P.A.C., Thompson Papers, Vol. 289, Thompson to Annie Thompson, November
21, 1886.
[31] *Ibid.*, Thompson to Annie Thompson, November 28, 1886.

Outside of Parliament the party lines at parties were rather loosely drawn. While it is improbable that Sir John Macdonald would entertain Alexander Mackenzie at a private dinner party, other Conservatives could and did. Alonzo Wright, the grandson of the founder of Hull, was Conservative M.P. for Ottawa County from 1862 to 1891. He and Mackenzie lunched together every so often, and on at least one occasion Mackenzie's speech in the Commons afterward (May, 1880) revealed both an asperity and a humour that bespoke Alonzo Wright's luncheon champagne.[32] The gaiety of Cartier's house in Ottawa, with its Saturday night stag parties, was legendary, with the rooms so crowded, as Liberal James Young described it, you could scarcely find room to stand.[33] One can see Cartier still, well into the evening's hilarity, perched on the edge of the dining-room table, driving his voice and his paddle (not a real paddle but getting more real all the time) through "Youpe! Youpe! sur la rivière," and the company roaring with laughter.

Adolphe Caron, in 1874 a man of 31, in this respect bade fair to succeed Cartier. He and some others, mainly Conservatives, devised a group called the Jim-Jam club, which met at Caron's boarding house in Ottawa, served and run by an old Communist, from Belleville, of all places. Senator R. W. W. Carrall, of British Columbia, was "Chief Poisoner." Caron's wit and good manners, and the ridiculousness of others, like James Domville, or Theodore Robitaille, J. B. Plumb, et al. made the thing go. The account of this club comes from George Casey, M.P. for Elgin County, Ontario, and one-time Liberal whip, who remarked on the rousing good time he had there.[34]

The cheerful flamboyance of Canadian society in manners and morals was to be somewhat more contained as the nineteenth century drew to its close, but it still flourished vigorously in the 1870s and 1880s. Not far from Brantford is the village of Brockton,

[32] Coyne Papers, Macdonald to Coyne, May 14, 1872.
[33] James Young, *Public Men and Public Life in Canada* (Toronto, 1912), II, pp. 163-64.
[34] Coyne Papers, Casey to Coyne, March 22, 1875

and there in 1869 took place a great cock-fight, for heavy stakes, a
contest between London and Toronto. Around the cockpit seats
were arranged for the more aristocratic portion of the audience,
while behind these were gathered two or three hundred of the
"fancy."

> . . . they were a motley crew. For the most part they were
> roughs and rowdies of the purest breed — Toronto, Lon-
> don, Buffalo and Detroit were all represented by as scound-
> relly a looking gang as it is possible to produce anywhere.
> First of all, there were the "fancy" pure and simple, with
> their bullet heads, small yet rough features, and the in-
> evitable drab coats and neck-ties. Then there were the tag
> rag and bob-tail. . . . To these were added a number of low
> tavern keepers, who are always found where anything
> mean and foul is going on. And above all, there was the
> aristocratic element. First among these was . . . a veritable
> Alderman of the City of Toronto. . . .
> "Five—ten—fifteen—twenty dollars that the London bird
> wins," shouted a miserable ragamuffin, who did not look as
> if he was worth five cents. "Make it a hundred and I take
> you," was the reply of a highly adorned young gentleman.
> "Done," said the ragamuffin, and he pulled from the
> pocket of his ragged trousers, a bundle of bills amounting
> to several hundred and the bet was made. "Twenty-five
> cents on the Toronto bird," cried a miserable looking little
> old man; but the idea was altogether so low that down
> came a hand on the crown of his hat, and he was in-
> stanteously extinguished.

Who does not think on reading this of Dickens? It is fair to add,
however, the *Globe* concluded that the affair was "a disgrace to the
civilization of our times. . . ."[35]

Grip is one of the most interesting sources for the social history
of Ontario in the latter nineteenth century. It was biased, of course.
It professed occasionally to be above politics; it would poke fun at
Blake and Cartwright and Mackenzie; but its sympathies were

---

[35] *Globe*, April 24, 1869. I have quoted this account in full in "The Cock-pit, 1869,"
in *Ontario History*, 1966, pp. 89-92.

clearly for the many causes that the Liberal party espoused. That also included Oliver Mowat, whom *Grip* affectionately portrayed as the little Cromwell of Ontario. It clearly enjoyed Mowat's battles with Macdonald. The only thing that seemed to mitigate *Grip*'s admiration for Mowat was his apparently inexplicable interest in, and his tenacious grasp of, the Roman Catholic vote. *Grip* was also fiercely prohibitionist. Notwithstanding these penchants, it had a remarkable range of comment and information, written with verve and a sharp sense of humour. There are many things in *Grip* I would enjoy quoting, but let one suffice. It is a description of a Toronto horse-car, on a rainy evening in April 1889. As a vignette of social history it is hard to beat.

> It was a damp, depressed day. I was ditto, only more so and hungry and tired to boot. With three miles before me, and no umbrella, no mackintosh, and no goloshes, I made one of a group of woe-begone individuals who stood at the corner of King and Yonge streets and craned their necks in the direction of the approaching cars. After waiting eighteen minutes by Ellis's clock opposite . . . I had the melancholy satisfaction of seeing my car being dragged leisurely along and filled like to the Black Hole of Calcutta. However, I was not to be balked of my ride, whatever the crush. . . . Before I had time to squeeze myself past the crowd of men clinging to various portions of the rear platform—some half sitting on the dripping railing chewing cigar stumps, some leaning carelessly against the door absorbed in the perusal of the six o'clock *Telegram*—the vehicle started with a jerk that very nearly precipitated me back into the street I had so hardly left. But I was fortunate enough to slip into a small space, by courtesy called a "seat", within a space of I suppose about twenty-five minutes.
>
> In the cold dampness of the day, the breath of each person was plainly visible. . . . Packed close, and each grudging his or her neighbor every inch of room, the occupants of this lugubrious public conveyance seemed like two hostile forces. . . . The windows rattled jarringly . . . the wet cushions exhaled a thick and odoriferous moisture. . . .

Opposite me was a red-haired girl with no eyebrows and a front of triple brass. The expression of her face seemed to indicate that she was prepared then and there to give with compound interest an answering smirk to any of the opposite bench who might have the hardihood to open up a flirtation with her. I did not dare look in her direction at all events. Turning my head I saw beside me two other young women, gay and gaudy despite the weather. Evidently their aim in life and in that car was to attract attention—perhaps even to make a chance acquaintanceship with some young man after their own heart—which, by the way [judging by appearances], must have been an insignificant portion of their anatomical structure. . . . Then came the conductor for the fares, which occasioned a great deal of awkward tucking in of long legs, holdings aside of bedraggled silk skirts and bespattered white, or once white, petticoats . . . for the required five cents. When this commotion had subsided there entered a corpulent and asthmatic woman of uncertain age, but of very certain weight and dimensions, who had a greasy face and a hairy mole on the upper flat of a two-storied chin. She breathed out threatenings and slaughter upon all around her in the shape of enormous chestfuls of peppermint-loaded breath. The car grew perceptibly heavier. . . . This was the last straw. I confessed myself vanquished, and, tottering to the door, plunged once more into the muddy street. . . .[36]

It is a pity we do not know more about the distaff side of society. There are a few tantalizing glimpses. The governor general's military secretary issued strict instructions for a presentation for the Princess Louise that was to take place in November 1878, in Montreal. The instructions about dress were, to say the least, unequivocal: "Ladies are to wear low-necked dresses. . . . Ladies whose health will not admit of their wearing low-necked dresses may, on forwarding to the A.D.C.-in-waiting, a medical certificate to that effect, wear square cut dresses. Dresses fastening up to the throat are not to be worn."[37] One of the funniest letters Alexander

---

[36] *Grip*, Toronto, April 20, 1889.
[37] Goldwin Smith, "Papers of a Bystander, No. 1," *Canadian Monthly and National Review*, January 1879, p. 118.

Mackenzie ever wrote was his description of a similar affair in
Toronto in September 1879. His Grit egalitarianism was touched
by the sheer amusement of the spectacle.

> Many of the number walked in evidently unable to see who
> the Princess was . . . and bowed to the wrong person or did
> not bow at all. Husbands in the hurry to get through
> trampled on wives dresses. . . . [A] stupendous woman a
> head taller than me and three times as thick went through
> with the preliminary movement to a curtsey. . . . Some
> one whispered, "is that whole woman to be presented at
> once". . . . One sedate judge was so flustered that he stepped
> on three or four feet of his wife's dress just as they passed
> me. She was about to commence bowing to the Marquis
> [of Lorne] when her husband's rear attack compelled her
> to bow backward. She managed, however, to cast a look
> backward which said as plainly as possible "Wait till we
> get home." A sudden move of one hand shewed that some
> tackling had given way, and she retired precipitately to
> repair damages. . . .[38]

Social history can have, as this paper shows, helical habits. What
I have been trying to set down, in this discursive and rambling account, has been a series of vignettes of Canadian society in the later
nineteenth century, strung together on a thread of argument. I
have tried to show that it was lively, raucous, and occasionally
brutal. It may not have been a very pretty society; but it cannot
be described by the adjective "Victorian" except in its temporal
relation with the reign of Queen Victoria.

It may just be that this stereotype of Victorian Canada is a product of the interests of some of our historians who were writing
between 1914 and 1945 about nineteenth-century Canada. They
asked their sources different questions; they necessarily got different answers. Political and constitutional issues interested them
profoundly; and they may still be right in their assumption that
the neatest and most telling indicators of a country's history is the

[38] Queen's University, Mackenzie Papers, Mackenzie to his daughter Mary, September 25, 1879.

range, character, and issues of its politics. But our interests, in the
1970s, have been made much wider, as our politics have been, and
we ask our sources new questions, and still further, we look for
sources that tell us new answers. I don't want in any way to deni-
grate the historians of fifty years ago. They often wrote superb
history. We, in our rather more picayune way, nibble at this and
that, and set it down in English often devoid of that one essential
quality that makes any history live: vitality.

It is easy to exaggerate the differences between that time and
ours, and thus to exaggerate their significance. It is proper, I think,
to be suspicious of any theory of society that strains too far the
basic consistency of human nature. Surely the essence of the
timelessness of history rests here. Aristophanes and Sara Jeanette
Duncan are both writers commenting on their own society. As
Ranke once observed in a miraculous phrase, all generations are
equidistant from eternity. The people of Aristophanes' time, or of
Miss Duncan's, were ourselves, just writ in a slightly different
script. Who does not recognize himself in Sara Jeanette Duncan's
description of September 1886, on the great return of September
after a summer's disporting in the country?

> They are coming back, the summer nomads. One meets
> them at every turn on King and Yonge Streets: bronzed
> young men, and freckled maidens, middle-aged dames
> with a sensible increase in avoirdupois since last one saw
> them, and old gentlemen with that indescribable dissarray
> of apparel and air of sun-seasoned jocularity. . . .[39]

Ottawa still has its couples strolling lovingly on Parliament Hill;
as Sara Duncan described them in 1888, "that happy parliament of
two in which the Government for the time being finds no Opposition, and the budget estimates are all undisputed. . . ."[40]

[39] *The Week*, "Saunterings," Toronto, September 16, 1886.
[40] *Ibid.*, "Ottawa Letter," May 10, 1888.

Part One

Oliver Mowat: Nineteenth-Century Ontario Liberal

A. MARGARET EVANS

Oliver Mowat has sometimes been described as a life-long Liberal, probably because of his association with the eminent George Brown in pre-Confederation Canada West, his skilful guidance in the late nineteenth century by which Liberalism reached its pinnacle of success in Ontario, the many years that he led the provincial party, and the importance which he attained in the national party. The fact is that the description is incorrect. The excerpt which Professor Frank Underhill liked to quote from Gilbert and Sullivan about boys and girls all being born "little Liberals" or "little Conservatives" does not apply to Mowat.

His interest in the politics of the Province of Canada was slow to develop. When it did emerge during the breakdown of the old parties and the regroupings of the 1850s, he thought that he would remain an Independent. Linked neither with the opposition nor with the government, he would be free to strive for his own views "where they differed from those of the Ministry and to condemn their misdeeds as occasion offered." But Mowat, always realistic, came to feel that such a position was "impracticable": "Neither party would care for me. I should be subject to misrepresentation by each." In the moulding of policy an independent was handicapped; he lacked party backing to make him "more useful as a friend—more powerful as an antagonist." Mowat reached the conclusion that "the only principle on which free government appears to be capable of being worked" is the "distinction of parties," and therefore every man "must take a side."[1]

The Conservative side was the one which Mowat might have been expected to take. There was a strong strain of conservatism in his nature. His family in Kingston, with whom he maintained a warm relationship, were traditionally Conservatives. He had read law for four years in the Kingston office of John A. Macdonald, and for a fifth year in the Toronto firm of James McGill Strachan, a son of the bishop. He had practised law in partnership with a leading Conservative, Philip VanKoughnet. Mowat's continuing friendship with Macdonald had been a help in his professional career, for Macdonald recommended his appointment as a Queen's Counsel in 1855 and as a commissioner for the consolidation of the provincial statutes in 1856.

Nevertheless, Mowat said, "One must not shape one's political course by friendship," nor should one be "carried away" by the historical names of parties:

> If you read English history . . . you will find that the Tories have sometimes been the democrats against the Whigs, and the Whigs sometimes the democrats against the Tories. . . . So again, the one party has sometimes had most virtue on its side, and the other party has had it at other times. The choice of a party must be made *as parties stand when the choice is made* [*sic*], and not as they stood at some former period; and, once it has been made, an upright man must do his best to keep his party right, as well as to obtain for it success.

[1] C. R. W. Biggar, *Sir Oliver Mowat: A Biographical Sketch* (Toronto: Warwick and Rutter, 1905), I, pp. 76-77, Mowat to Alexander Campbell, January 16, 1858.

In 1857, when Mowat, now thirty-seven years of age, was ready at last to ally himself with a political party, he chose not the Conservatives but the Clear Grits. In the general elections of that year, his support of George Brown's planks of representation by population and non-sectarian schools won him a seat in Ontario South and started his rapid ascent to a foremost place among the Reformers. But it was not so much agreement with Brown on these two specific questions which brought Mowat to his decision in 1857 as it was the conviction that the stamp of "reprobation" must be placed upon the ministry. He believed that Macdonald, Van-Koughnet and their colleagues had abandoned their former principles and adopted their opponents' measures merely to get and retain office "with its prestige and its power." Their "objectionable" course disentitled them to "public confidence." In the mode of William Ewart Gladstone, who was prone to see public issues in a moral light, Mowat inquired of his friend, Alexander Campbell, "Has virtue died?" "Can we not have again men of the moral character of Baldwin, or Bidwell, or Lafontaine, or Robinson?"[2]

Thus Mowat, when a man of mature age, became a Liberal by deliberate choice. J. C. Dent wrote that "His growing leanings toward Liberalism were the outgrowth of the time, and of his own study and reflection."[3] If, as his letters to Campbell indicate, the choice was made primarily because he considered it a "duty" to be anti-ministerialist, the Liberalism for which he stood in post-Confederation Ontario was a positive program. A study of it must be based largely on his actions as party leader and premier from 1872 to 1896, for he did not set forth views on Liberalism, as Edward Blake, Wilfrid Laurier, W. L. Mackenzie King or Lester B. Pearson have done. Mowat was essentially practical. When on occasion he spoke of his ideas, the result was likely to be not political, but social philosophy with a strongly religious tone. His research into comparative religion began in the 1840s, the years of his expanding law practice, and continued into his retirement from

---

[2] *Ibid.*, I, pp. 74-75, 77-81, Mowat to Campbell, January 16, January 24, January 26, February 1, 1858.
[3] J. C. Dent, *The Canadian Portrait Gallery* (Toronto: Magurn, 1880), II, p. 88.

active politics after 1897. It persuaded him, the staunch Presbyterian, that the "progress of Christianity includes both Roman Catholics and Protestants," and that no one creed has "a right in this country to predominate."[4] His religious humanitarianism led him many times to express a special interest in the workingmen:

> They have a smaller proportion of the comforts and advantages of life than the rest of the community. Then there is our common manhood which binds us all together. In a Christian country, one cannot help remembering that the great Saviour of the world, when He came into the world, lived and worked with mechanics, with humble toilers, and it was for the poor as well as the rich that He laid down his life. In a right state of society there ought to be no antagonism between the various classes of which the community is composed. I am glad to believe that there is little antagonism between the different classes in this glorious Province, but if there is antagonism, my sympathy and that of my colleagues is with the masses rather than with the classes.[5]

Neither of the phrases often used of Mowat—"Christian statesman" and "practical politician"—is a misnomer.

Mowat always paid tribute to Blake for having rescued the government of Ontario "from the enemy." He himself had "held the fort," but Blake had "enabled the Liberal party to *have* [*sic*] 'the fort' to defend."[6] Although Blake had cut Sandfield Macdonald's majority in the elections of 1871 and defeated him in the Assembly on a vote of want of confidence—by a majority of only one—there was no sign, when Blake turned over the premiership to Mowat a year later, that their party possessed an advantage such as would

[4] Mowat, *Christianity and Its Influence* (Toronto: Hunter, Rose, 1898), p. 11; *The Fraser Banquet* (n.p., [1879]), p. 14.
[5] This was part of Mowat's reply to an Address presented to him by the Knights of Labor of Woodstock, quoted in the *Globe* (Toronto), May 13, 1890. Cf. Mowat, *Christianity and Some of Its Evidences, Popularly Stated* (new rev. ed.; Toronto: Briggs, 1901), pp. 41-42.
[6] Ontario Department of Public Records and Archives, Edward Blake Papers, Mowat to Blake, March 7, 1884; March 3, 1891.

keep it in power for another thirty-three years. It was Mowat, without any doubt, who welded the provincial Liberals into the party as impossible to dislodge as that of John A. Macdonald at Ottawa. What, then, was the nature of Mowat's Liberalism?

The *Empire* maintained that Mowat constructed the strength of the Ontario Liberals on "flagrant" redistributions of the electorate and a "cohort of office holding and fee nurtured partisans," all "working like beavers" through the province.[7] One of Macdonald's friends wrote of the premier: "He is a poor stick himself as I have ever come across. . . . He needs a plunge in Jordan at least to cleanse him."[8] Mowat did, indeed, excel in attention to party machinery and tactics. When changes in the boundaries of constituencies were to be made, he said candidly that if there were two arrangements for representation which were equally good, party considerations aside, he did not see why the government should not choose the one more in its favour. And when positions were open, he asserted his intention of appointing persons primarily for their efficiency, but did not deny that Liberals would be selected. "Everything else being equal, no administration was in the habit of preferring their opponents to their friends."[9] Yet, however much Mowat's penchant for patronage and failure to rise above the political mores of nineteenth-century governments are to be deplored, he does not seem to have filled the province with corrupt or incompetent officials. His alterations of electoral districts, when examined in principle and effect, do not, except for a brief trial of minority representation in Tory Toronto, possess the unscrupulous manipulative qualities of a gerrymander. Mowatism embraced much more than the free use of the weapons of influence which are at the disposal of the party in power.

It has been the fashion with the historian to treat "provincial rights" as the core of Mowat's Liberalism and to depict the regret-

[7] *Empire* (Toronto), June 4, June 22, 1894.
[8] Public Archives of Ontario, Sir Alexander Campbell Papers, J. B. Plumb, Niagara, to Macdonald, November 23, 1883.
[9] *Globe*, May 5, 1894, report of proceedings in the Legislative Assembly, May 4, 1894; and January 21, 1876, report of proceedings in Assembly, January 20, 1876.

table results for the Dominion from his victories in some half-
dozen legal contests with the government of Macdonald. The
interpretations by the two men of the position of the provincial
legislatures could scarcely have been more at variance. To the
Canadian prime minister they were "but one-horse concerns":

> . . . the General Government or Parliament should pay no
> more regard to the status or position of the Local Govern-
> ments than they would to the prospects of the ruling party
> in the corporation of Quebec or Montreal.[10]

In contrast, Mowat wrote to John S. D. Thompson, with whom
he always had a very cordial relation:

> I dare say that as Attorney-General of one of the Provinces
> [Nova Scotia] you hold as I do that . . . the Provincial
> Governments of all parties should always diligently watch
> over and maintain the rights of the Provinces by all lawful
> and constitutional means. . . . the ground on which those
> Supreme Court Judges proceeded who held the Provincial
> Legislation as to Q.C. [*sic*] to be ultra vires, was that the
> Provinces have no authority in matters of prerogative. Now
> this doctrine goes enormously farther than the question of
> precedence amongst the lawyers in our courts.

In the same letter Mowat took exception to infringement of
provincial rights by imperial legislation:

> It is surely for the Provinces and not for the Imperial Par-
> liament to say who may practise medicine within their
> boundaries and to determine whether or not English
> Practitioners should have that right without passing the
> examination here required of our own students. It will not
> do to submit if we can help it to either unfavourable deci-
> sions of our Courts, or to Imperial interference. . . .[11]

[10] Sir Joseph Pope, ed., *Correspondence of Sir John Macdonald* (Toronto: Oxford
University Press, n.d.), p. 75, Macdonald to Brown Chamberlain, October 26, 1868;
p. 245, Macdonald to Goldwin Smith, October 1, 1878.
[11] P.A.C., Sir John S. D. Thompson Papers, Mowat to Thompson, November 5,
1880. Cf. *ibid.*, Mowat to Thompson, January 7, 1881: "Constitutional questions
are too important to have them decided behind the back of the Provinces."

The definition in *Hodge* v. *The Queen* of the coordinate authority of the provincial legislature with the federal, each in its own sphere, was substantially Mowat's concept of the constitution. Still, the portrayal of Mowat as the "Defender-in-Chief" of provincial rights and the weakener of the national fabric is oversimplified. It looks too exclusively at Ontario, probably because of the greater number of legal disputes with the Dominion in which that province under Mowat was involved, and because of the invariable vindication of his stand by the Judicial Committee of the Privy Council. "What luck" he has had "with the P.C.," Macdonald once remarked.[12] The dominance of the central government in the first thirty years after Confederation was challenged, however, not merely by the Mowat-inspired resurgence of old sectional loyalties in Ontario, but also by economic stresses, renewal of racial and religious discord, and grievances in the Maritimes, Quebec and the West against federal policies. The Interprovincial Conference of 1887 made very clear that provinces other than Ontario, though for different reasons, were prepared to assert their rights in opposition to Macdonald's centralism. Mowat's contention was that the successful working of Confederation required the careful observance of provincial autonomy, and the events of that generation seemed to bear him out.

The clash of constitutional theories, moreover, was only one side of the friction between the Ontario and Canadian governments. The personal antagonism of Mowat and Macdonald, which Mowat claimed began with his adoption of the Reform cause in the 1850s, reached a peak in the 1880s. At the opening of the provincial session of 1882, Macdonald complained that Mowat was "thoroughly hostile."[13] The Ontario premier must have had the same feeling about Macdonald when the latter, in fine style, expressed his scorn at the Conservative convention of the same year:

> Mr. Mowat, with his little soul rattling like a dried pea in
> a too large pod—what does he care if he wrecks Confedera-

---

[12] Campbell Papers, Macdonald to Campbell, December 18, 1888.
[13] *Ibid.*, Macdonald to Campbell, January 14, 1882.

tion and interferes with the development of Canada so long as he can enjoy his little salary as Attorney-General. . . ?[14]

The stubborn determination of these leaders throughout the Dominion-provincial contests was partly motivated by their antipathy for each other.

But more important than the personality conflict was the fact that, in the various controversies, practical issues of immediate political advantage or disadvantage were at stake. The roles which the two men took were therefore cast for them to some extent by the positions which they occupied. For example, since the authority to grant liquor licences included the control of large sources of patronage, it was to be expected that Macdonald would try to keep the power for the Dominion and Mowat for the province. Similarly, Mowat's government derived a good deal of revenue from timber limits, the value of which would be seriously diminished if a person was allowed exclusive right to a stream by virtue of having made a dam or slide along its lower part. If for no other reason than concern about the reduction of lumbering operations in the province, Mowat could not overlook the disallowance of his Rivers and Streams Act by Macdonald in 1881, 1882 and 1883. Most of all, in the tangled legal questions of the north-west boundary, though no constitutional position was endangered, the people of Ontario could gain or lose over 100,000 square miles of territory. Even the Toronto *Mail*, looking back at the protracted boundary struggle, conceded in 1886 that Mowat had done nothing "which any other premier, Liberal or Conservative, would not have done for Ontario." As for his defence of the provincial right to the resources of the disputed territory, the paper continued, W. R. Meredith, the leader of the Conservative opposition, "were he premier, could not, and, it is certain, he would not do otherwise."[15]

The story of Mowat's relations with the Dominion is thus a complex one, but one which is not necessarily central in a discussion of his Liberalism. The assumption that the "provincial

[14] *Mail* (Toronto), September 14, 1882, report of the convention.
[15] *Ibid.*, December 27, 1886.

rights" movement was politically rewarding to his party in Ontario is not sustained by a close examination of electoral campaigns and results. Popular interest is not evoked by constitutional strife over such matters as the lieutenant-governor's powers respecting escheats, or appointment of Queen's Counsel, or the prerogative of pardon. The insurance cases, it should be noted, were between the province and two insurance companies, not between the provincial and Canadian governments. If there were political profits in the defence of Ontario's liberties, Mowat would surely have reaped them in 1883, the only election in which he appealed on the platform of provincial rights. The manner of exercise by the Dominion of the right of disallowance, Macdonald's threat to remove provincial control over liquor licences, and his delay in ratifying the boundary award, were all put before the voters at every Liberal meeting and filled the columns of the party press. Yet Mowat was more nearly defeated that year than at any other time. It was as if Ontarians put their confidence in the temperateness and the carefulness which were his habitual qualities, but felt apprehension at his adoption in this campaign of a hard line and uncharacteristically vehement tone. Had the provincial rights cry been as popular as is usually suggested, the astute premier would undoubtedly have raised it again in the next elections, especially since in the meantime his return from England after brilliantly arguing and winning the boundary case had been greeted by mammoth receptions and excitement unusual in sedate Ontario. The bulky Liberal campaign pamphlet in 1886, however, gave only two pages to a factual statement of his triumphs in the courts after describing in detail his achievements for the internal development of the province.[16] These, to which the traditional historian has given little notice, were what absorbed most of the attention of Mowat and his ministers and won him repeated favour at the polls. Possibly a revisionist will some day show him to have done more to upset the intention of the Fathers by his contributions to ex-

---

[16] *The Mowat Government: Fourteen Years of Liberal Legislation and Administration* (n.p., [1886]), pp. 70-72.

pansion of the economy and of social services in the central province than by the famous legal cases.

Mowat's domestic policies, in which it is here argued the essence of his Liberalism is to be found, carried on the Reform tradition of Canada West, which had reflected the interests of the primary producers, especially the farmers. Mowat declared at the outset of his Liberal leadership that agriculture could not receive too many benefits from the government considering that it was "our great source of wealth, upon which our whole population depended."[17] Under him expanded grants to agricultural societies and the regular publication of statistics by the newly founded Bureau of Industries helped this "basic" Ontario industry to increase its efficiency. Improved communications brought markets to the farmer's door. Drainage schemes made wet lands fit for cultivation. Ontario became the pioneer in Canadian agricultural research and education when the Agricultural College and Experimental Farm were opened at Guelph in 1874. The provincial Department of Agriculture, created in 1888, also the first in Canada, encouraged farmers to seek greater prosperity through diversification. The priority which Mowat gave to the farmers, if their wishes clashed with others' in the community, was obvious when he was persuaded to exempt them from liability under the Workmen's Compensation Act in 1892. The principle established then was altered only at the beginning of the year 1966.

Even though Mowat built on foundations laid by the Reformers before 1867, his Liberalism had many new emphases to suit the altering circumstances. Whereas the older Liberalism had stressed freedom from government, he began to move away from laissez faire toward provincial control even in his agricultural measures, notably in regulations to combat the spread of weeds, injurious insects, and animal and plant diseases. Mowat saw, too, the rising social problems and the need for regulatory policies in public health and welfare. The Board of Health, established in 1882, made

---

[17] *Globe*, November 30, 1872, report of Mowat's speech at the nomination meeting in Woodstock, November 29, 1872.

possible provincial research into causes of disease, effective steps to prevent epidemics, and supervision over municipal water and sewer systems. Provincial inspection of hospitals promoted higher standards in buildings, management and nursing. A series of enactments showed provincial concern for the unfortunate members of society—the mentally ill, the neglected children, the destitute and aged, the inmates of reformatories. The departure from laissez faire was particularly noticeable in Mowat's legislation for urban labour, an element in the province which became increasingly important with the rising industrialism of the late nineteenth century. He and his government accepted the responsibility for regulating conditions and hours of work in factories and shops, for aiding in the adjustment of trade disputes, for safeguarding the earnings of labourers by liens, and for providing protection for employees injured at work.

The qualities of Mowat's Liberalism are well illustrated in these labour laws. They were very conservative in comparison with the novel social theories put forward by the radical *Palladium of Labor* in Hamilton in the 1880s, or *Labor Advocate* in Toronto in the 1890s. At the same time, they were progressive for the day. They represented an extensive growth of intervention by the provincial government in the relations between capital and labour, and were generally commended by the moderate workers. In 1891, the Ontario Committee of the Canadian Trades and Labor Congress reported that "organized labour may fairly congratulate itself" on the legislation in the province.[18]

Mowat not only weaned the Liberal party from its predominant agrarianism; he also erased the anti-Catholic tradition of earlier Grittism. Amid the Protestant–Catholic tensions in Canada and Ontario in the late nineteenth century, it was a task of tremendous difficulty to steer a middle course which would not alienate the Protestants, who made up five-sixths of the provincial population, and would regain the Catholic support lost to the Conservatives in the 1850s. Step by step Mowat found the middle path. He with-

---

[18] Ontario, Bureau of Industries, *Annual Report, 1892*, Part VI, p. III.

held from the Orangemen the special acts of incorporation, which to the Catholics amounted to endorsement of a hostile secret society, but by passing a general act he recognized the right of Orange lodges to be incorporated. When in turn the *Mail*, the Equal Rights Association, the New Party, the Conservatives, and the Protestant Protective Association, assailed separate schools, Mowat declared that these schools were "a fact in our Constitution, and we have to accept it whether we now like it or not." He said he conceived it his duty to curtail none of the privileges accorded them in 1867, and to see that they functioned efficiently as did public schools. In this spirit, and with the desire to be fair to all creeds and to respect the rights of both the minority and the majority, which he termed "true Liberalism," his government passed a number of separate school amendments which were acceptable enough except to the ultra-Protestants.[19] He agreed with Archbishop Lynch of Toronto that a second Roman Catholic inspector was needed in the province, but not that a deputy minister should be appointed for Catholic schools. He made no move toward a complete system of Catholic education through the establishment of Catholic high schools, colleges and normal schools. Pressed by the opposition to impose a secret ballot for the election of separate school trustees in order to end clerical "intimidation" of voters, he compromised with an optional ballot. In addition, when attacked for permitting the use of French in the schools of eastern Ontario, he and George Ross, his Minister of Education, refused to crush the language by immediate anglicization; but they did appoint a commission to study how the teaching of English might be improved, and acted upon its recommendations. By such means Mowat rebuilt the Ontario Liberals as a party based on cooperation between Protestant and Catholic, English and French; and laid the groundwork for Laurier's success in unifying the national Liberal party.

In still another respect, Mowat's Liberalism was comprehensive.

---

[19] See Mowat, *The Sectarian Issues, History of the Separate School System in Ontario and Quebec*, and *Proposed Amendments to the Act Relating to Separate Schools*, Provincial Politics, nos. 1, 2 and 4 (Toronto: Hunter, Rose, 1890).

Whereas the Clear Grits, with their agrarian strength in western Ontario and under the metropolitan leadership of Brown and the *Globe*, had had no claim to be a province-wide party, Mowat drew support from all sections of Ontario. This end was accomplished partly by his additions to the cabinet of men from eastern Ontario, but mainly by developmental projects for all segments of the economy. His was not the simple and cheap government of the earlier Reformers or of Alexander Mackenzie at Ottawa. When Mowat appeared at many meetings with Mackenzie in 1877, their platform on the surface was the same—honest, efficient and economical government. But there was a significant difference: Mowat in his speeches made economy subsidiary to "progress" and to "improvement" of all parts of the province.[20] Besides the costly new services for agriculture, labour, and the well-being of society, his government spent money on constructing railways, roads and other public works, including new Parliament Buildings; on stimulating immigration and the opening of the Shield; on a pioneer farm in Western Algoma; on the encouragement of mining; on measures to protect the forests from fire; and on the establishment of provincial parks for conservation and recreation. These expenditures were not in Mowat's eyes wastefulness, for which he had a thorough Scottish aversion; they were the proper use for posterity of the surplus which Ontario in her favourable financial position managed to have practically every year. Mowat lacked the dynamic qualities of Macdonald, but he was like Macdonald in sensing the aspirations of the people for material growth, and in lending generous government assistance to it.

Mowat's Liberalism developed empirically. He was quick to borrow practices from other countries which seemed suited to his province. His own intense Britishism was most manifest when talk of unrestricted reciprocity, commercial union and political union with the United States, filled the air in both rural and urban Ontario. In 1891 Mowat vied with Macdonald in avowal of loyalty:

[20] *Globe*, July 3, July 14, July 17, July 26, October 1, October 4, October 17, October 22, November 5, November 9, 1877, printed the full texts of Mowat's speeches at the Reform demonstrations.

"A British subject I have lived for three-score years, and something more—I hope to live my life a British subject and as a British subject die."[21] The annexationists went too far when they arranged a meeting for Mowat's own riding. He sent out a call for "friends of British connexion and the old flag."[22] The gathering, packed with his followers, declared by a vote of twelve to one against annexation. Mowat told Laurier that he would leave the national Liberal party if its policy was to be that of the continentalists, left-wing Richard Cartwright and Edward Farrer, chief editorial writer of the *Globe*. In 1892, Mowat made a very patriotic speech at Niagara: "I hope that when another century has been added to the age of Canada it may still be Canada, and that its second century shall like its first be celebrated by Canadians, unabsorbed."[23] Against this background of loyal attachment, he accepted a knighthood on the twenty-fourth of May, the Queen's birthday.

It is not surprising, then, that there was a strong infusion of Victorian English Liberalism in his legislation. The *Mail* even compared Mowat's method of handling a deputation on the controversial question of prohibition to that of Mr. Gladstone, "that great master of political tactics, who can make in a most definite way statements which upon close investigation frequently mean very little."[24] Among the many measures patterned on English legislation were the Ontario act of 1884 providing for the safety and health of workers in factories, and the Free Libraries Act of 1882, which was the first step in Canada toward the provision of libraries for everyone's use.

The most striking examples of English influence were Mowat's electoral and judicial reforms. England's experience in adopting the secret ballot in 1872 and admitting new groups to the electorate

[21] Cited in G. P. deT. Glazebrook, *A History of Canadian External Relations*, rev. ed. (Toronto: McClelland and Stewart, Carleton Library No. 27, 1966), I, p. 157.
[22] Biggar, *Sir Oliver Mowat*, II, pp. 582-85, Mowat to Dr. Angus McKay, M.P.P. for South Oxford, November 23, 1891.
[23] Sir John S. Willison, "Sir Oliver Mowat," *The British Empire Review*, V (1903), p. 20.
[24] *Mail*, February 8, 1894.

in 1867 and 1884 helped educate Ontarians away from open voting and toward a more democratic franchise. Mowat's successive extensions of the franchise were timed to the advance of provincial opinion, and in the English tradition of moderate reform, carried out gradually. But it has to be added that he introduced full manhood suffrage for Ontario in 1888, a point which Great Britain did not reach until 1918. The common law and equity courts of the province were practically the same as those in the mother country, which were in the process of being reformed by the Gladstone government when Mowat became leader. The *Mail* feared that he might be so "old fogyish" that he would not "move abreast of the times," or that, as a barrister, he might not like to see the courts shorn of any of their privileges.[25] Mowat, as lawyer and judge, however, had had first-hand knowledge of the anomalies of the rival proceedings, and he was ready to imitate the English law reformers as quickly as the profession and the public in Ontario could be prepared for change. His Judicature Act of 1881 united the superior courts of the province, but retained the principles of equity to enrich the common law by means of a clause worded identically with one in the British Judicature Act of 1873:

> Generally in all matters not hereinbefore particularly mentioned, in which there is any conflict or variance between the Rules of Equity and the rules of the Common Law with reference to the same matter, the Rules of Equity shall prevail.[26]

Sometimes deference to British models made Mowat's measures very limited in their effect, as in his first attempt to legislate for the settlement of industrial disputes in 1873. His act was almost worthless because it gave to boards of arbitration similar powers to those in England, and these did not include authority in disputes arising over wages, the most common cause of all. Sometimes, too, Mowat incurred severe criticism by looking to Britain for prece-

[25] *Ibid.*, January 9, 1873.
[26] *Statutes of Ontario*, 1881, c. 5.

dents. He defended his adoption of a numbered ballot of the English type as necessary for the detection of fraudulent votes. But the Conservative opposition denounced the numbered ballot as a device which made possible an "infamous espionage" by the Liberal government.[27] Generally, though, the measures which reflected the ideas and the gradualism of Victorian England were popular in the loyalist province.

Even if Mowat's Liberalism gave preference to the British way over American democracy, he did frequently find value in the example of the states across the border. Farmers' institutes for the exchange of agricultural information were copied from the United States. The success of kindergarten classes in St. Louis, Missouri, led to the authorization of the first Canadian public kindergartens in 1887 in Ontario. A bill of 1873 for profit-sharing agreements between masters and workmen was based on an act in Pennsylvania. The experience of Adirondack Park helped in the formulation of rules for Algonquin Park. The superiority of the protective services for fish and game in adjacent American states spurred Mowat on to a stiffening of the provincial law. His introduction of effective legislation for compulsory school attendance in 1891, which had been delayed because it meant interference in the domain of the family, was preceded by a careful look at compulsory education in the United States, Britain and continental Europe. Also, Mowat's observation of legislation in European countries, the sister dominions, and provinces of Canada yielded useful suggestions which he applied in his own province in such diverse fields as forestry, social welfare, the safety of miners, and the collection of statistical information.

Although many of the ingredients of Mowat's Liberalism came from England and other parts of the world, it was he who selected them, decided on the proportions, and mixed with them elements indigenous to the province. The latter he took from many sources: the ranks of his own party and his friends; the press; the clergy and judiciary; the temperance and humanitarian societies; the rep-

[27] *Free Press* (London), November 9, 1892; *Empire*, February 22, 1893.

resentations of farmers, labour unions, manufacturers, municipal bodies, and sportsmen; the reports of provincial and federal commissions. And, according to Hector Charlesworth, Mowat cleverly "whipsawed" Meredith by accepting any constructive proposal from the opposition.[28] The product was distinctively Mowat's and Ontarian. Can it rightly be called "Liberal"?

Mowat was quite accustomed to such labels as "timorous" and "a Tory of the old school," and such charges as "inertia" and "fossilism" from his contemporaries.[29] At his death in 1903, the *Canadian Law Times* wrote that "Sir Oliver all his life posed as a . . . Reformer."[30] Even so, like Mackenzie King in his sensitivity to the mood of the people, Mowat had performed competently the "function of a Liberal minister" as Blake outlined it in the Aurora Speech:

> to say nothing in advance of the popular opinion of the
> day, to watch the current of that opinion, and when it has
> gathered strength, to crystallize it into Acts of Parlia-
> ment.[31]

Furthermore, Mowat did not always temporize. At every level of education, for instance, his government introduced innovations and expanded services without waiting for popular support. He went ahead of most rural opinion when he set up the College and Experimental Farm to give leadership in improving agricultural methods. And when he made the further provision for degrees in agriculture, even the *Globe*, understanding public sentiment, objected:

> It would strike a farmer as a ludicrous thing to have his
> son come home a full blown "Doctor of Agriculture," or
> "Master of Artificial Manures," or "Bachelor of Livestock."
> The unfortunate young man would be apt to become the

[28] Charlesworth, *Candid Chronicles* (Toronto: Macmillan, 1925), p. 169.
[29] E.g., *World* (Toronto), May 22, 1893; *Empire,* May 26, 1893; January 13, February 15, 1894.
[30] "Sir Oliver Mowat," *Canadian Law Times*, XXIII (1903), p. 181.
[31] *Globe*, October 7, 1874, text of Blake's speech at Aurora.

butt of all the small wits of the neighbourhood. . . . If he obtained a cent less for his oats than some untitled neighbour did, a broad grin at the expense of scientific farming would diffuse itself around.[32]

Mowat's wariness and pragmatism were clearly compatible with creative and province-building programs. As Liberal leader and premier for twenty-four years, he set the pattern for Ontario's politics of common sense and moderation with their particular blend of conservatism and reform, of caution and advancement.

[32] *Ibid.*, January 23, 1880.

Disagreement at the Commencement: Divergent Ontarian Views of Federalism, 1867-1871

BRUCE W. HODGINS

Premier Sandfield Macdonald, in July 1867, claimed to the electors of Pickering Township that he was "the most obstinate man in existence except George Brown and yielded his opinions to nobody." He was still not convinced that the new constitution would solve past "ills." Nevertheless, he had agreed to form a coalition administration. He, not John A. Macdonald or anyone else, was master of the Ontario situation, and he would remain a Reformer; the Conservatives had come to him and not he to them, and he would keep them in line. Not to have formed a coalition would have meant submitting to the "extreme wing of the Reform party."[1] This, he said a few days later in London, would have arrayed Ontario against the "General government" of "our new Dominion," and this isolation he was not prepared to see.[2] Instead,

[1] *Globe*, July 25, 1867.
[2] *Leader* (weekly), August 2, 1867.

he said, it was necessary to "harmonize" the local regime with the general regime.

"Monstrous,"[3] retorted George Brown's *Globe*. In a federal system the unit governments had to be independent of the central government; otherwise "their existence would be useless." It would be "as improper" for the "Confederate Government" to interfere in provincial affairs as for the imperial government "to dictate to our Confederate Government"; behind the Ontario premier was John A. Macdonald who, in the first month of its operation, had seriously violated the constitution.[4] The two chief ministers, argued the *Globe*, had brought "our system of government into contempt."[5]

Yet one year earlier, Brown had declared, over objections from John A. Macdonald and even Sandfield, that the full responsible cabinet system was unnecessary at the local level, that department heads need not be in the legislature and that the model should be the contemporary county councils.[6] Sandfield had thought that the central appointment of lieutenant-governors might reduce local responsible government and that perhaps the electorate should have some say in their selection, but Brown had disagreed.[7] Speaking in camera at the Quebec Conference in 1864, Brown had expressed even more centralist sentiments. Upper Canadians did not want expensive local (provincial) governments nor ones that would take up "political matters." Fixed legislative terms for a unicameral body and centrally appointed lieutenant-governors "would bring these bodies into harmony with the General Government." He proposed the direct election of executive officers with fixed terms, probably subject to removal; they would serve as a council actually presided over by the lieutenant-governor without any premier. Full responsible government was unnecessary, considering "how

---

[3] *Globe*, July 30, 1867.
[4] July 25, 1867.
[5] July 20, 1867.
[6] Canada, Legislative Assembly Debates, August 3, 1866, in *Globe*, August 3, 1866, and Canadian Library Association microfilm, *Parliamentary Debates*, August 3, 1866.
[7] *Leader*, July 28, 1866, and *Globe*, July 28 and August 3, 1866.

insignificant are the matters agreed at Charlottetown to be left to the local Governments."[8] Then during the Canadian debates on the Quebec Resolutions in February 1865, Brown argued that complete legislative union was not administratively practical nor would it produce justice in taxation; besides, politically it could not have been secured. Yet the proposed scheme had "all the advantages of a Legislative union and a Federal one as well." The major responsibilities, especially in the economic sphere and concerning the appointment of judges, were "retained" at the central level; the divisive issues were "thrown over on the localities." By central supervision of local measures, he asserted, "we have secured that no injustice shall be done without appeal in local legislatures."[9] Important powers were central powers and in the central legislature representation by population would finally be secured, thereby bringing "complete justice" at last to Upper Canada. The securing of that in the plan "alone, renders all the blemishes averred against it utterly contemptible in the balance."[10]

The Grit leader was able to accomplish such a phenomenal transformation in his approach toward federalism without any discernible protest either from those of his lieutenants who remained loyal to him or indeed from his rank and file supporters. Several reasons made this possible. Confederation was a predemocratic achievement accomplished by a relatively small non-democratic political elite,[11] although, as Professor Peter Waite has shown, it had a genuinely popular side.[12] The English-Canadian part of this elite, mainly conservative but including the liberal but non-democratic leadership of Toronto, wished to create a structure as similar to the legislative union of the United Kingdom of Great

[8] G. P. Browne, *Documents on the Confederation of British North America* (Toronto: Carleton Library, No. 40, 1969), pp. 113-15.
[9] P. B. Waite, ed., *Confederation Debates in the Province of Canada, 1865* (Toronto: Carleton Library, No. 2, 1963), pp. 73-74.
[10] *Ibid.*, p. 64.
[11] See Bruce W. Hodgins, "Democracy and the Ontario Fathers of Confederation," *Profiles of a Province* (Toronto, 1967), pp. 83-91.
[12] *Life and Times of Confederation: Politics, Newspapers, and the Union of British North America* (Toronto, 1962).

Britain and Ireland as circumstances permitted, knowing that the French-Canadian elite had to be assured of the *survivance* of its culture. To the Canadian Fathers, Confederation involved a nation-building device which would deliver them from their political paralysis, enable them to avoid democracy, create an economically progressive union which would ultimately be transcontinental, and mitigate against dreaded annexation by the United States. The English-Canadian Fathers had to abandon any lingering commitment to Durham's plan to assimilate the French or to the American melting-pot concept of majoritarian conformism. The resultant anti-continentalist "Macdonaldian" constitution[13] is best described as "subordinate federalism," with limited biculturalism. "Due subordination" was not a denigrating but an ennobling relationship and as S. F. Wise has recently shown, was, with a particular view of "rational liberty," at the historic core of Canadian conservative thought.[14] The "provinces" of the new entity would have something similar to the status of New South Wales, old Canada and old Nova Scotia as provinces in the British Empire, with the crucial distinction that the citizens of the provinces would participate in the government of the whole entity and indeed would make up the population of that entity, though that entity would remain a colony of the British Empire. As the Montreal *Gazette* asserted, the scheme would achieve "legislative union with a constitutional recognition of a federal principle."[15] It would also avoid the "Tocquevillian implications of majority tyranny,"[16] and secure the North-West for the business communities of Montreal and Toronto and the prolific farmers of western Upper Canada before the Americans could get it. Yet neither the centralist aspects of the scheme (apart from the glorious long-awaited achievement

[13] W. L. Morton, "Confederation, 1870-1896: The End of the Macdonaldian Constitution and the Return to Duality," *Journal of Canadian Studies*, I (May 1966), pp. 11-24.
[14] S. F. Wise, "Conservatism and Political Development: The Canadian Case," *South Atlantic Quarterly*, LXIX (Spring 1970), pp. 232-33.
[15] September 9, 1864.
[16] Kenneth McNaught, *Pelican History of Canada* (London, 1969), p. 137.

of representation by population), nor the full implications of the commitment to the French elite, were emphasized or even adequately explained in Grit Upper Canada.

To most of the Grit voters, Confederation meant deliverance from French and Montreal dominance, a potential for greater progress, representation by population, cheaper and more honest administration, the restoration of Upper Canadian self-government, a vague national destiny and, to those land-hungry who were interested, the imminent acquisition of the North-West. Confederation was an elitist achievement. Yet in Upper Canada, concepts and assumptions of political democracy were growing, and they emphasized localism. The bulk of the Grit rank and file or, perhaps more accurately, the local leadership seems always to have favoured local self-government, both municipal and for Upper Canada. These people seem hardly to have been aware of Brown's extreme centralism of 1864-66. During those years Brown and the two Macdonalds were all centralists, though Sandfield opposed the Quebec scheme as too "federal," that is too decentralist. Oliver Mowat, William McDougall and William Howland do not appear to have dissented. The Grit followers who stuck with Brown in 1867 were hardly aware of his centralist utterances in 1864 and had been preoccupied with other aspects of his position in 1865 and 1866. In 1867 George Brown, the long-time liberal opponent of democracy, frustrated by the two Macdonalds, McDougall and Howland and by the "ruse" of continued coalition, and already angered by concessions to the Maritimes at the London Conference, "joined" his followers. Building on the deep Upper Canadian commitment to self-government and local authority and the developing grass roots concept of majoritarian populist democracy, he and other Reform leaders began to articulate the relatively alien doctrine of classical federalism.

The "Genesis of Provincial Rights," therefore, lies much further back in the social history of Upper Canada than even Norman McL. Rogers asserted.[17] In this genesis, the concept of local

[17] *CHR*, XIV (1933), pp. 9-23.

decision-making was central. This localism was a part of the thought of William Lyon Mackenzie; in 1850 it formed a major component in the programme of the original Clear Grits. It probably owes very little to the frontier. It was not completely alien to the Loyalists. It owes quite a bit to the practice and theory of self-government in various Presbyterian, Congregational, Baptist and Methodist denominations and to the pragmatically successful operation of Baldwin's Municipal Government Act of 1849 in the organic structure of small town and rural Upper Canada. Chartist and other British radical ideas entered the amalgam, especially at the journalistic level, and American state experience and theory were never very far away.

Elwood Jones has argued convincingly that at the Great Reform Convention of 1859 delegates talked localism, and a large majority favoured separatism or something fairly close to it.[18] The words then of Malcolm "Coon" Cameron, who bridged the Mackenzie era, the years of the original Clear Grits and later the early Mowat years, were not atypical. He wanted to cut old Canada into "three or four provinces," and was not afraid of direct local taxation because "the smaller the districts within which the taxes are expended, the more narrowly do the people look at the expenditure." The old Home District had been divided into sixty municipalities, "but do the people grumble at the increased expenditure?"

> I early discovered the fact that it is only when the money raised on taxes is spent directly under the eye of the tax-payers, that economy can be enforced, for I observed that it was only Prince Edward and some of the smaller districts where they kept out of debt.[19]

John Smith of Mornington, also favoured dissolution and direct taxation (and sounded more like Michel Brunet than Pierre Trudeau): "When two countries were united together, which had

[18] "Ephemeral Compromise: The Great Reform Convention Revised," *Journal of Canadian Studies*, III (February 1968), pp. 21-28, and "The Great Reform Convention of 1859" (Ph.D. thesis, Queen's University, Kingston, 1971). The author is indebted to Elwood Jones for helpful suggestions on various aspects of this topic.
[19] *Globe*, November 10, 1859.

scarcely any similarity with regard to their feelings, language, religion, and occupations, one country must inevitably dominate over the other"; only local government could preserve public morality. Though Hope Mackenzie from Sarnia opposed pure dissolution because of fears over access to the St. Lawrence, he argued for local legislatures controlling "entirely their own local affairs" with a small common unicameral body picked by the local legislatures on a representation by population basis, merely to handle "our joint interests—our railways, canals and other public works."[20] The only people who opposed dissolution, argued the *Markham Economist*—and much of the most intense expression of localist philosophy was expressed by delegates from York and other central counties—were placeholders and men who opposed efforts to have the ordinary people influence legislatures, men who in the past had opposed the uprooting of the Family Compact, the secularization of the clergy reserves and the development of the public school system, municipal institutions and local courts.[21]

During the 1865 Canadian legislative debates on the Quebec scheme, several Grittish opponents expressed, with somewhat different emphases, sentiments similar to those of 1859. Although they tended to emphasize the need for a democratic referral to the "people" on the matter of a fundamental change in the constitution, they complained that the public did not yet really understand the exact nature of the proposed union. They also complained of the probable cost of taxation by aloof authorities, and of the arbitrary nature of the proposed upper house. They noted the danger of continued concentrated power in the hands of the executive as well as the centralized nature of the plan—often they were not against the idea of a carefully considered limited confederacy. Nearly all of their complaints were subtly related to the question of localism.[22]

For his part Sandfield opposed the Quebec scheme not because of

[20] *Ibid.*
[21] October 20, 1859.
[22] Canada, *Parliamentary Debates on the Subject of the Confederation of the British North American Provinces* (Quebec, 1865), e.g. speeches by James Currie, pp. 269-84, David Rees, pp. 327-33, and Joseph Rymal, pp. 933-36.

localism but because he opposed disrupting the political unity of the St. Lawrence valley. He was not against the eventual union of British North America. In some respects he was the last prominent provincial Canadian or political Laurentian. Furthermore, he rejected the arbitrary, unpopular way in which the conservative-dominated coalition was attempting to implement a drastic constitutional reorganization; he was closer to being a democrat than was either Brown or John A. But he also opposed the idea of centrally enforced constitutional guarantees for minorities, because such guarantees violated responsible government and would look like tempting forbidden fruit to future majorities. The Canadian problem, he argued, was not the present constitution but "demagogues and designing persons."[23]

In December 1865 Brown resigned from the cabinet, no longer able to abide coalition. But his Reform colleagues, McDougall and Howland, remained. During the 1866 unsung last session of the provincial legislature of Canada, the one which considered the constitutions for Ontario and Quebec and dealt with their respective minority school situations, a triangle of tension among the three great Upper Canadian political leaders, Brown and the two Macdonalds, was much in evidence. In 1867, with Sandfield's personal animosity for Brown known to be greater than his distaste for John A., the haughty Baldwinite became particularly valuable to the master politician who was about to become prime minister of the new union. McDougall and John A. successfully worked out arrangements for continued coalition at the federal level, but McDougall and his friends alone were not enough to make continued coalition in Ontario credible, both federally and provincially. But the addition of Sandfield, the official leader of the old opposition and the last Reform premier of Canada, might. Sandfield would not serve under John A. But he was persuaded to head a genuine coalition regime for Ontario. As a result, the opponent of turning the eyes of the Upper St. Lawrence and the Ottawa valleys on Toronto rather than Montreal, became the province's first

[23] *Ibid.*, p. 654.

premier. That the coalition ceased to be more than a façade in the 1870s does not in any way make its formation and limited success in 1867 any less real or legitimate. Nor did the appointment of Sandfield as premier violate either the Macdonaldian system or indeed the principles related to the initiation of responsible government. John A. and Brown had served in a coalition to achieve the new scheme, and Brown considered such action upright and moral though it meant deserting his fellow liberals in Lower Canada. John A. and Sandfield headed two different coalition regimes to launch the new ship of state, and Brown sincerely considered it unjustified and immoral. To Brown it violated the constitution, which he now chose to interpret deductively from an abstract federal model rather than inductively and pragmatically as he had done when he was an innovator. Many Reformers, especially in eastern Ontario and, strangely, those under the influence of the *London Free Press*, stuck with Sandfield and McDougall. "Hunting in pairs," the coalitions easily won the elections. But the Liberal party of Ontario was created around those Grits who remained loyal to George Brown; the abstract model rather than the plan of the Fathers better suited their own deep-seated and practical sentiments and traditions. The development of political democracy amid the reappearance of culturally divisive issues and the precarious state of John A's own support in Ontario, dependent as it was in so many ridings on members of the Orange order, ensured the destruction of the initial dispensation.

Sandfield Macdonald endeavoured to make the Macdonaldian system work. He was never a flunkey for Sir John A. or anyone else. Indeed, he fought Sir John A. on several crucial issues and significantly expanded the power and prestige of the Ontario jurisdiction. His regime was dynamic and highly progressive. But neither premier nor prime minister tried effectively to sell the system to the people of Ontario. Perhaps it was unsaleable.[24]

---

[24] The author elaborates on this theme in his *John Sandfield Macdonald: 1812-1872* (Toronto: Canadian Biographical Studies, 1971), chapter VI, and his "The Plans of Mice and Men: An Introduction to a Comparison of Early Australian and Canadian Federalism," *ANU Historical Journal*, VII (November 1970), pp. 16-25.

In 1868, the prime minister asserted that, with the growth of Canadian maturity, supervision by Whitehall was rapidly declining. Because the people of the provinces were first and foremost citizens of the Dominion, however, supervision by Ottawa and the use of disallowance would continue permanently; this would correct local mistakes and promote the national interest (read, the central Canadian imperial interest). The Ontario premier did not object to the prime minister's examination and private comment and criticism of Ontario legislation. The exchange of private and official correspondence between them is rather voluminous. The prime minister had the governor general disallow only two Ontario acts, but he often urged the premier to amend or repeal certain laws. Occasionally Sandfield was persuaded by the logic of the argument, often he fought back. Frequently he emerged victorious. The prime minister complained to others (he frequently talked behind Sandfield's back) that the premier "paddles his own canoe" and was much too independent-minded and that his legislation was often too "radical."[25]

Politically, Sir John A. did not give sufficiently realistic attention to the problems of coalition; by not doing so he undermined the rationale for Sandfield's position and increased his own unpleasant dependence on the Orangemen who, like the Grits, never really accepted the implications of the Quebec scheme. Elections just prior to Confederation had shown that in Upper Canada Reform voters, though disunited, were in a clear majority. This, Sir John A. seemed to forget. Sandfield was thoroughly annoyed in 1868 when, without consultation, Sir John A. had Howland, the federal Coalition Reformer, appointed lieutenant-governor of Ontario. The prime minister still regarded lieutenant-governors as subordinate federal officials. It was, therefore, only with great reluctance that Sandfield finally agreed to accompany Sir John A. on his delicate

---

[25] Numerous letters in PAC, Macdonald Papers (Macdonald to R. Stephenson, October 8, 1871, refers to the canoe and Macdonald to Macpherson, February 7, 1871, refers to the radicalism), in PAC, John Sandfield Macdonald-Langlois Papers, and in W. C. Hodgins, *Correspondence, Reports of the Minister of Justice and Orders-in-Council upon the Subject of Provincial Legislation, 1867-84* (Ottawa, 1888).

mission to Halifax to neutralize or win over another truculent Reformer, Joseph Howe. In this, Sandfield's role was quite significant, and personal relations improved. Then Sir John A. appointed McDougall, the federal Coalition Reform leader, as lieutenant-governor of the North-West Territory. Strains reappeared when the prime minister, in a move which is incomprehensible from a political point of view, had old Sir Francis Hincks, recently returned from British Guiana, appointed Minister of Finance and "Reform" leader in the federal cabinet. One of the few matters of Reform politics that Brown and Sandfield agreed upon was that Hincks was an unscrupulous spendthrift and the man who in 1854 had destroyed the old Reform party.

Meanwhile Sandfield was holding firm on Ontario's right to supplement the salaries of certain federally appointed judges who were assigned special tasks and to remove county judges under certain circumstances. Sir John A. had the offending act disallowed. Even before this took place and with the acquiescence of the prime minister, the premier had the legislature pass bills which reconfirmed Ontario's assertions but moderated the form.[26] Sandfield continued to feud privately with Hincks. Then McDougall, after being challenged by Louis Riel on the Red River and deserted by the prime minister, returned to the Commons to sit with A. T. Galt, who was also alienated, on the opposition side. Despite Grit denunciation, the coalition was still working in Toronto, although it was wearing pretty thin in Ottawa. Admittedly, Sandfield's only really capable cabinet colleagues, Matthew Cameron and John Carling, were Conservatives. His own position depended on the credibility of the coalition and, as it turned out, the viability of the Macdonaldian system depended to a considerable degree on the political isolation of the Grits for a few more years. Sandfield's stand on federalism was further undermined by the unpopularity in Ontario of the "Better Terms" for Nova Scotia and the federal government's allegedly incompetent handling of the Red River

[26] JSM Papers, Macdonald to JSM, December 14, 1868 and January 20, 1870; and Macdonald Papers, JSM to Macdonald, November 6, 1869, Macdonald to JSM, November 18 and December 18, 1869.

troubles, including its negotiations with alleged revolutionaries. Although personal relations between the two first ministers were cordial in late 1870 and early 1871, Sandfield's political position had badly deteriorated, despite some good administration and the continuing surge of significant legislation.

Meanwhile the *Globe* and the Grit opposition, building on genuine feelings for local self-determination and on Upper Canadian prejudices and frustrations with the direction of the administration in Ottawa, were developing the doctrines of classical federalism. But the ingredients were all there in 1867. As early as July 31 of that year the *Globe* had claimed that federation gave the Ontario legislature and government "within its own limit independence of the General Government altogether." Sandfield, it then pointed out on August 7, really wanted a legislative union and that was what the coalitions were now seeking; in a federation there could be no coercion. On August 14 it claimed that Sandfield was a much more severe threat to Confederation than Joseph Howe because Howe opposed what he claimed was a legislative union while Sandfield thought provinces were useless. Sandfield's behaviour in Ottawa—he was also a federal member—was that of "the veriest dummy and the most slavish ministerialist in the House," the *Globe* wrote on December 6. Later, on June 11, 1869, it claimed that Sandfield was actually plotting to undermine the Ontario government and legislature to create a legislative union. He was bringing "them into contempt" to pave the way for the curtailment of their power and the ultimate "dispensing with them altogether." So vehement was Edward Blake's opposition in 1869 to the federal government's granting of "Better Terms" to Nova Scotia that although Sandfield beat back twelve resolutions against the move, on the thirteenth, calling for a constitutional measure to prevent future bilateral fiscal deals, he had his own forces support the vote to prevent major desertions.[27] Yet Blake himself was inconsistent in that he had the year before persuaded Sir John A. to disallow an Ontario Act—which he thought gave

[27] *Globe* and *Leader*, November 24, 1869.

legislatures too many privileges,[28] and in 1871 he introduced a
motion censuring the federal government for its handling of the
murder of Thomas Scott. In the latter case M. C. Cameron himself
was able to be classically federal with a successful counter motion
condemning the murder but arguing that the province should not
interfere in federal affairs.[29] Confederation was designed, the
Globe claimed on April 4, 1870, "to give us all control over local
Provincial matters, as far as that is compatible with national unity."

Of course the Opposition and its press also attacked Sandfield
substantively. Like Baldwin before him, Sandfield openly and
rather crudely used the legitimate Victorian tool of patronage to
reward the faithful. For this he was castigated. Yet some condemned him for not giving enough jobs to his fellow Catholics. He
was damned for parsimony. He was accused of overemphasizing
the role of the executive and of prodigality in persuading the
legislature to grant the cabinet an undifferentiated sum of $1.5
million from the huge Ontario surplus to aid in the construction
of northern development railroads. Finally, the *Globe*'s endorsa-
tion of classical federalism became merged with its vitriolic personal attacks on the Premier:

> Petulance, bad temper, a garrulous, half-wandering inco-
> herent style of speech, a littleness and total want of dignity
> of bearing and expression; a shabby, shuffling way of
> wandering out of it; a reckless style of assertion and a
> strange forgetfulness today of what may have been the
> utterance of yesterday; this, without the least exaggeration
> is a fair description of Mr. Sandfield Macdonald as the head
> of the Government and leader of the Legislative Assembly
> of Ontario. The question that a stranger instinctively asks
> himself is, by what strange freak of fortune this queer
> caricature of a practical statesman has been elevated to a
> prominent position in the politics of his country.[30]

By the time of the provincial election in the spring of 1871,

[28] Macdonald Papers, Blake to Macdonald, November 30 and December 28, 1868.
[29] *Leader*, February 3, 1871.
[30] *Globe*, December 21, 1871.

Sandfield's overthrow and the achievement of justice for Ontarians had become for the *Globe* a crusade requiring God's help. Sandfield was nothing more than "a puppet" who could "dance to any tune the Macdonald of Kingston likes to start."[31] A vote for Sandfield meant a vote for "French domination at Fort Garry" and, it seemed, everywhere in Canada.[32] The coalition lost ground severely, but within it the Conservatives, suffering from Irish defections, both Orange and Green, lost more than Sandfield's Reformers.[33] Sir John A., however, complained that Sandfield had made insufficient partisan use of the railway fund. On October 3, the *Globe* argued that the "old gang" and the French Canadians still ruled over the affairs of Canada and hence Ontario, with Ontario paying the bills and Quebec doing the spending. When the legislature met in December, the opposition, with the help of a few procedural tricks, marginally outvoted the government. Although a new dispensation would not be clearly evident until 1896, the Macdonaldian system had been defeated in the pivotal province of Ontario. As the new premier, Blake announced that his government, unlike his predecessor's, would insist that the provincial and federal levels "be absolutely independent of the other in the management of its own affairs"; all "interference" in Ontario's business would be protested.[34] The *Globe* went further and implied that interference simply would not be accepted.[35] In the molding of the new system Oliver Mowat, who became premier in 1872, would play the leading role.

Back in 1864 John A. had successfully argued in favour of subordinate federalism, with provincial bodies having only those powers strictly needed for "local purposes" and to provide for "sectional prejudices and interests." The powerful central authorities would protect minorities and achieve "constitutional liberty as opposed to democracy."[36] And he admitted privately to M. C.

[31] *Globe*, February 15, 1871.
[32] *Globe*, March 14, 1871.
[33] Macdonald Papers, JSM to Macdonald, March 24, 1871.
[34] *Globe*, December 23, 1871, report of proceedings of December 22.
[35] *Ibid.*
[36] Browne, ed., *Documents*, pp. 94-95.

Cameron, soon to be in Sandfield's cabinet, that he expected in his lifetime to see provincial organs "absorbed in the General Power."[37] He had not reckoned on the development of populist democracy in Upper Canada, on Ontario's deep commitment to localism or on his Toronto political opponents' ability to capitalize on that sentiment. After 1867 he grossly underestimated his need to lean on the Reform elements within his coalition, and he allowed himself to become overly dependent upon Orange support. Little elitism existed in the Orange order, and while Orangemen were not articulating a doctrine of classical federalism, one suspects that deep down they were as anti-centralist as the Grits, but with a weaker, more pragmatic philosophical base. As Lovell Clark has shown, this became obvious by 1896.[38] As early as 1868 Sir John A. was somewhat redefining his federalism in light of political realities. Nevertheless, in 1870 he accepted a Quebec-style constitution for Manitoba, and for this and his softness toward the Métis he was severely chastised by Orangeman as well as Grit. When in the next year the New Brunswick schools question surfaced, he seems to have been convinced that because of Ontario views he could not safely act. Through sophistry he found excuses which repudiated his 1864 stand on behalf of provincial minorities. This time he was lucky in that Cartier and his followers stuck with him. The Acadians were expendable. Yet partly because of this, Cartier was personally defeated in 1872. There would later be trouble in Quebec. Meanwhile, if the role of the central government in the protection of minorities was weakened, perhaps irretrievably, its role in national development was preserved. While Manitoba became technically a province, it received a kind of special status in reverse. Land and other natural resources remained under the control of central authorities. Canada could thus develop the North-West in an imperial way not too unlike the colonial way Lord Durham, thirty years previously, had wanted Upper Canada developed, a way Upper Canadians of all shades of political opinion

---

[37] Macdonald Papers, December 19, 1864.
[38] "The Conservative Party in the 1890's," Canadian Historical Association *Report*, 1961, pp. 58-74.

had rejected.[39] This crucial violation of provincial rights was not much objected to by the Liberal elite of Toronto. In fact some of its young bloods, deeply Ontarian and verging on racist but rather disturbed by Brown's acceptance of localism, formed their little Canada First movement and then, with some exceptions, in a few years were attracted into Conservatism by this National Policy of Macdonald. It would be transplanted Ontarians with their deep commitment to localism who would have to take on the battle in Manitoba itself. In twenty years these transplanted Ontarians would display their social heritage by overthrowing the minority guarantees of the Manitoba Act. The reverberations from that action would help decisively to secure the final triumph of the classical federalism first advanced by the Grits in 1867. But it would take sixty years and many regional protests in the face of more "imperial" policy before the prairie provinces would secure control over their lands and resources. Although one side of the Macdonaldian system, the centralist role in preserving "constitutional liberty," had a very short life, another side, the economic imperial side, with Ottawa as the joint agent of the rival Toronto and Montreal elites, lived on.

Meanwhile Ontario Liberalism, in endorsing development, provincialism and classical federalism, abandoned any commitment to major reform. This basically suited the empire-building leaders of Toronto. "Better," wrote the *Globe*, "that a few individuals die of starvation than that a pauper class should be raised up with thousands devoted to crime and the victims of misery."[40] Sandfield, in contrast, had argued that public charities would in the future have to be supported by the state. "The Reform party," the *Globe* noted approvingly in 1878, "is the party of economy, retrenchment and free trade." Premier Oliver Mowat was more positive than that. He rarely had to discuss provincial rights; with its deep origins it had become a part of the value system of the grass roots Grit. Instead, Mowat could maintain a broad, pragmatic, mildly

[39] Lewis H. Thomas, *The North-West Territories: 1870-1905* (Ottawa: CHA Booklet No. 26, 1970).
[40] February 24, 1874.

progressive developmental regime. This regime gradually extended the franchise and nurtured the local option approach concerning prohibition, while securing the warm and wet support of the Irish Catholics, many of whom with careless inconsistency continued federally to support Sir John A.

Mowat, Laurier and the Federal Liberal Party, 1887-1897

CARMAN MILLER

Oliver Mowat's relations with the federal Liberal party under Laurier's leadership resembled the relations which exist between an honourable member of the opposition and the government: Laurier accepted Mowat's opinions, counsel and criticisms only if they suited his plans and party strategy. The personal and political divisions among Ontario Liberals, which to a certain extent explain Laurier's elevation to the national leadership, enhanced his position and gave him considerable control over the Ontario party. Even Mowat, "the most influential Liberal in a position of power in Canada,"[1] could not effectively challenge his control.

Mowat, during Blake's leadership, enjoyed considerable influence in the councils of the federal party. In January 1887, just before the federal elections, Blake, discouraged and ill, had even offered Mowat the national leadership, because he believed Mowat's power

[1] Paul Douglas Stevens, "Laurier and the Liberal Party in Ontario," unpublished Ph.D. thesis (University of Toronto, 1966), p. 73.

and prestige would bring support at the polls, particularly in Quebec, where Mowat retained a high reputation because of his stout defence of Ontario separate schools and his amicable relations with the Roman Catholic Church. Mowat initially accepted Blake's offer on the condition that Blake enter the cabinet if Mowat formed a government. When Blake refused Mowat withdrew his acceptance, pleading insufficient personal means. Mowat's change of mind may have been caused less by poverty than by Blake's cooling ardour. Sometime during the Blake–Mowat negotiations Blake began to doubt the practical wisdom of Mowat's move from Toronto to Ottawa. Moreover, the Liberal party's electoral success in the province of Quebec vindicated Blake's controversial policy of "wooing Quebec," strengthened Laurier's position in the party, and convinced Blake that Laurier, not Mowat, could and must lead the Liberal party.

Mowat, like many prominent Ontario Liberals, discounted Laurier's promotion to the party leadership in June 1887. Mowat, a shrewd, canny weathercock of Ontario public feeling, at first carefully avoided too close an association with the French-speaking Catholic leader, a fact he demonstrated all too vividly during Laurier's 1889 speech at Toronto's Horticultural Pavilion. Laurier, despite the forebodings of seasoned party strategists, went to Toronto to explain his position on Mercier's Jesuit Estates Bill and the Equal Rights Association. The audience was noisy and hostile. Mowat, sensing the mood of the meeting, refused to deliver the prepared speech he had planned praising the new leader and asked Willison to withhold a letter he had written to the *Globe* in a similar vein. The next day, however, when Mowat learned of the personal success with which Laurier's remarks had met in Toronto, he lavished praise on Laurier in full measure.[2]

Mowat simply regarded Laurier as a temporary caretaker until Blake, "the favourite leader and profoundest thinker of the Liberal party,"[3] returned, or some other Ontario Messiah arose to lead the

[2] John Willison, *Reminiscences* (Toronto, 1919), p. 170-74.
[3] Margaret Evans, "Oliver Mowat and Ontario 1872-96: A Study in Political Success," Ph.D. thesis (University of Toronto, 1967), p. 6.

party to victory. But Laurier had come to stay, a fact which Mowat could scarcely have predicted in 1887. Nor could Mowat have foreseen his own loss of influence on the federal party which Laurier's leadership entailed.

Mowat knew Laurier relatively little. In 1882 Laurier had generously defended Ontario's position on the Manitoba boundary dispute. He had also campaigned for Mowat during the 1886 provincial election among the Franco-Ontarians of the eastern counties. Yet their relationship remained on a formal, polite level, in contrast to the warm, friendly relations Mowat enjoyed with Blake. Moreover, Laurier's leadership represented a significant shift in the party's power balance away from Ontario to Quebec, a shift which Laurier's leadership symbolized rather than created. Laurier, preoccupied initially with restoring party unity, often ignored Mowat's opinion.

Laurier believed that a precise and popular economic policy would rally the dissident ranks of his demoralized party, diffuse the explosive racial-religious issues agitating Canadian politics, and rout the crumbling Conservative party. During the early years of Laurier's leadership, however, the magic success formula escaped his grasp, owing partly to the dissension within his party.

Blake's resignation and the subsequent search for his replacement revealed at least two distinct factions in the Liberal party. Sir Richard Cartwright, a firm, unrepentant, free-trade advocate, quite naturally considered himself a candidate for Blake's succession. On the other hand, Blake and his followers, including the Ontario premier, disliked Cartwright's personality, his policies and his blue-ruin, denunciatory oratory. Cartwright had never been happy under "Master Blake's" tutelage. He disapproved of his strategy of wooing Quebec, placating the fears of the manufacturers and making peace with the Canadian Pacific Railway. David Mills, the former Minister of the Interior in Alexander Mackenzie's government, seemed a possible compromise candidate. Mills, known as "a Blake man," also believed in unrestricted reciprocity, even commercial union with the United States. But he possessed no following and remained aloof, academic and unpopular, ever the "philosopher of Bothwell." Laurier, the Ontario leaders soon realized, had one very important qualification which none of the Ontario aspirants could claim: he was the man who divided them least.

In 1887, Sir Richard Cartwright later recalled, the Liberal leadership "was not an enviable position."[4] During Laurier's first four years he faced three serious problems. First there was Blake, who could not lead and would not follow, and who retained a devoted body of supporters and continued to sulk on the sidelines. Second, the Liberal party, like the government, remained deeply divided on the racial-religious issues of the day, the Jesuit Estates Bill, the Equal Rights Association, the Protestant Protection Association and the Manitoba school issue. Third, an articulate and influential body of Ontario Liberals remained dissatisfied with Blake's trade policy to which they had adhered for seven unhappy years.

These personal and policy divisions enabled Laurier to remain the arbiter of the Ontario section of his party. Laurier knew that success came not from excluding but including and accommodating as many diverse elements as possible. While he frequently deferred to Cartwright's opinion on economic matters, at least until 1891, Cartwright's pronounced Protestant opinions and lack of sympathy for French Canada challenged Laurier's policy of moderation. The Blake wing, with but a few early exceptions, had a sounder record on issues of race and religion. Laurier, therefore, when dealing with these issues depended on it, and particularly on J. D. Edgar, its apparent leader in Blake's absence, who had been educated in Quebec, spoke French and had no tolerance for Protestant extremism. Edgar was Laurier's chief contact with the Toronto industrial and financial community, sat on the *Globe* board of directors, served as the Ontario party fundraiser and generally performed functions which Cartwright could not, owing to his opinions or reputation. In 1888 Edgar organized Laurier's tour of Ontario, accompanied him and advised him on the subjects and tone of his speeches. It was Edgar who denounced

---

[4] Richard Cartwright, *Reminiscences* (Toronto, 1912), p. 274.

the Equal Rights Association, initiated procedures to relieve J. D. Cameron of his post as editor of the *Globe*, and replaced him with J. S. Willison. Laurier also urged Edgar and Mills to help negotiate Blake's return to the party, a task which Cartwright could never do, owing to the strong antipathy existing between the two men.[5]

Laurier carefully avoided becoming the creature of any faction. He followed Blake's example and ruled the party through a small steering committee composed of Cartwright, Mills, Louis Davies, William Patterson and C. W. Weldon, which met every Saturday the Commons was in session and formulated policy and strategy. He placed Mills in charge of constitutional matters and confirmed Cartwright's position as chief financial critic. But Laurier frequently sought advice outside the confines of the parliamentary caucus. In Quebec Ernest Pacaud, editor of *L'Evénement*, plied Laurier with valuable information and advice. In Ontario Laurier relied increasingly on the sound, sensible opinion of J. S. Willison, whom Laurier had made editor of the *Globe*, despite the reservations of Mowat and Cartwright.[6]

But Laurier's most pressing priority as leader was to find a policy to unite the dissident elements of his party. It was either that "or go to pieces,"[7] Sir Richard Cartwright informed Laurier. The Ontario farmers, particularly in eastern Ontario, Cartwright wrote, were restless and demanding freer trade relations with the United States.[8] Laurier, suppressing his earlier protectionist sympathies, agreed that trade ought to become the party's central issue, that is, if he could bring his party to agree.

While Laurier, Charlton, Mills and Cartwright argued for a radical departure from traditional party policy, Blake and his followers, Edgar, William Mulock, James Young and James Sutherland, refused to move beyond a negotiated reciprocity treaty. The Blake wing, in the words of James Young, the editor of the

[5] W. R. Graham, "Sir Richard Cartwright and the Liberal Party, 1863-96," unpublished Ph.D. thesis (University of Toronto, 1950), p. 260.
[6] Stevens, *op. cit.*, p. 107.
[7] P.A.C., Laurier Papers, Cartwright to Laurier, 17 September, 1888.
[8] *Ibid.*, 8 July, 1887.

Galt Reformer, considered unrestricted reciprocity, which they equated with commercial union, "utterly anti-Canadian and subversive of the idea of an independent future."[9] They felt that unrestricted reciprocity implied a common tariff, discrimination against British goods, and a loss of revenue which could be supplemented only by direct taxation, a policy which received little support outside the editorial board of the *Globe.* They agreed with the reputed comment of James Blain, the American Secretary of State, "the privilege of a free market is the prerogative of citizenship."[10] Laurier, faced by stolid opposition from Blake's men, seriously considered abandoning the trade issue.

Then J. D. Edgar suddenly changed his mind. In October 1887, Joseph Chamberlain, speaking in Belfast before he left Britain for Washington to serve on a Joint High Commission to settle outstanding Canadian-American differences, condemned the idea of commercial union, declaring that it simply meant separation from Britain. Chamberlain's speech offended Edgar's sensitive sense of Canadian autonomy, and thereafter Edgar became more tractable on the trade issue. Meanwhile Cartwright, faced with the defeat of commercial union candidates in by-elections in Haldimand, East Northumberland and Shelburne in December 1887, moderated his position and agreed to accept the safer course of unrestricted reciprocity. The principal difference between unrestricted reciprocity and commercial union, the party now maintained, was that reciprocity did not require a common tariff and hence preserved Canada's fiscal autonomy. Laurier, taking advantage of this consolidation of opinion, laid the issue squarely before the annual Liberal caucus meeting just before the beginning of the 1888 session and received the unanimous support of the members present. But Blake was absent and adamantly opposed.

After Edgar's capitulation, the strongest opposition Laurier encountered from within the party, apart from Blake, came from Mowat and the Ontario government, whom Cartwright blamed

[9] *Ibid.,* James Young to Laurier, 19 November, 1887.
[10] Moreton Frewen, *Melton Mowbray* (London, 1924), p. 267.

for the continued "timidity" of some of his prominent federal colleagues. Mowat, Cartwright and Laurier agreed, had made his peace with the manufacturers and railways and drew his political support from similar segments of society to Macdonald. Laurier, therefore, ignored their opposition. "They are in power," he wrote to Cartwright, "and they do not want to see a question raised which might perhaps disturb the smooth surface of the waters in which they sail. They can afford to rest where they are."[11] There was, however, another reason for Mowat's reluctance to "move onwards." He realized that Blake would accept neither unrestricted reciprocity nor commercial union and he feared that the Liberal trade policy would alienate Blake permanently from the party. Laurier and Cartwright rejected Mowat's reservations, confident that "gradually we can, I believe, bring everyone to fall in,"[12] including Blake.

The unanimity of the federal caucus soon crumbled shortly after Cartwright proposed, in the House of Commons, his motion calling for unrestricted reciprocity. The final vote revealed an embarrassing lack of support from Liberal members. While the government mustered a full contingent to defeat the resolution, the Liberals counted only sixty-seven out of a possible ninety-two members in support of the motion. Laurier recognized the failure of his party's trade policy but refused to abandon it immediately. In subsequent sessions he simply relegated it to a position of secondary importance. In the 1889 session the Liberals made commercial autonomy, Canada's right to negotiate and sign its own commercial treaties, the centrepiece of their policy. And in 1890 the Liberals decided to make the last session before a general election a farmers' session.

Mowat, of course, approved of Laurier's new more pragmatic approach to party policy. "As regards Dominion politics," he wrote Laurier in August (?) 1890, "I think that your course in the H of Commons has been all that could be desired and that perseverance in it will be the best policy." Mowat naturally feared

[11] Graham, *op. cit.*, p. 162.
[12] *Ibid.*

and wished to prevent the revival of the contentious trade policy, which he knew remained a sacred creed among many influential members of Laurier's caucus.

Mowat's fears were confirmed later that year when Cartwright, anticipating a general election, suggested holding an Ontario convention to demonstrate Ontario's loyalty to Laurier. Laurier, after consulting some, but not all, of his Ontario colleagues, agreed to Cartwright's plan and called a convention for mid-January 1891. Mowat objected strongly to the proposed convention. He feared Cartwright would press for a more radical stand on the trade issue, which would drive Blake farther from the party. He immediately wrote Laurier a letter, which Blake persuaded him not to send, outlining his opposition, a position he declared most of his Ontario colleagues shared. Mowat's chief objection seemed sound: "If Mr. Blake should feel it his duty to make public his difficulties, the Convention would involve disaster."[13] Fortunately Macdonald resolved the Liberals' dilemma by announcing an election before the Ontario convention assembled.

Macdonald, having failed to secure a reciprocity treaty with the United States, fought the 1891 election on the Liberal trade policy of unrestricted reciprocity, their policy of treachery and veiled treason. During the election Mowat, a loyal party man, endorsed unrestricted reciprocity, but as the campaign continued he became increasingly unhappy with the policy and began to lace his speeches with firm declarations of loyalty to his British birthright.[14]

To many federal Liberals, Macdonald's victory, closely followed by Blake's West Durham letter, which Mowat advised Blake to delay until after the election, seemed serious setbacks. But Cartwright, Charlton and the *Globe* took comfort in Ontario's support for their policy. In Ontario the Liberals had obtained 51.1 per cent of the popular vote and had taken forty-four seats. "It is manifest,"

---

[13] P. A. C., Blake Papers, Oliver Mowat to Blake, 14 January, 1891. I would like to thank Christopher Armstrong, York University, for generously providing me with photocopies of Mowat correspondence found in the Blake Papers.

[14] Graham, *op. cit.*, p. 130.

J. S. Willison wrote in the *Globe*, "not merely that unrestricted trade has come to stay but that, in spite of a temporary check, it is here to win."[15] Some supporters, encouraged by the Ontario success, began to agitate for the "more advanced" policy of commercial union.

Mowat, and the more conservative members of the party, were both discouraged by the party's national failure, and alarmed at the subsequent success of the agitation to adopt an even more radical policy. "What is to be done to meet the difficulty?" Mowat wrote James Young in the summer of 1891. "In my position, I have not the time, nor have I now the energy which would be needed."[16] When no-one emerged to lead the crusade against commercial union, Mowat found both the time and energy.

Even before Mowat began his crusade against commercial union Laurier had made some efforts to quell the simmering revolt in the Ontario section of the party. On the eve of the election he had received letters from prominent Ontario supporters protesting Cartwright's predominance in the party's councils. Soon after the election Laurier named James Sutherland, a staunch opponent of Cartwright and a close ally of the Ontario premier, the chief party whip. Later that year Laurier demonstrated his growing caution on the trade question. He had accepted an invitation to speak in Boston in November 1891. The continentalists, Cartwright, Farrer and even Edgar, whom Laurier had sent to Washington to sound out the American government on the Liberal policy of unrestricted reciprocity, urged Laurier to endorse discrimination against British goods. John Ryan even suggested that Laurier should commit the party to political union.[17] Laurier, however, refused their advice, and in his Boston speech rejected the idea of political absorption and repudiated a policy of discrimination against British goods.

While Laurier was still in Boston he received a letter from Cartwright announcing an incipient revolt in the party. Cartwright

---

[15] *Globe*, 7 March, 1891.
[16] James Young, *Public Men and Public Life in Canada* (Toronto, 1912), vol. II, p. 431.
[17] Laurier Papers, John Ryan to Laurier, 2 November, 1891.

wanted Laurier to settle the dispute by a return visit via Toronto.
The immediate difficulty seemed to centre around Mercier's demands for more federal subsidies, which the *Globe* threatened
to denounce. The problem, however, probably lay in the deeper
discontent with party policy. "So far as I can judge at present,"
Cartwright wrote, "our parliamentary supporters from Ontario
are reasonable and will do nothing (knowingly) to dampen or
embarrass you. . . . The truth is, I fear, that there are occult and
dangerous influences at work from a quarter you can guess at and
I have already mentioned the entire surroundings at Toronto are
unfavourable to a consideration of this difficult issue."[18]

Goldwin Smith was more explicit. He wrote Laurier urging him
not "to bring up on any sure anchorage short of political union."[19]
Mowat, Smith warned, "and those whom he can control will recoil,
but Mr. Mowat has long been at heart a Tory."[20] Smith continued,
"If I read aright between the lines he does not desire unrestricted
Reciprocity much more than Political union." Mowat's loyalty cry,
Smith confessed, might frighten "a few timorous people from our
side. The rumour here is that Mr. Mowat desires to retire on a
knighthood. This may be the merest gossip; but it is the impression
naturally made by his attitude for some time past. I suspect you
have in him something not very far removed from a political
opponent."[21]

Smith's prediction proved correct: Mowat had decided to fight
the annexationists in the Liberal party, using all the means at his
disposal. He began his open attack on the annexationists in late
November 1891. Solomon White, a Conservative member of the
Ontario legislature for North Essex and an avowed commercial
unionist, announced a meeting in Woodstock for November 24 to
discuss the trade issue. Mowat immediately dispatched Dr. Angus
Mackay, M.P.P. for South Oxford, to refute Solomon's thesis and
declare the Liberal party's loyalty. Mowat had decided "in case a

---

[18] *Ibid.*, Cartwright to Laurier, 11 November, 1891.
[19] *Ibid.*, Goldwin Smith to Laurier, 27 November, 1891.
[20] *Ibid.*, 19 November, 1891.
[21] *Ibid.*, 27 November, 1891.

pro-annexation resolution should be carried at this meeting, to resign his seat for North Oxford and appeal again to the constituency
on the straight issue of British Connection vs. Annexation."[22]
Mowat, however, had planned well. According to Goldwin Smith,
scarcely an impartial observer, "Mr. Mowat sent down his secretary [S. T. Bastedo] to Woodstock and packed the meeting." Although the *Globe* reported that White's motion had been defeated
decisively by a vote of twelve to one, Smith informed Laurier that
"there was tampering with the Globe's report [and that the votes]
... instead of being twelve to one against the resolution, were pretty
evenly balanced."[23] Mowat could scarcely have ignored White's
meeting in the heart of his own constituency. It also gave Mowat
an opportunity to warn Cartwright, whose constituency was in
South Oxford, and his commercial union cohorts of the possible
political dangers inherent in their reckless course. The Woodstock
victory, Colonel G. T. Denison later extravagantly claimed, "delivered a death-blow to the annexation movement."[24]

The following month, Mowat wrote an open letter to Alexander
Mackenzie, which appeared in the *Globe* on December 14, denouncing commercial union and affirming publicly his British
loyalty and sympathies. The *Globe*'s editorial staff replied to
Mowat's letter reminding him that trade with the United States
need not entail discrimination against Britain. Mowat, annoyed
at the *Globe*'s rebuttal, appealed directly to Laurier and Cartwright, complaining that the *Globe* was "creating an annexation
party out of members of the Reform party." He also called upon
Laurier to repudiate the commercial unionists in the party and
promised "to join in any particular movement having that object."
The alternative, Mowat solemnly warned, would be "an open
division of the party."[25]

Laurier replied at once to Mowat's charges, politely soliciting his

[22] C. R. W. Biggar, *Sir Oliver Mowat: A Biographical Sketch*, 2 vols. (Toronto, 1905), p. 586.
[23] Laurier Papers, Goldwin Smith to Laurier, 27 November, 1891.
[24] George T. Denison, *The Struggle for Imperial Unity* (Toronto, 1909), p. 189.
[25] Laurier Papers, Oliver Mowat to Laurier, 26 December, 1891.

further opinions, to which Mowat responded in a milder but equally forthright manner. Laurier, he reiterated, must define publicly Liberal trade policy so clearly and emphatically "that there could be no cavil as to its meaning." Political union was "a price too great to pay for unrestricted reciprocity." He also advised Laurier to rein in the *Globe* and its most prominent continentalist writer, Edward Farrer. But these things, Mowat continued, "would not alone undo the past, or prevent future propagandism against our nationality."[26] More was required.

Mowat had decided that "Cartwright was no longer to be trusted,"[27] an opinion confirmed by Cartwright's recent speeches. Mowat had written to Cartwright the same day he penned his first protest to Laurier, but Cartwright, who was leaving Kingston to deliver a speech at Almonte, had only acknowledged receipt of the letter. In the meantime Mowat read in the *Globe* an account of Cartwright's speech which he considered distinctly disloyal. The year before, in Boston, Cartwright had spoken of Canada providing a whole new tier of northern states.[28] To Mowat this was clearly treason. Cartwright was "contemplating and desiring political union" and must be stopped. Mowat terminated his second letter to Laurier with the resounding threat: "If that is to be the policy of the Dominion Liberal party I cease to be a member of it."[29]

Laurier, however, paid surprisingly little heed to Mowat's threat and all during 1892 Mowat continued to attack the annexationist element in the party. In May 1892 he dismissed Elgin Myers, a Dufferin county attorney, who had written and spoken publicly in favour of annexation. Mowat determined to warn all provincial employees that he considered annexationist sentiments "inconsistent with the holding of a public office."[30] That same month Mowat accepted a K.C.M.G., as Goldwin Smith had earlier predicted, to

[26] *Ibid.*, 31 December, 1891.
[27] Graham, *op. cit.*, p. 275.
[28] *Ibid.*, p. 260.
[29] Laurier Papers, Oliver Mowat to Laurier, 31 December, 1891.
[30] Biggar, *op. cit.*, p. 607.

demonstrate "his sympathy with those members of his own and the Conservative party who desired to accentuate in every way their adherence to the British institutions and British connection."[31] On July 16, 1892, Mowat spoke at Niagara-on-the-Lake, at the centenary celebrations commemorating the creation of the Province of Upper Canada, and turned his speech into a thinly veiled attack on a speech Cartwright had delivered some months previously to a similar celebration and in which he had referred slightingly to the Loyalist contribution. "I am glad to know," Mowat told his Niagara audience, "that Canadians of the present day are, as a body not disposed to say of the sturdy self-sacrificing men who were the first settlers of our province that they were blunderers and wrongdoers in the sacrifices which they made of property and prospects and material interests generally, and, in so many cases, of life also."[32] Mowat had determined to drive the commercial unionists from the Liberal party.

Laurier continued to display little interest in Mowat's crusade. He refused to repudiate Cartwright and he waited until June 1893 to announce a revised trade policy.[33] Even Louis Davies' resolution during the 1892 session calling for preferential treatment on British goods probably originated more from pressures inside the party than from without; but Mowat's campaign doubtless assisted. Although the retirement of Edward Farrer from the editorial staff of the *Globe* in the summer of 1892 might be considered Mowat's doing, Willison informed Laurier that "Mr. Mowat is not at all responsible for his resignation."[34]

The great Liberal convention of June 1893 provided Laurier with the opportunity to announce the party's revised trade policy. Willison had suggested a convention as early as the summer of

---

[31] *Ibid.*, p. 608.
[32] *Ibid.*, p. 619.
[33] Stevens, *op. cit.*, p. 78. Stevens seems to suggest that Laurier retained the contentious trade policy to divide Blake from the party and enhance his own leadership. In Stevens' opinion, the announcement of the revised trade policy owed more to Blake's decision to leave Canada in June 1892 than to Mowat's campaign.
[34] Laurier Papers, J. S. Willison to Laurier, 4 August, 1892.

1892 and Laurier began immediately to plan for the gathering. Laurier, despite his protestations, closely controlled the proceedings, largely through James Sutherland, who planned and managed it from start to finish.[35]

Soon after the convention commenced, Laurier nominated Mowat chairman. W. S. Fielding, the Nova Scotia premier, became chairman of the important resolutions committee, which re-shaped the Liberals' trade policy. The first two of ten resolutions endorsed by the eighteen hundred official delegates dealt with trade. The first, moved by Laurier, called for closer trade relations with Britain and the United States. In the second, moved by Louis Davies and seconded by John Charlton, the Liberal party retreated from the dangerous ground of unrestricted reciprocity with the United States to the safer territory of a negotiated trade treaty, the policy of the party under Blake. This convention and the program it endorsed may well have "confirmed the triumph of the conservative Liberals led by Mowat" over the continentalists led by Cartwright, but it was not a total victory. It had been done in the best style of Laurier. It gave the revised trade policy a democratic imprimatur, lent a certain grace to Cartwright's retreat and helped save the reputations of all its original authors.

After the convention, relations between Mowat and Laurier improved considerably. Mowat requested Laurier's advice, for example, before he spoke at an unveiling of a monument to John A. Macdonald in Hamilton. Mowat feared that "Sir John Thompson, who is to be the principal speaker and other Conservatives, will no doubt say a great deal to which I could not assent." Mowat decided to attend only if Laurier concurred. His letters glowed with good will. He generously complimented Laurier for "those speeches which have been so justly commended and done so much good."[36] Laurier responded in kind, requesting Mowat to visit Montreal and address a Quebec audience. Their relations, nevertheless, remained formal and Laurier often used Alexander Smith,

---

[35] J. W. Lederle, "The Liberal Convention of 1893," *Canadian Journal of Economics and Political Science* (February 1950), p. 50.
[36] Laurier Papers, Oliver Mowat to Laurier, 11 October, 1893.

the secretary of the Ontario Liberal Association, to negotiate with Mowat on delicate matters, for example, party patronage.[37]

Still Laurier astutely refused to repudiate Cartwright or to allow Mowat to humiliate him. Nor did Laurier desire to become Mowat's political protector, which, given the turbulent Ontario political situation, may have proved extremely maladroit. During the early nineties Mowat's policies came under strong attack from two political factions, the Protestant Protection Association, based principally in the Liberal stronghold of south-western Ontario, and the Patrons of Industry, which drew much support from eastern Ontario. In the centre the McCarthyites had all but severed their relations with the Conservative party under Thompson's direction. They also deplored Mowat's friendly entente with the Catholic Church and his defence of separate schools. The Patrons, on the other hand, while friendly to the federal Liberals, directed much of their attention toward Mowat, especially his refusal to permit the election of municipal officials which would have destroyed the effect of Mowat's elaborate patronage network.

The formidable opposition Mowat faced during the June 1894 provincial election caused Laurier considerable concern. He agreed with Tarte that "Elle sera beaucoup plus difficile quand M. Mowat aura été vaincu dans Ontario ou qu'il aura été affaibli."[38] In January 1894 Laurier wrote apologetically to Mowat suggesting that he might draw the fire of Protestant protest by conceding the ballot to separate school elections,[39] a suggestion which Mowat accepted. He also sent J. D. Edgar and other federal Liberals into the political arena to help Mowat.

But Laurier also hoped to reap the benefit of Protestant wrath against the federal Conservatives' Catholic proclivities and the Patrons' and McCarthyites' sympathy for Liberal tariff policy. He therefore had to avoid too close an association with Mowat's provincial regime. Moreover, Laurier was carefully considering an electoral strategy which was certain to arouse the ire of Mowat's

[37] *Ibid.*, Alexander Smith to Laurier, 7 December, 1894.
[38] *Ibid.*, I. Tarte à Laurier, 30 janvier, 1894.
[39] *Ibid.*, Laurier to Mowat, 29 January, 1894.

men. The federal Liberals, Cartwright had first suggested, must appease the P. P. A. in order to hold south-western Ontario. In central Ontario they had to cooperate quietly with the McCarthyites, a policy Laurier began as early as January 1894. In the Conservative eastern counties, where Cartwright enjoyed a certain popularity with the Patrons, he advocated a "saw-off" which would deliver a death blow to Thompson's party.[40] In October 1894 Cartwright, with Laurier's consent, published a letter to the Patrons of Lennox county attempting to convince them to aid the Liberals.

Mowat and his followers were furious that Cartwright should negotiate with their political opponents so soon after a hard-fought and bitter provincial election. He decided therefore to drive him from public life. Although Alexander Smith, Simeon H. Janes, a retired Woodstock merchant living in Toronto, and James Sutherland led the movement, Mowat was undoubtedly the master mind.[41]

In November 1894 Smith appealed to Laurier to repudiate Cartwright's dealings with the Patrons.[42] When Laurier refused, Smith, Janes and Sutherland decided to force his hand. In late November the Liberals of South Oxford, Cartwright's constituency, anticipating an early election, called a nominating convention. Janes, supported by Sutherland whose constituency, North Oxford, bordered on Cartwright's, decided to contest Cartwright's nomination. Rumours that Janes and Sutherland carried Laurier's blessing gained considerable credence in the constituency and Cartwright's alarmed supporters called upon Laurier to deny the charge.[43] Laurier first attempted to negotiate, but Janes agreed to withdraw only if Cartwright promised to retire from public life before the next election, leaving the constituency open to Janes,[44] a condition Laurier could scarcely accept. Instead, he simply wrote to John Williams, the president of the constituency organization, endorsing Cartwright as a candidate and colleague.

[40] *Ibid.*, Richard Cartwright to Laurier, 22 October, 1894.
[41] Graham, *op. cit.*, p. 287.
[42] Laurier Papers, Alexander Smith to Laurier, 26 November, 1894.
[43] *Ibid.*, J. Williams to Laurier, 2 November, 1894.
[44] *Ibid.*, S. H. Janes to Laurier, 18 January, 1895.

Mowat's rather crude plan had clearly failed. But Janes gathered considerable support for his candidacy and Laurier, had he wished, might have rid himself of Cartwright simply by a policy of neutrality. Laurier, despite these Ontario pressures and the admonition of Israel Tarte to abjure Cartwright and all "des diminutifs de George Brown, dont ils n'ont, grâce à Dieu, ni la force ni le talent,"[45] refused to abandon him. He always retained a certain affection for Cartwright. Moreover he realized that success in Ontario would come not by rejecting Cartwright or Mowat but, if possible, by utilizing the talents of both. And Cartwright still possessed considerable political utility, a fact which the 1896 election demonstrated when eleven Liberal candidates retired in favour of Patrons and twelve Patrons withdrew to support Liberals.

Laurier continued to rule the Ontario section of the party not through one man but through many. Sutherland remained party whip and accompanied Laurier on his 1893 tour of Ontario. William Mulock, who paid one-third of the expenses of Laurier's western Canadian tour in 1895, became a close adviser and confidant.[46] J. S. Willison continued to enjoy Laurier's favour.

It is probably misleading to speak of only two wings in the Ontario Liberal party, the Mowat and the Cartwright wings, as though everyone fitted neatly into one or the other. J. S. Willison, for example, regarded neither Mowat nor Cartwright as acceptable leaders. Mowat, Willison felt, had lost his reforming zeal[47] and Cartwright could never win. In 1892 Willison confided to Laurier, "Hatred of Sir Richard keeps the Conservatives a solid body." David Mills, on the other hand, a one-man party, frequently objected to everything everyone said, especially the "cutthroats of *the Globe*."[48] There was, in fact, much truth in Alexander Smith's candid comment to Laurier: "More than ever you are the Ontario leader."

The high regard Laurier retained in Ontario became particularly

[45] *Ibid.*, I. Tarte à Laurier, 17 janvier, 1894.
[46] Graham, *op. cit.*, p. 330.
[47] Laurier Papers, J. S. Willison to Laurier, 19 January, 1894.
[48] *Ibid.*, David Mills to Laurier, 26 March, 1895.

evident soon after Sir John Thompson died in December 1894 and Laurier, ill, discouraged and doubtful of his ability to lead the party, placed his resignation in the hands of Charles S. Hyman, chairman of the Liberal caucus.[49] Although Laurier recited the same reasons for his resignation he had often used before, poverty, health, race and religion, the latter two now seemed to disturb him most. He feared that, with Thompson's death, the Protestant Ontario support he had so carefully cultivated would vanish. "Your origin & creed will be a more prominent factor," Mulock reminded Laurier, "now that your Catholic opponent is gone."[50] Moreover, the Judicial Committee of the Privy Council's final judgment had just been made public, enabling the government to introduce remedial legislation ordering Manitoba to restore separate schools. For many months Cameron, Cartwright, Sutherland, Mulock and Willison had pressed Laurier to declare the Liberal party's position on the controversial Manitoba schools question. Israel Tarte and the Quebec Liberals, equally anxious to make their party's position acceptable to the majority in their province, demanded from Laurier a firm statement supporting separate schools. Laurier himself maintained a moderate stand, which threatened to disappoint both provinces. He supported remedial legislation if the dispute could not be settled first by amicable negotiations with the Manitoba government. While Laurier may seriously have considered resignation, he may also have threatened to resign to strengthen his hand during the difficult months ahead.

Ontario leaders would not hear of Laurier's resignation. The Tories, Alexander Smith wrote, "have no personality and this brings to the minds of the electors, with greater force, your own standing with the people of Ontario."[51] Mulock, too, added his objections. The Tories might try to use Laurier's religion against him but, he added, "You are too well known here now for much success to attend such manoeuvres."[52] Later that year, after the

---

[49] *Ibid.*, Laurier to Charles Hyman, 28 March, 1895.
[50] *Ibid.*, William Mulock to Laurier, 14 December, 1894.
[51] *Ibid.*, Alexander Smith to Laurier, 3 April, 1895.
[52] *Ibid.*, William Mulock to Laurier, 14 December, 1895.

Liberals lost two by-elections in Ontario, John Willison reported on Laurier's reputation in Ontario. The party, Willison felt, "is not in the least danger of disintegration." He regretted that Laurier's Ontario colleagues were weak. We are, he wrote, "handicapped somewhat in Ontario in that we have not yet a leader with a following. Sir Richard is able but he is not popular. Mr. Mulock is unknown. Mr. Mills is doing nothing. Mr. Patterson, too who has popular qualities does not seem to have the ambition for leadership. Mr. Sutherland, Mr. Hyman and Mr. Gibson are good men but are not leaders. The truth is that we have no leader in the province and that we must suffer some in consequence."[53] Willison, however, remained optimistic about the party's future. Laurier's race and religion, he reported, had no effect and the only criticism he had to offer was partly complimentary: Laurier's failure to be in the constituencies. Laurier's popularity in Toronto in 1896 was such, Willison later recorded, that "Sir John Macdonald himself never could have had a more tumultuous welcome in the Orange and Protestant stronghold of Canada."[54]

As the Conservative party moved closer to imposing remedial legislation on Manitoba, Laurier feared the dissolution of the Catholic wing of his party, and in Laurier's eyes Mowat's political stock began to rise. To retain credibility among conscientious Catholics he began to court the support of Mowat. Mowat's active electoral support promised Laurier several assets: Catholic confidence, the good-will of Protestants aware of Mowat's sound reputation on provincial rights, and the support of Mowat's more vigorous Ontario colleagues. Moreover, Mowat and his provincial colleagues, George Ross and Richard Harcourt, agreed with Laurier's stand on the Manitoba school question. They too believed that provincial educational autonomy had been abridged by section 93 of the British North America Act, granting the right of an aggrieved minority to appeal for redress to the Governor-General-in-Council. They also admitted that the Catholics of Manitoba had a legitimate grievance but it was one which they, like Laurier,

---

[53] *Ibid.*, J. S. Willison to Laurier, 27 December, 1895.
[54] Willison, *op. cit.*, p. 255.

believed could be remedied through conciliation rather than coercion.[55]

In March 1895 James Young informed Blake that some newspaper had "started a story that in case of Laurier winning, Mowat might be offered the position of Minister of Justice." At the time Mowat's colleague, A. S. Hardy, dismissed the rumour saying that Mowat was not strong enough to take "such a trying position."[56] Yet Young remained skeptical, confident that some approach had already been made.

Little more than a year later, on the eve of the federal election, Laurier asked J. S. Ewart to try to persuade his uncle, Oliver Mowat, to join the federal party. Mowat, Ewart reported, seemed tempted by "the very laudable ambition to play a part in a larger sphere,"[57] but hesitated to agree for three reasons. He feared the physical strain which a new cabinet post might entail. He was not entirely happy with the Liberals' electoral program; it lacked clarity on two principal points, the Manitoba school question and the tariff.[58] But primarily he disliked disrupting his family home in Toronto, the gathering place of his children and grandchildren. Ewart felt that ultimately old age and family considerations would triumph over ambition. If Laurier insisted, however, Ewart suggested he might offer Mowat the premiership, permit him to bring "such of his present colleagues as he might think it advisable to carry with him," and induce other prominent Liberals to write Mowat insisting on his joining the federal party.[59]

Mowat's price, it seemed, was high, but Laurier appeared ready to pay part of it. "The question of the premiership," Laurier generously replied, "can easily be settled. I would most gladly make way for Sir Oliver."[60] A syndicate of Toronto capitalists, headed by George Cox and S. H. Janes, were also prepared to guarantee Mowat an annuity for the rest of his life. Laurier hesitated, however, to

[55] *La Patrie*, 25 avril, 1896. See also Biggar, *op. cit.*, pp. 652-53.
[56] Blake Papers, James Young to Blake, 14 March, 1895.
[57] Laurier Papers, J. S. Ewart to Laurier, 17 April, 1896.
[58] *Globe*, May 4, 1896.
[59] Laurier Papers, J. S. Ewart to Laurier, 17 April, 1896.
[60] *Ibid.*, Laurier to J. S. Ewart, 20 April, 1896.

agree to the inclusion of some of Mowat's Ontario colleagues. "This," he explained, "would arouse a good deal of objection and, I think ought not to be insisted upon."[61]

Laurier undoubtedly wished to secure Mowat's services. "The interest which I take in the Manitoba School question and my desire to see it settled in a way that will give satisfaction to the minority," Laurier wrote Ewart, "are so great that it would be a pleasure for me to make any sacrifice in order to induce Sir Oliver to enter federal politics."[62] But Laurier scarcely contemplated surrendering the leadership to Mowat. If Mowat's health was too fragile to support the duties of a cabinet minister how could he assume the more arduous responsibilities of chief? Moreover, if Mowat accepted the leadership Laurier had no right to object to his selection of Ontario colleagues. Presumably Mowat, as prime minister, could choose whom he wanted.

Laurier needed Mowat for one particular purpose: to settle the Manitoba school question. Laurier had no intention of making Mowat his Ontario lieutenant in the sense of retaining one acceptable Ontario spokesman and adviser to whom he would always defer on questions pertaining to that province. Mowat, Laurier explained to Bourassa, could scarcely play "une part aussi active à la lutte, à cause de son grand âge, bien que j'ai la promesse de son concours actif pour le réglement de la question des écoles dans le cas où nous serions appelés à la régler."[63] The terms upon which Mowat agreed to abandon provincial politics were limited in nature and time. Laurier promised Mowat four things: that he should not have to contest a seat but would receive a Senate appointment; that he would serve as government leader in the Senate; that he should be granted an important cabinet post; and that he could leave the cabinet and return to Toronto as soon as the position of lieutenant-governor of Ontario should become vacant.[64] (Many newspapers of the day claimed that Tupper also

[61] *Ibid.*
[62] *Ibid.*
[63] Bourassa Papers, Laurier à Henri Bourassa, 18 avril, 1896.
[64] W. T. R. Preston, *My Generation of Politics and Politicians* (Toronto, 1927), p. 210.

offered Mowat the lieutenant-governorship to prevent him from joining the Liberal campaign.)[65] Laurier felt he needed temporarily Mowat's prestige, his familiarity with school legislation and his capacity to draft sound legislation.

Laurier realized, however, that Mowat would be of little active assistance during the electoral campaign. He was seventy-six and in poor health; his eyesight had deteriorated, he had difficulty walking and his voice was weak and easily tired. Since the early 1890s his cabinet colleagues had relieved him of tiresome committee work. He found it impossible to attend evening sessions, and since his wife's death had become increasingly absorbed in religious subjects. During the election he spoke only five times outside Toronto;[66] twice he had to cancel speaking engagements in Quebec. When Laurier made his tour of Ontario in early June Mowat attended only one meeting, in London, where he addressed the rally. His voice, however, gave out and he had to cut short his speech.[67] Devoted friends like David Mills complained they had scarcely heard a word of Mowat's address.

Mowat's electoral strength lay more in his name and reputation. His decision to abandon provincial politics to join Laurier's campaign created a considerable impact, particularly among Catholics in Quebec.[68] Laurier's promise in St. Roche on May 7 that if he were elected Mowat would lead a commission to investigate Catholic ills in Manitoba received wide coverage in the Quebec press. *La Patrie* also traded on Mowat's good relations with the Ontario hierarchy to convert Quebec Catholics.[69]

It is possible, however, to exaggerate Mowat's contribution to Laurier's victory. The initial impact of Mowat's entry into federal politics died relatively quickly, and each province soon became absorbed in local issues, personalities, scandals or, in Quebec, the government's decision to purchase new guns for the militia.

[65] *Herald*, May 5, 1896; *La Patrie*, 5 mai, 1896.
[66] Blake Papers, Mowat to Blake, 25 June, 1896.
[67] *Herald*, June 5, 1896.
[68] *La Patrie*, 24 avril, 1896; 4 mai, 1896; 12 mai, 1896.
[69] *La Patrie*, 8, 9, mai, 1896; 9 mai, 1896; 6 mai, 1896; 1 mai, 1896.

Mowat's name became conspicuous more by its absence in the Quebec press. Sir Henri Joly, a Protestant, whom papers tagged Laurier's Quebec lieutenant, retained a reputation for justice and fair play almost equal to that of Mowat.[70] Whatever the *Globe* may have written about Mowat becoming a co-premier, *La Patrie* had no such illusions:

> Nous avons eu dans le passé le gouvernement Baldwin–Lafontaine, celui de Hincks–Morin, celui de Macdonald–Cartier et de Mackenzie–Dorion, mais n'avons jamais eu le gouvernement Lafontaine, ni le gouvernement Morin, ni le gouvernement Cartier, ni le gouvernement Dorion. Voici que les Anglais, obéissant à un beau mouvement de tolerance et de fraternité, veulent donner au pays le gouvernement Laurier.[71]

The (Montreal) *Herald* agreed: "Mr. Laurier is to-day the one striking personality in Canadian politics."[72]

Once the election was won, Mowat lacked any real influence in Laurier's cabinet. Laurier, contrary to John Charlton's peevish charge, chose his own cabinet, including the Ontario section. For several months Mowat was unable to secure a place in the cabinet, the Commons or the Senate for his old friend David Mills. Laurier also rejected Mowat's suggestion that James Lister, M.P. for Lambton West, be considered for a cabinet post, after himself and Cartwright.[73] Laurier ignored Mowat's advice to have no dealings with McCarthy. At first, Laurier even tried to pawn off on Mowat himself a minor cabinet post, the Post Office or Presidency of the Privy Council.[74] Louis Davies had set his heart on the Ministry of Justice and tried to convince Laurier that Mowat's appointment to Justice "would be simply ruinous," since he held no seat in the

[70] *La Patrie*, 8 juin 1896. Joly announced that his primary purpose for returning to public life was to settle fairly the Manitoba school question. The *Herald*, May 11, 1896, simply considered Mowat "an additional guarantee of fair settlement."
[71] *La Patrie*, 30 mai, 1896.
[72] *Herald*, April 24, 1896.
[73] Stevens, *op. cit.*, p. 156.
[74] Laurier Papers, G. W. Ross to Laurier, 7 July, 1896.

Commons and was old and lacked sufficient strength for an important department.[75] When Mowat refused flatly to consider any position other than the Ministry of Justice and threatened to retain his post as premier of Ontario, Laurier capitulated.

Mowat remained in Laurier's cabinet from July 13, 1896, until November 18, 1897, although he had ceased effectively to carry out his ministerial duties two months before he retired. He found ten hours of work a day exhausting and burdensome, and during the last month he remained in office the Solicitor General, Charles Fitzpatrick, relieved him of many of his routine duties. His chief contribution to the government had been his settlement of the Manitoba school question, for which, Laurier wrote Ernest Pacaud, Mowat "a le plus contribué à obtenir du gouvernement du Manitoba les concessions que nous en avons."[76] Yet when the lieutenant-governor's position became vacant Mowat, quite naturally, appeared reluctant to leave. He knew, he confided to Blake, that the lieutenant-governor's post meant he would "become a cipher in politics for the rest of my life, and, old as I am, I do not like the prospect."[77]

But Mowat's time in active politics was finished. His health was poor and, almost a year after he became lieutenant-governor he suffered a paralytic stroke which impeded his speech. Moreover, once the Manitoba schools issue was settled, Mowat had outlived his usefulness to Laurier's administration. He never wielded much influence with Laurier but now, old, feeble and stripped of any real power, he simply became Laurier's ward.

[75] *Ibid.*, L. H. Davies to Laurier, 6 July, 1896.
[76] Pacaud Papers, Laurier à Ernest Pacaud, 24 novembre, 1896. Mowat generously returned the compliment.
[77] Blake Papers, Mowat to Blake, 1 July, 1897.

The Mowat Heritage
in Federal-Provincial Relations

CHRISTOPHER ARMSTRONG

Sir Oliver Mowat deserves the title, "father of the provincial rights movement in Canada." It was he who challenged Sir John Macdonald upon the use of the power of disallowance, over the granting of "better terms" to some provinces without the others being consulted, and over the functions of the lieutenant-governor. He took a hand in the calling of the first Interprovincial Conference, which dutifully passed a number of resolutions he had drafted demanding for the provinces sovereign control of their affairs within their sphere of jurisdiction. He appeared personally before the Judicial Committee of the Privy Council with conspicuous success and persuaded them to accept his contentions in a number of important constitutional cases. All in all, he made it certain that the provinces would be far more than the glorified municipalities which some Fathers of Confederation, not least himself, had envisaged.[1]

---

[1] All students must be indebted to J. C. Morrison's study, "Oliver Mowat and the Development of Provincial Rights in Ontario: A Study in Dominion-Provincial Relations, 1867-1896," in *Three History Theses* (published under the auspices of the Ontario Department of Public Records and Archives, 1961), *passim*.

Some might say that Canadians have little reason to be grateful to Mowat for his efforts. It must be admitted that the conduct of federal-provincial relations seems to bring out the worst in our political leaders. In the intervals between delivering long-winded speeches, most of which are no more than platitudinous humbug, premiers and prime ministers alike have engaged in back-biting and name-calling on a grand scale. Witness, for example, Mackenzie King's description of Howard Ferguson as a "skunk," or Sir James Whitney declaring that the federal minister of Justice, " 'Baby' Aylesworth, . . . is without exception the most infantile specimen of politician or statesman that ever came to my notice," or that master of invective, Mitchell Hepburn, reviling King in 1941 as an "assassin of Confederation," fiddling with the Canadian constitution while London burned.[2] None of this has raised the tone of our political life, and such bitterness might be said to have retarded the growth of Canadian national feeling.

Mowat, of course, can hardly be blamed for the whole unedifying spectacle. What should be remembered is that during almost twenty-five years as premier of Ontario he defined the objectives of the province's external policy, of its relations with the federal government and with the other provinces. These his successors continued to pursue long after his retirement. He recognized that Ontario occupied a unique place in the Canadian federation owing to its size, its wealth and its population. The poorer provinces might look upon federalism as a means of overcoming regional disparities, but Ontarians, loyal to the Clear Grit tradition, valued separation more than equalization. The province wished to be left on its own to develop its bountiful resources without outside interference. Mowat sensed that "Empire Ontario" must have its emperor, and during his premiership did his best to enhance the province's power and influence along with his own.[3]

[2] King Diary, June 17, 1930, quoted in H. B. Neatby, *William Lyon Mackenzie King*, vol. 2, *1924-1932, The Lonely Heights* (Toronto, 1963), p. 337; Public Archives of Ontario, Whitney Papers, Whitney to R. L. Borden, September 11, 1907; *ibid.*, Mitchell F. Hepburn Papers, draft of speech to Dominion-Provincial Conference, January 1941, p. 12.
[3] I am indebted to Professor Nelles' essay in this volume for this concept.

Mowat's first objective then was to secure the fullest control over the province's economic development. Federal policies which threatened to restrict this must be strenuously resisted. Indeed, there developed a sort of dialectic in federal-provincial relations: any "interference" by Ottawa was opposed by provincial politicians, almost as a conditioned reflex. Whenever federal policies failed to meet Ontario's needs, or threatened to work against her best interests, the province tried to substitute its authority for that of the federal government. More often than not, it should be noted, the dynamic force which provoked such clashes was a private interest group, attempting to use whichever level of government best met its needs and desires. The province would take up the cudgels on behalf of its clients, whose opponents were usually pressing just as hard for Ottawa's aid.

Because of its vast domain Ontario was rich enough to resist the efforts of the federal government to bully it or bribe it into line. While the other provinces clamoured for "better terms," Ontario held aloof. Since almost half of federal tax revenues were supplied by Ontarians, any increase in federal transfer payments to the other provinces held a limited appeal for them. When the other premiers went cap in hand to Ottawa, Mowat could afford to stay at home and denounce any changes made in the financial relations between the Dominion and the provinces without consulting him. Occasionally, however, Ontario might wish the support of the other provinces for some demand it was making upon the federal authorities. Then the premier could unbend a little and ensure the necessary backing by approving the demands of the poor relations for increased subsidies.

Sir Oliver was quick to realize that both of these objectives could better be attained if Ontario were to secure a veto over constitutional change. He could not only torpedo those amendments of which he disapproved but demand favours in return for his assent. Since the British North America Act contained no formula for its own amendment, there was no statutory basis for such a demand, but the "Compact theory" of Confederation, which explained the constitution as a treaty between the provinces, offered a historical and conventional justification for this claim. Mowat early became an ardent exponent of the theory, and while his efforts bore little fruit during Macdonald's lifetime, his successors reaped the benefits.

Only a few illustrations can be offered here of the way in which Mowat and his successors pursued these aims, but they are sufficient to show that the premiers of Ontario, regardless of party, have been surprisingly faithful to them. As a result the Mowat heritage in federal-provincial relations long remained a vital part of our national life.

The most serious threat to the Ontario domain during Mowat's premiership arose from Macdonald's determination to cut the province down to size by handing over a huge area west of the Lakehead to the new province of Manitoba. To the *Globe* the issue was a simple one:

> Shall Ontario be deprived of the railway terminus on Lake Superior, with the city which is certain to spring up there?
> Shall Ontario be robbed of 60,000 acres of fertile land?
> Shall Ontario lose the revenue of $125,000,000, the sum which the pine timber alone, to say nothing of other valuable timber on the disputed territory, is computed to be worth?
> Shall Ontario be defrauded of a mineral region the wealth of which may exceed anything else in the known world?

Mowat threw himself vigorously into the fight; in 1882 he went so far as to threaten secession, boldly stating that

> if they could only maintain Confederation by giving up half their province, then Confederation must go . . . and if they could not demand the large amount of property to which they were entitled without foregoing the advantages of Confederation then it was not worth maintaining.[4]

[4] *Globe*, May 20, 1882, quoted in Morrison, "Mowat and Provincial Rights," pp. 147-48, 296.

Eventually the matter was fought out before the Judicial Committee. With Mowat personally arguing the province's case, Ontario won its point. He returned home to a hero's welcome, and while touring the province the premier told the crowd at a reception in Niagara Falls,

> I rejoice to know that the one great cause, the principal cause of your enthusiasm, is that you love Ontario as I love it. The display that you have made this night shows that you are for Ontario, and that you are for those who maintain Ontario's cause.[5]

When Macdonald continued to claim the timber and minerals in the disputed area, Mowat entered another suit to establish full possession. In 1888 the Privy Council again upheld him, and a settlement with the Dominion was finally arrived at in 1889.

The way in which private interest groups could create tension between the Dominion and the province was also dramatically demonstrated in Mowat's time by the row over the Rivers and Streams Act. The significant fact was that one of the lumbermen involved in the dispute was a Grit, the other a Tory. The Grit naturally turned to the provincial government for help, while the Tory hitched his fortunes to the government in Ottawa. Four times the legislature passed the act and three times it was disallowed by Macdonald. The two levels of government were drawn into serious conflict through a private quarrel. Neither premier nor prime minister emerged from this fracas with an enhanced reputation, but a pattern had been fixed which would frequently be repeated in future.[6]

Macdonald was convinced that Canada's economic development could best be achieved through the National Policy. So long as it seemed to promote the fullest development of Ontario resources and the creation of an industrial base there, the province's

---

[5] *Globe*, September 16, 1884, quoted in K. A. Mackirdy, "Regionalism: Canada and Australia" (unpublished Ph.D. thesis, University of Toronto, 1959), p. 186.
[6] For an analysis of the conflict over the Rivers and Streams Act, see Morrison, "Mowat and Provincial Rights," pp. 206-15.

politicians were content to accept its benefits. But as soon as Ontario's interests seemed threatened, the province stood ready to challenge federal policies, to substitute an "Ontario policy" of its own. The need did not arise during Mowat's premiership, but in 1897 the Dingley Tariff imposed a duty of $2 per thousand board feet on Canadian pine lumber, while the unprocessed raw material, pine sawlogs, was admitted free to the United States. Ontario lumbermen were naturally upset at the closing of the huge and profitable American market. They pressed the federal government to impose an export duty on sawlogs to force the McKinley administration to negotiate. But Sir Wilfrid Laurier was reluctant to act, not only because the Dingley Tariff included certain retaliatory provisions, but because he had fixed his hopes for freer trade on the pending negotiations aimed at settling all Canadian-American differences.

Unable to get relief in Ottawa, some Ontario lumbermen turned to the provincial government and demanded that it require the sawing of all Ontario pine in Canada. They succeeded in convincing the public and both political parties that Ontarians would become mere "hewers of wood and drawers of water" for their richer, industrialized American neighbours if they failed to act. Facing a provincial election in 1898, Mowat's successor and long-time subordinate, Arthur S. Hardy, bowed to this skilfully promoted public clamour and inserted a manufacturing condition in all timber licences so that the exportation of pine sawlogs cut on crown land was forbidden.[7]

American lumbermen who owned limits in Ontario protested both to Washington and to Ottawa. Secretary of State Day suggested that the federal government might disallow the export embargo legislation. Premier Hardy began to fear that the federal government might do so in order to persuade the McKinley administration to accept a reciprocity agreement. Laurier refused, however, to interfere with the provincial policy, for Hardy had warned that this would seriously damage the Liberal party's

[7] See Professor Nelles' essay for a more detailed analysis of the manufacturing condition.

prospects in Ontario. Efforts were then made by the American lumber interests to have prohibitive duties imposed on lumber and other Canadian imports. Meanwhile, the Colonial Office urged Laurier to persuade Hardy to suspend the embargo until the courts decided whether it was a regulation of trade and commerce and, hence, a federal responsibility. The premier stood firm in the face of pressure from Washington, London and Ottawa. He refused to suspend the act or to join in a reference to the courts, and eventually the embargo was declared valid by the Judicial Committee in a private suit.

As Professor Nelles has shown, the government of Ontario wished to force companies exploiting the province's natural resources for sale in the United States to do their processing in Canada. This was intended to create jobs as well as capital investment in plant. The success of the sawlog export embargo in forcing the relocation of a number of American sawmills in the province led the government to extend the manufacturing condition to pulpwood, nickel ore and hydroelectricity too, though with varying degrees of success. Ontario sought, then, to impose her own development policy, which sometimes clashed with the consistent federal policy of seeking to secure free access to the American market for Canadian raw materials.

The mediating influence of party loyalty, both Hardy and Laurier being Liberals, had helped to prevent any open federal-provincial conflict over the sawlog embargo. With the election of the Conservative Whitney administration in 1905 this influence disappeared. Over the next half-dozen years bitter rows between the two levels of government over development policy were frequent. Technological innovations in the fields of transportation, hydroelectricity and pulp and paper held out the lure of such large profits that one observer was moved to declare, "If Solomon were on hand today, he would say, 'With all your getting, get a water power and a lighting and electric railway franchise'."[8] Astute entrepreneurs were quick to take note of these opportunities;

[8] P.A.C., Willison Papers, Alex. Smith to J. S. Willison, October 2, 1905, 27826-7; Smith was the secretary of the Ontario Reform (Liberal) Association.

owing to the vagueness of the B.N.A. Act about the division of authority to incorporate companies,[9] men like James Conmee became convinced that they could play a kind of game and evade provincial control by obtaining federal charters. Attempts at regulation by the Ontario government could then be denounced as attacks upon vested interests and the sacred right of private property.

Conmee himself was specially favourably situated as a Liberal Member of Parliament, able to call upon the government to back his schemes. But others were quick to follow his lead in seeking to obtain at Ottawa what they were denied at Toronto. So complaisant did the Laurier administration prove in meeting the demands of company promoters, that Whitney was forced to retain the services of a watchdog in Ottawa to alert him to trouble ahead.[10] A good deal of time and energy was spent by both provincial and federal Conservatives in denouncing charter-mongering by the Liberals, though their protests usually fell upon deaf ears. A reservoir of ill-will built up which did much to embitter the relations of the province and the Dominion as long as Laurier remained in power.

Ontario's single most valuable resource was hydroelectricity, the province's only domestic power source. For over thirty years Mowat's successors resisted federal attempts to take control of the electrical industry. Here, too, the conflict was rooted in a constitutional ambiguity. While the province owned its lands and

---

[9] The provinces could charter companies "with provincial objects," but it was not clear whether this phrase was to be construed territorially, so that only concerns operating within one province were covered, or jurisdictionally, so that any company with objects covered by Section 92 was included. The federal government could incorporate companies whose objects were covered by Section 91, such as banking and shipping concerns, and also claimed the right to charter any company whose works were declared to be "for the general advantage of Canada." The province contested the latter claim and pressed for the jurisdictional interpretation of provincial objects.

[10] The provincial agent was an Ottawa lawyer, R. G. Code; see the Code-Whitney correspondence, 1905-10, in the Whitney Papers.

natural resources, the B.N.A. Act gave the Dominion control of navigation. The greatest hydro potential lay on navigable rivers like the St. Lawrence and the Ottawa. If the existing canals were improved, creating new waterpowers, the federal government might claim them as "incidental" to navigation. Or else it might block the construction of provincially owned generating stations indefinitely as impediments to shipping. Once the province had taken the decision to develop all its power through an arm of the provincial government, the Hydro-Electric Power Commission, conflict between Ontario and the Dominion seemed unavoidable.

The First World War produced an enormous upsurge in the demand for electricity, and by the mid 1920s the H.E.P.C. was casting longing eyes at a share of the two million horsepower potential of the International Section of the St. Lawrence. This development obviously required the cooperation of the United States government which was ready to support the construction of the St. Lawrence Seaway as a joint power-navigation project. However, Prime Minister Mackenzie King was determined that if there was to be a Seaway it should be paid for through the sale of power and not from federal revenues. Should the federal government establish control over this development, it would have sufficient leverage to establish a national electricity policy.

Premier Howard Ferguson of Ontario was equally determined to prevent this. The very idea of a national electricity policy was repugnant to his government, and he rejected the notion that the H.E.P.C.'s customers should finance the Seaway through higher electricity rates. To bolster its position the province fell back upon the Compact theory of Confederation:

> Canada was created by the act of the separate provinces. They established a federal union, yielding to the union the rights and functions appropriate to the national endeavour. Navigation went to the federal authority in the interests of national trade and commerce. . . . On the other hand, it was only natural that the more local aspects, the more particular property rights, the power, the domestic and sanitary uses [of waterways], which physically are applic-

able only to local industry and endeavour and should be
retained within the sphere of the Provinces.

Ottawa's claim that power was "incidental" to navigation was

> a concealed assault upon the provincial position under our
> federal system. In effect, if admitted, it would mean that
> federal action could completely oust the province from all
> benefits whenever a stream could be made navigable.

Such tactics "could slowly convert Canada from a federal union
into a legislative union under supreme control of the Parliament
at Ottawa."[11]

Efforts to clarify the constitutional position through a reference
to the Supreme Court in 1928 proved abortive, for the learned
judges confined their replies almost entirely to vague hypotheticals.
Efforts to negotiate a settlement during the next two years were
equally fruitless. During the federal election campaign of 1930
Ferguson and King traded insults over who was to blame for the
delay. The new prime minister, R. B. Bennett, was more enthusiastic about the Seaway than his predecessor; and a fellow-
Conservative, George Henry of Ontario, proved more cooperative
once it was clear that Bennett was prepared to concede the province's demands. By the Canada–Ontario agreement, which preceded the St. Lawrence Deep Waterway Treaty of 1932 with the
United States, the federal government agreed to pay the entire
cost of works required for navigation alone plus 30 per cent of the
cost of joint navigation and power works. The remaining 70 per
cent, about $37.7 million, along with the $66.5 million to equip the
powerhouses, was to be met by the province. The H.E.P.C. would
own all the power.

The treaty failed to get approval in the United States Senate,
but Ferguson's struggle had not been in vain. When the Roosevelt
administration persuaded Mackenzie King to take up the Seaway

---

[11] Unsigned memorandum entitled, "Federal and Provincial Rights in Waterways,
Georgian Bay Canal Charter and Dominion Lease of Carillon Rapids to National
Hydro Electric Company," February 24, 1927, p. 8, in P. A. O., Howard Ferguson
Papers.

project again in the late 1930s, it was simply assumed that Ontario would control Canada's share of the power. Under the St. Lawrence Basin Agreement of 1941 the province's share of the cost of joint works was also reduced from 70 per cent to 62.5 per cent. Just as Mowat had done in the case of the Manitoba boundary, his successors successfully defended the province's control of a vital resource on which its industrial base and future prosperity were heavily dependent.

The second part of Mowat's legacy was opposition to increases in federal transfer payments to the provinces. As early as 1869 Edward Blake led the Ontario Reform party in denouncing the grant of better terms to Nova Scotia as a violation of the Confederation compact. Ontario's first premier, Sandfield Macdonald, accumulated such a large surplus that the provincial government weathered the depression of the 1870s with relatively little difficulty. However, when the Mowat administration found itself faced with large deficits in the early eighties, his ministers turned their fire upon Macdonald's habit of soothing discontented provinces with financial titbits taken from the pockets of Ontarians. Christopher Fraser, the Commissioner of Public Works, told the legislature in 1885:

> [W]e who have charge of Ontario affairs would be recreant to our trust, if in the face of what we see going on, and what is absolutely certain to occur again, we made no sign, and did not indicate that Ontario would not continue submitting to these raids by the other Provinces. . . . We do not care to get these indirect and unwarranted grants, and that Ontario shall be the milk cow for the whole concern.[12]

When Honoré Mercier suggested an Interprovincial Conference in 1887, Mowat at once agreed that federal encroachment on provincial autonomy must be resisted, but added pointedly that Ontario "was satisfied with the provisions of the British North America Act, and would still prefer them to any changes if the

[12] *Globe*, February 23, 1885, quoted in Morrison, "Mowat and Provincial Rights," pp. 260-61.

principle on which they are based were faithfully carried out by the Dominion Parliament with the approval of all the provinces."[13] Yet he realized that subsidy increases were the chief concern of Mercier and the other premiers. In what would become a classic ploy for Ontario leaders, he agreed to throw his weight behind their demands, despite his reservations, in return for the backing of the other provinces in his demand for greater provincial autonomy. The conference called for hefty increases in the scale of grants to civil government (in Ontario's case involving a rise from $80,000 to $240,000 per year), and proposed that the annual per capita subsidy of 80 cents be tied to the current census figures rather than the 1861 ones. Such a "basis for a final and unalterable settlement" meant, of course, that the Mowat administration would get the tidy sum of $600,000 a year to dispose of.[14]

Macdonald simply ignored the resolutions passed at the conference. The subsidy question was not raised again until 1900 when the Liberal premiers of Quebec and the Maritime provinces secured better terms. Premier George W. Ross of Ontario immediately protested to Laurier "about the reopening of questions of public policy which were considered settled years ago."[15] The other provinces were insistent on an all-round subsidy increase, however, and an Interprovincial Conference met in December 1902. Ross, who was occupied with a crucial series of by-elections, did not even bother to attend or to send an Ontario representative. In a memorandum read to the delegates, he simply reaffirmed support for all the resolutions passed in 1887, although he did suggest more generous grants for the support of civil government. Premier S. N. Parent of Quebec, by contrast, wanted the per capita subsidy fixed at $1. In the end the delegates merely repassed the earlier resolutions.

[13] *Globe*, March 31, 1887, quoted in Morrison, "Mowat and Provincial Rights," p. 263.
[14] The deliberations of this conference, and the subsequent ones, may be studied in *Dominion Provincial and Interprovincial Conferences from 1887 to 1926*, and *Dominion-Provincial Conferences, November 3-10, 1927, December 9-13, 1935, January 14-15, 1941* (Ottawa, 1951). See also J. A. Maxwell, *Federal Subsidies to Provincial Governments in Canada*, (Cambridge, Mass., 1937), *passim*.
[15] P. A. C., Laurier Papers, Ross to Laurier, May 14, 1901, Private, 56180-1.

Laurier showed no more inclination to act upon these demands than had Macdonald, but as the federal surplus mounted the provinces became increasingly restive. By 1904 even Ontario faced a deficit of $800,000 on ordinary account, although the proceeds from the sale of timber limits covered this. Ross was still convinced that piecemeal grants of better terms were a poor way to cope with financial difficulties. Nevertheless, the financial pinch made him less high-minded; he pleaded with Laurier for a subsidy of $6,400 per mile for the provincially owned Temiskaming and Northern Ontario Railway. Laurier refused, however, to treat the province like "an ordinary railway company," opening the way for a flood of similar demands from the other provinces.[16]

The election of Whitney's Conservative government in 1905, ending almost thirty-five years of Liberal rule, saw no reversal of the province's policy on transfer payments. When Premier Lomer Gouin of Quebec sought the new premier's support for another Interprovincial Conference, Whitney agreed coolly that "fixity of arrangement between the Federal Government and the Provinces . . . would, for more than one reason, be very desirable. . . ."[17] It was left to the Liberal premiers to persuade Laurier to call a meeting in October of 1906. Whitney recognized that the original subsidies had become quite inadequate. The 1887 proposal to tie the per capita subsidy to the growth of population had several attractions. It had been twice approved by Interprovincial Conferences. The subsidy would automatically increase through time, so that periodic revisions would be unnecessary. Such an arrangement would be both elastic and yet permanent. Last but not least, the largest province would get the biggest increase. Whitney therefore decided to propose that the conference simply endorse the 1887 subsidy resolution once more.

The other premiers were prepared to agree to this, but insisted that each province should have the right to demand additional special allowances. Whitney fought a stubborn rearguard action against this, but was eventually overborne. He then proposed that

[16] *Ibid.*, Laurier to Ross, February 29, 1904, 82607-12.
[17] Whitney Papers, Whitney to Gouin, September 18, 1905.

British Columbia, the most importunate in its demands, should receive a special grant of $100,000 annually for ten years. An attempt by the other western provinces to obtain similar grants was turned down largely at Whitney's insistence. Laurier agreed to accept these terms as a "final and unalterable" settlement of the subsidy question, and the B.N.A. Act was amended the following year.

The steadily increasing demand for provincial services like highways and education soon absorbed these increases completely. The years immediately before the First World War found even a rich province like Ontario sufficiently hard-pressed that its opposition to greater federal transfer payments was again relaxed somewhat. The election of Robert Borden in 1911 was the signal for the repayment of a number of political debts owed to Conservative premiers like Whitney, Rodmond Roblin and Richard McBride. The boundaries of both Ontario and Manitoba were extended, and conditional grants to agricultural education and highway construction proposed. Still provincial spending mounted inexorably. In 1913 another Interprovincial Conference was held to consider the subsidies. Whitney and the other premiers approved a resolution demanding that 10 per cent of federal tariff revenue be channelled into subsidies. Grants to civil governments were to be increased 50 per cent to $2,610,000, while the remaining $10,710,000 (for 1913) would be distributed according to population. The beauty of this scheme, from Whitney's point of view, was that it would return to Ontarians a fairer share of the money which the federal government would collect from them in any case, so that any increase in transfer payments financed by the province would be comparatively small. Despite strongly worded pleas from Whitney, Borden refused to consider this ingenious suggestion, which would have made every tariff revision the occasion for a federal-provincial donnybrook.

In 1927 there came another occasion when the Mowat ploy proved effective. A Dominion-Provincial Conference was called by Mackenzie King in the midst of his dispute with Howard Ferguson over the control of waterpower on navigable rivers.

Since the prime minister was content to drag his feet, to refuse to negotiate seriously, Ontario faced a severe power shortage with no prospect of early development of either the St. Lawrence or the Ottawa rivers. Ferguson and Premier L. A. Taschereau of Quebec were confident that the courts would uphold the claims of the provinces, but a reference case required the consent of the federal cabinet. The conference provided a heaven-sent opportunity for forcing King's hand.

Both the Maritimes and the western provinces wanted better terms. When the question of subsidies was raised, Ferguson seized his chance. He reminded the delegates that Ontario paid the largest amount into the federal treasury, yet he supported the demands of the poorer provinces. "He did not," he said,

> intend . . . to cavil about small things. He regarded it as supremely important to bring about a situation which would be satisfactory to all the provinces.
>
> The basis of financing laid down by the British North America Act could not be regarded as permanent and must be subject to readjustment. . . . The big problem was to promote satisfaction and prosperity by giving fresh inspiration to those who needed help. . . . The expenditure of a few hundred thousand dollars was nothing if optimism, harmony, and industry could be inspired.[18]

Lest the other premiers forget their duty, he suggested that the power question should be eliminated from the agenda and referred to the courts. Despite an invitation from the prime minister to discuss this matter the other premiers remained quiet as mice. Doubtless they were too busy savouring the "fresh inspiration" of "a few hundred thousand dollars." Outmanoeuvred, King gave way and allowed the matter to go to the Supreme Court, though not without taking care to frame the questions so as to render most of the answers irrelevant.

[18] "Precis of Discussions, Dominion-Provincial Conference, November 3 to 10, 1927," p. 25, in *Dominion-Provincial Conferences, 1927, 1935, 1941.*

The Compact theory of Confederation, the third element in the
Mowat heritage, provided an underpinning for the other objectives. It could be called into play to defend Ontario's interest
in controlling its development or in the financing of the federal
system. To insist upon consultation concerning constitutional
change proved the surest defence of provincial rights against
federal encroachment. The grant of better terms to Nova Scotia
had been attacked by Edward Blake in 1869, on the grounds that
the assent of all the provinces was required to change the financial
terms of the B.N.A. Act. As Blake's successor, Mowat quickly
adopted the Compact theory as a weapon in his disputes with
Macdonald.

The Interprovincial Conference of 1887 was represented as the
reconvening of the Quebec Conference of 1864, at which the
original compact had been agreed to. Under Mowat's influence,
the 1887 meeting resolved that the provincial legislatures "should
at the earliest moment take steps with a view of securing the enact-
ment by the Imperial Parliament of amendments to the British
North America Act. . . ." In return for his agreement to support
an all-round subsidy increase, the premiers gave their support to
Mowat's proposals to widen the powers of the provinces and make
them even more immune to federal interference.

Mowat's successors were equally loyal to the Compact theory.
George Ross declared that it was

> quite evident that in every stage of its progress it [the
> B.N.A. Act] was regarded by its framers as a treaty under
> which the Provinces agreed to transfer a certain portion of
> their sovereignty to a central Government, which would
> undertake to discharge the duties common to all, while at
> the same time leaving the residuum of their sovereignty
> intact and unimpaired. . . .
>
> Now is it not clear that a trusteeship so formed cannot
> be dissolved, or its powers abridged or increased without
> the consent of the parties by whom it was made?[19]

[19] Sir George Ross, *The Senate of Canada, Its Constitution, Powers and Duties
Historically Considered* (Toronto, 1914), pp. 31-32.

By the turn of the century, indeed, politicians of both parties paid lip service to some version of the Compact theory. The influence of Blake and Mowat remained strong within the Liberal party, and Robert Borden admitted that,

> In very many matters touching the everyday life of the people, the policy and aims of any provincial administration are of the greatest possible interest and importance. The Liberal-Conservative party for many years past has been inclined to regard Provincial issues as of somewhat minor consequence.

This he now promised to change.[20]

Nevertheless, the provinces did not succeed in establishing a firm conventional right to be consulted about constitutional change. The 1907 subsidy revision was agreed upon at the Interprovincial Conference, and its recommendations accepted by Laurier, but later amendments were not the product of consultation. However, at the 1927 Dominion-Provincial Conference Ernest Lapointe laid before the delegates an amending formula for the B.N.A. Act, declaring that

> The Government has taken the ground that the B.N.A. Act is an agreement between different parties and that no substantial change should be made without consulting the contracting parties. The B.N.A. Act is the charter of the provinces in which powers have been fixed and determined between the Dominion and the provinces. Consequently, the provinces have the right to be consulted about establishing a new procedure to amend it.[21]

Lapointe's plan would have allowed amendments concerning exclusively federal matters to be made without reference to the provinces. Changes concerning education, the use of French, the administration of justice, property rights and the like, would have

[20] P. A. C., Borden Papers, Borden to W. B. A. Ritchie, June 15, 1909, 6646-7.
[21] P. A. C., Bennett Papers, Precis of Discussion, Dominion-Provincial Conference, 1927, 16298-312.

required unanimous provincial consent, and other changes could be made with the consent of any six of the nine provinces.

The dangers inherent in this proposition cannot have escaped Ferguson. Federal powers could now be altered without any reference to the provinces. More important, on all but a few matters, any six provinces could join with the federal government to approve an amendment even if both Ontario and Quebec opposed it. Better to allow the existing confusion to continue, meanwhile loudly claiming the right to be consulted about every alteration, than to tie oneself up in such an unsatisfactory arrangement. Ferguson felt the change might "affect the fundamental structure of our constitution" and declared that he could "see no substantial reason in favour of it." Strong support for this stand came from Premier Taschereau, and Lapointe had to abandon his efforts.

In 1930 the problem recurred. Newly elected, R. B. Bennett prepared to depart for London and an Imperial Conference to approve a draft of the Statute of Westminster, which would have repealed the Colonial Laws Validity Act of 1865 insofar as the Dominions were concerned. Thereafter, British legislation would apply to Canada only if the Dominion expressly requested that it should do so. But the B.N.A. Act was a British statute. Could the division of powers between Dominion and province be altered at the request of the federal Parliament alone once the Statute of Westminster took effect leaving the provinces with no recourse?

Premier Ferguson was much upset, and suggested to Taschereau

> that the provinces should enter a vigorous protest against what is being done without the original parties to the Confederation agreement being consulted. . . . [W]e should at least be consulted about it before representations are made to the Imperial Parliament. I have made strong protest to Mr. Bennett in one or two discussions I have had with him, and at his suggestion I am putting my views in writing and have asked him to give voice to them at the Conference.[22]

[22] Ferguson Papers, Ferguson to Taschereau, September 10, 1930.

The premier put his position in an open letter to Bennett.[23] Confederation had been "brought about by the action of the Provinces," and the constitution was "the crystallization into law . . . of an agreement made by the provinces. . . ." Accordingly, Ferguson claimed the right to veto any changes: "The Province of Ontario holds strongly to the view that this agreement should not be altered without the consent of the parties to it." He protested vigorously against the proposed statute and demanded that nothing be done until "the parties to the original compact" had been consulted and were satisfied. Any other course, he warned, would "not only greatly disturb the present harmonious operation of our Constitution, but I fear may seriously disrupt the whole structure of our Confederation."

In an accompanying memorandum the Compact theory of Confederation was further explained. First came a number of bald assertions: "the Quebec resolutions . . . were in the nature of a treaty between the provinces . . ."; "the Dominion was . . . created at the instance of the provinces. . . ." Then came the "proof": Macdonald, Cartier and Brown had all referred to the agreement as a "treaty" at various times. Moreover, the federal Parliament had not been given the power to amend the constitution; if it had had such power "the long and hitherto successful controversy [*sic*] as to the constitutional rights of the provinces would have had a very different outcome, because at any stage of the struggle the Dominion Parliament would have had the power to enact legislation setting aside the pretensions of the provinces." Skating lightly around the difficult question of who was now party to the compact, the memorandum merely insisted that all the provinces, even those created since 1867, had the same rights. The fact that the provinces had only been formally consulted about a constitutional change on one occasion was dismissed; it simply showed the perfidy of the federal authorities. After all, Ontario had been demanding to be consulted since 1869. A new era had begun in

[23] This letter and the accompanying memorandum were published as a pamphlet entitled *Amendment of the Canadian Constitution, Statement and Protest by the Prime Minister of the Province of Ontario* (Toronto, 1930).

1927, when Lapointe had at last admitted that the provinces had a right to be consulted. There could be no turning back now, and Ontario would bring all its influence to bear to prevent the power to amend the constitution unilaterally being handed over to Ottawa by the British parliament.

Coming from the Conservative premier of the largest province, this protest proved effective. The Imperial Conference was adjourned "until an opportunity has been given to the provinces to determine whether their rights would be adversely affected. . . ."[24] In April 1931, a Dominion-Provincial Conference met and Bennett somewhat reluctantly agreed that the statute should be amended so that it conferred no new powers upon either the Dominion or the provinces to amend the B.N.A. Act or to alter their legislative jurisdiction. The broader question of an amending formula was ignored. The outcome satisfied Premier Henry of Ontario, since provincial powers had not been reduced.

Pressure for constitutional amendment was naturally increased by the Depression. The fashion of the day in many quarters was to insist that the federal government should assume full responsibility for unemployment and for relief. Not surprisingly, however, neither the Henry government nor the Liberal administration of Mitchell Hepburn was enthusiastic about such a constitutional change. Both premiers suspected that proposed amendments would simply be designed to place all effective power in federal hands. Arthur Roebuck, Hepburn's attorney general, was alarmed by Bennett's aggressive attitude towards the provinces: "Wherein lies the need for immediate revision?" he asked J. W. Dafoe. "The tory-minded would like to centralize power. The Divine Righters always did, and every battle for freedom has been directed to decentralization." In any event, Roebuck added, nothing should be done until the provinces all agreed upon an amending formula.

---

[24] Bennett Papers, Bennett to George S. Henry, Feb. 23, 1931; Ferguson had been succeeded by Henry upon the former's appointment as Canadian High Commissioner in London by Bennett. J. W. Dafoe greeted the news this way: "What a gift for Ontario but imagine him at Canada House! Part of the harvest of the regime of bunk, blather, bluster, blasting, braggadocio, Bennett—a swarm of B's." P. A. C., Dafoe Papers, Dafoe to Harry Sifton, November 29, 1930.

He was confident that tactical skill in these negotiations could "head off a Dominion grab."[25]

In 1935 Mackenzie King accepted the recommendation of a Select Committee of the Commons that an amending formula should be discussed at a Dominion-provincial conference. Roebuck insisted that any method must be "satisfactory to all provinces."[26] Some progress was made; he and W. J. Major of Manitoba proposed that all the constitutional statutes should be consolidated and divided into four categories, each with a different amending procedure. Matters exclusively federal, like disallowance or the creation of new provinces, could be handled by Parliament alone. Changes concerning the Dominion and some, but not all, the provinces could be made if the provinces concerned concurred in amendments approved by Parliament. All ten legislative bodies would have to approve changes in minority rights. The remainder of the constitution, in particular the distribution of powers under Sections 91 and 92 of the B.N.A. Act, could be altered with the consent of Parliament and two-thirds of the provinces if they represented 55 per cent of the population.

A number of meetings of a committee of attorneys general were held to discuss this plan during 1936. It was approved in principle, although fears expressed by Maritimers that the other six provinces might gang up on them were met by treating "property and civil rights" and "all matters of a merely local or private nature" in the same way as minority rights. Moreover, a province was to be permitted to opt out of any amendments and to retain its exclusive jurisdiction. Ontario certainly supported this formula; with one-third of Canada's population, its veto would operate unless all the other provinces united against it. The attraction of the formula, as the province's deputy attorney general pointed out, was that, "This method definitely recognized the compact or contract theory. Changes cannot be made without the consent of the provinces affected, and this settles for all time the question as to whether the

[25] *Ibid.*, Roebuck to Dafoe, January 7, 1935.
[26] "Dominion-Provincial Conference, 1935, Record of Proceedings, Ottawa, December 9-13, 1935," p. 50, in *Dominion-Provincial Conferences, 1927, 1935, 1941.*

provinces should be consulted or not."[27] The long struggle begun under Mowat and carried on by his successors had apparently been won.

Unfortunately, it proved impossible to secure the unqualified assent of all the provincial governments to the formula. Mackenzie King's announcement in the spring of 1937 that a Royal Commission would be appointed to study Dominion-provincial relations led to the suspension of negotiations pending its report. Premier Hepburn considered the Rowell-Sirois Commission a waste of time and money. Loyal to the Compact theory he bluntly told the Commissioners: "I have always regarded Confederation as the outcome of a conference. . . . If there is to be a change in Confederation, it can be brought about only by renewed conference of the representatives of the people and with unanimity of approval."[28] The *Report*, therefore, realized his worst fears. Already at odds with Mackenzie King over his handling of the war effort, the Premier drafted a blistering speech for delivery to the Dominion-Provincial Conference in January 1941. He described the Commission's recommendations as "a scrapping of Confederation, that robs the provinces of their fiscal independence and of their full autonomy." When the conference opened he immediately declared that he would not be a party to "national vandalism," to the handing over of the constitution to the tender mercies of any "mushroom government that may in future take office at Ottawa. . . ." When Premier John Bracken of Manitoba suggested that the Ontario leader should show the same breadth of vision that George Brown had displayed in joining the Great Coalition of 1864, Hepburn was defended by his Highways Minister, T. B. McQuesten: "[I]n taking the attitude he has, Hon. Mr. Hepburn has been living up to the tradition of Brown and has defended and upheld all that Brown stood for, and is safeguarding the rights and responsibilities vested in the separate

[27] I. A. Humphries, *Observations on a Proposed Method of Amending the British North America Act* (n. p., n. d.), pp. 17-18.
[28] Royal Commission on Dominion-Provincial Relations, *Statement by the Government of Ontario* (n.p., 1938), Book I, Statement by Premier M. F. Hepburn, pp. 3-4.

provinces by Confederation."[29] In the face of such opposition the conference hastily adjourned. Hepburn's performance, if not his manners, had been firmly in the Mowat tradition, and the aim of securing provincial consultation concerning constitutional change had at last been achieved.

Although the illustrations given here cover only the period up to the Second World War, there is evidence that Mowat's legacy retains its vitality. Premier William Davis has declared that if federal action is not forthcoming to offset the effects of the 10 per cent surcharge on imports, imposed by President Richard Nixon in August 1971, upon Ontario businesses, then the provincial government will take independent action. Arthur Wishart, attorney general in the Roberts administration, expressed his belief in the Compact theory of Confederation on a number of occasions. And in April 1971, former Premier Roberts attacked the increase in the federal equalization payments drawn from Ontario taxpayers, which he claimed had risen from $1.4 billion in 1970 to $2 billion in 1971, or over 40 per cent in one year.[30]

Since the Mowat heritage has been so consistent and long-lasting, it seems proper to ask whether it has been a constructive force in Canadian development. Mowat's own achievements have not been kindly dealt with. He has been criticized for misleading the Privy Council, and they for heeding his arguments in favour of provincial rights. It has been pointed out, quite rightly, that Mowat was inspired as much by partisanship as by principle. More important, his heedless use of the provincial rights movement is said to have hindered the development of national feeling in Canada. As early as 1889 D'Alton McCarthy argued that

> The worship of local autonomy, which some gentlemen have become addicted to, is fraught . . . with great evils to this Dominion. Our allegiance is due to the Dominion of

---

[29] Mitchell F. Hepburn Papers, draft of speech to Dominion-Provincial Conference, January 1941, p. 14; "Dominion-Provincial Conference, Tuesday, January 14, 1941, and Wednesday, January 15, 1941," pp. 15, 76, in *Dominion-Provincial Conferences, 1927, 1935, 1941.*
[30] For Roberts' speech, see *Globe and Mail*, April 20, 1971.

> Canada. Our separation into provinces, the rights of local
> self-government which we possess, is [*sic*] not to make us
> less anxious for the promotion of the welfare of the Domin-
> ion.

Canada's uncertain response to the economic crisis of the 1930s
seemed to many to confirm that Mowat's legal and political guile
had subverted the intentions of the Fathers of Confederation. The
nation had been reduced to a collection of enfeebled but semi-
independent principalities, no longer capable of providing Canada
with a minimum level of social and economic services, and re-
sistant to the development of a strong and cohesive national
identity.[31]

Mowat and his successors were certainly partisans. They identified their possession of power with the public good. But the very
relentlessness with which they pursued their objectives in federal-
provincial relations suggests that they sensed a strong, deep-laid
Ontario particularism, on which they could draw. The Clear
Grits had expressed this feeling before Confederation, and it did
not disappear in 1867. Reinforced by Mowat's political skills and
legal successes, it became a resource upon which the politically
astute, the Whitneys, the Fergusons and the Hepburns, could depend. Ontarians resent being the "milk cow" of Confederation
just as much in 1971 as in 1941 or 1885. The Compact theory of
Confederation, however shoddy historically or legally, is important
as an expression of the province's self-consciousness.

Perhaps, however, sectional loyalties like this do pose a bar to
the development of strong national feeling. Certainly, it has usually
been assumed that they do so, but David Potter has recently
pointed out "the general similarity between nationalism and other
forms of group loyalty." The attachment of the citizen to his

---

[31] Sir Charles Tupper quoted McCarthy in Canada, House of Commons, *Debates*,
March 17, 1896, p. 3700; D. G. Creighton has severely criticized the trend towards
decentralization in his essay, "Federal Relations in Canada Since 1914," in Chester
Martin, ed., *Canada in Peace and War: Eight Studies in National Trends Since 1914*
(Toronto, 1941), p. 48; similar criticisms may be found in F. R. Scott, "The
Development of Canadian Federalism," *Proceedings of the Canadian Political
Science Association* (1931), pp. 231-58.

nation can be a by-product of loyalty to non-national groups and goals, for in Morton Grodzins' words, ". . . one is loyal not to nation but to family, business, religion, friends. One fights for the joys of his [*sic*] pinochle club, when he is said to fight for his country." Nationalism and sectionalism are not necessarily anti-thetical, though they may sometimes conflict. The editor of the *Globe* grasped as much when he wrote in 1883: "Only upon condition that Provincial rights are respected is there any hope of building up a Canadian nationality." National loyalty flourishes not by overpowering other loyalties but by subsuming them and keeping them in a mutually supportive relationship. Loyal Cana-dians can also be loyal Ontarians.[32]

Professor Maurice Careless has suggested that we should explore "limited identities" in Canada.[33] Big, rich and successful, Ontario has not hesitated to express its feelings, its distinctive identity. Indeed, its government has been the foremost crusader for pro-vincial rights. The cultural and ethnic distinctiveness of Quebec has made it particularist, too, yet French-Canadian politicians have never been able to ignore the existence of the minority outside Quebec. The Manitoba school question showed vividly how min-ority rights and provincial rights could collide. How, then, could French Canadians commit themselves fully to provincial rights for Quebec if this meant the sacrifice of the diaspora? Federal power, as they saw, could be called upon to serve ethnic ends, for the Official Languages Act has a lengthy pedigree. But Ontario's leaders have been hampered by no such ambivalence. They have

---

[32] David M. Potter, "The Historian's Use of Nationalism and Vice Versa," *American Historical Review*, vol. 67 (1962), p. 931; Morton Grodzins, *The Loyal and the Disloyal: Social Boundaries of Patriotism and Treason* (Chicago, 1956), p. 29; *Globe*, February 5, 1883, quoted in Morrison, "Mowat and Provincial Rights," p. 299; John Robarts remarked in the spring of 1971, that Ontario now had the "capability to devise and offer alternatives to major federal policies and programmes. While the alternatives are developed in Ontario, they cannot be based only on an Ontario standpoint. Rather, if they are to serve Ontario's interest, they must repre-sent national alternatives, and by national I do not mean simply federal. They must be based on a recognition of the fact that what is good for Canada is good for Ontario . . . ," *Globe and Mail*, April 20, 1971.

[33] J. M. S. Careless, " 'Limited Identities' in Canada," *Canadian Historical Review*, L (1969), pp. 1-10.

committed themselves fully to the cause of provincial rights and so given expression to Ontario's particularism or, as some might say, its imperial ambitions. In this they have reflected the desire of Ontarians to fasten their version of Canadian nationalism upon the rest of the country, making little copies of what they see as the "real" Canada.

Where Mowat led his successors have followed. He taught them all the moves: how to rally the other provinces against Ottawa; when to form accords and when to go it alone; above all, he revealed the value of persistence and tenacity. He was not an enemy of the national spirit, but one who understood how it would develop in a new country, by grafting itself onto older, deeper, loyalties. His vision of Canada's development was different from Macdonald's, but time has proved him more far-sighted. When the Ontario legislature met in 1897, that stubby, determined, myopic figure was absent from the premier's chair for the first time in a quarter of a century. Andrew Pattullo recalled his past triumphs for the cause of provincial rights. "In this long series of constitutional victories," Pattullo told the Assembly,

> lies perhaps Oliver Mowat's highest claim to enduring fame and everlasting gratitude of his countrymen. For it was essential to the stability and very existence of Confederation that the rights and privileges of the Provincial and Federal Governments should be clearly and justly defined. Without such just consideration and protection of the rights of the Provinces by the Privy Council, it is quite certain that the Provinces would not have remained in the same union.[34]

---

[34] *Globe*, February 12, 1897.

Part Two

Health, Emigration and Welfare in Kingston 1820-1840

MARGARET ANGUS

Oliver Mowat arrived in Kingston only five days after the arrival of one who was to become an even more famous Kingstonian—John Alexander Macdonald. Oliver, born on July 22, 1820, to John and Helen Levack Mowat, was a native Kingstonian. John A., then five years old, was an immigrant—or to apply the official term then in use—an Emigrant. It was typical of the imperial attitude that settlers were designated, not as coming into Canada, but as leaving the British Isles.

John A. was one of the fortunate immigrants. Although his father came with the hope of bettering himself and had no job waiting for him, the Macdonald family was welcomed into the household of well-to-do relatives, the Donald Macphersons. Oliver's father, too, had been an immigrant. He had served in Canada with the 3rd Buffs during the War of 1812 and, on procuring his discharge, returned to Canada to enter business in

Kingston.[1] John Mowat also followed the pattern set by many of the discharged soldiers who had served in Canada. He established himself in business before sending to the old country for the girl who became his wife.

There were, however, an increasing number who came to Canada with little or no knowledge of the country. They had neither friends nor relatives to greet them and no jobs awaiting their arrival. Great numbers of these immigrants were attracted by the promise of cheap land, which would give them, so they were told, a new life in contrast to the misery and hopelessness they had left behind. The British government not only encouraged voluntary emigration, but also pointed out to British parishes the wisdom of assisting the emigration of the parish paupers.

It was a way of ridding the country of "the suffering wants of the lower classes" who had been given enough "only barely to keep them in existence and quiet."[2] William Cattermole, who lectured on the subject in Colchester and Ipswich, said emigration "ought to be considered a far more rational mode of disposing of the young men, than by advising them to enter the army, generally rendering them useless in after life, and no actual relief to the country; while by emigration every pauper so removed, with reasonable industry, may become in 3 years from his landing in Canada, an occupier, instead of remaining a mill-stone round the neck of his native country."[3] He said further, "it is by no means to the interest of the mother country, that her small capitalists should emigrate, and that her unemployed able-bodied agricultural labourers (paupers), should be left at home."[4] Of course, it was not only the distressed agricultural workers who emigrated. There were also mechanics and labourers who dreamed of owning some land or, at least, looked for a better life in the new province. And a number of men who might have been called

[1] Robert McGill Mowat, *Genealogy and Story of the Mowat Family* (unpublished manuscript).
[2] William Cattermole, *Emigration; the Advantages of Emigration to Canada* (London, 1831), p. 114.
[3] *Ibid.*, p. 115.
[4] *Ibid.*, p. 124.

"small capitalists" joined the migration. But, "the introduction of English population into those colonies will tend in the end to furnish a very valuable market for the sale of the manufactures of this country. . . ."[5] So emigration, of whatever sort, would be beneficial to the mother country.

The great surge of assisted and voluntary emigration in this period did certainly relieve the mother country of "redundant population." And almost all of it was of consequent benefit to the emigrants and to Canada. The influence of immigration on Upper Canada in settlement, development, economics and politics has been the subject of many studies, usually general and fairly brief. But the effect of that immigration on a place such as Kingston has seldom been examined.

Urban life—if we can dignify it by that term—was generally neglected by contemporary writers. Many an English traveller included only brief mention of lake ports in what purported to be his definitive study of life in the provinces. The experience gained in a summer tour of Canada and the United States resulted in a sort of tourist's guide to bad roads, poor beds, worse meals and the horrors of republicanism. Some family letters gave intimate glimpses of domestic life in a larger settlement, but few mention anything but family affairs. It is the advertisements, editorial comments and brief local notes in contemporary newspapers that provide a view of the municipal scene. From these comes the story of Kingston's health and welfare problems created by the immigrants.

Immigrants destined for Upper Canada, with very few exceptions, came to or through Kingston. After a journey of five or six weeks by sea and river, Kingston must have seemed a welcome haven. A busy harbour, crowded wharves, glimpses of a church spire and substantial buildings were as attractive to the homesick and travel-weary immigrants as the feel of solid land beneath their feet.

In 1820, Kingston with a population of over three thousand,

---

[5] *Ibid.*, p. 128.

counting the garrison, had advantages—and problems—not found in other lake ports. It was the British naval base on the Great Lakes. Though that advantage had been diminished by the Rush-Bagot Treaty, the skills of the shipbuilders had been put to use on commercial vessels. Proximity to the American shore was sufficient reason for the defence construction which maintained a good level of employment and provided some competition with domestic building.

In the thriving commercial port, the ships kept the wharves occupied and the storehouses full. And trade also filled the pockets, or the credit columns in the account books, of the merchant-forwarders. Hoteliers and innkeepers prospered from the travellers who broke their journeys at Kingston. But the so-called "emigrant season" brought a different kind of traveller in numbers far beyond the capacity of the town's accommodation. The assisted, the voluntary, the provident or the improvident had to have a place to sleep, food to eat, water to drink. They also needed some sanitary facility, whether it was called "the usual offices," "the necessary house" or, simply, "the privy pit."

Not many of those needs could be easily met. Kingston, built in a compact area close to the wharves, was on a rocky promontory enclosed by water and by woods. Except for military and naval reserves and the clergy reserve plot, all land was privately owned. Only one swampy area near the Rideau (Cataraqui) River was available to temporary squatters. Most immigrants simply stayed on the wharves near their small piles of belongings until their transportation up the lake was arranged.

In the expanding community the sanitary provisions for the town itself caused problems. With limestone so close to the surface the residents had difficulty in any excavation, big or small. And too often the privy pits were close to the wells. The consequent seepage through cracks in the limestone polluted many wells. The main source of water was from the carters who filled their puncheons from the river or from the lake along the Front Road, west of the town limits. As long as the water looked clean and had no offensive taste it was considered to be safe to drink. Most households had a rain barrel and the bigger houses were equipped with a system of pipes to bring rain water from the eavestroughs into a cistern.

Those same big houses and the hotels and inns employed "night soil" carters to clear their "necessary houses." The dumping of night soil was controlled by the magistrates under the regulation that gave them authority over "slaughter houses and nuisances." They ruled that such night soil could be hauled in the summer only between the hours of 11 P.M. and 3 A.M. and it could not be dumped within the town limits. The carters easily complied with those provisions except in the winter months when they dumped the contents of their carts on the ice in the harbour, not very far from shore. A small sewer system was installed in the early 1830s and was extended in 1837.[6]

However, these conveniences were not available to the immigrants encamped on the wharves. The travellers who could not afford to stay or even to eat at a waterfront inn made use of the immediately available facilities—the water in the slips and under the docks. The resulting sickness probably became evident only after they were on their journey up the lake—that is, if transportation was soon available.

One of the assisted groups of immigrants was not able to continue its journey in time to avoid the health problem. In 1825, between the 2nd and the 30th of July, eight shiploads of Irish came to Kingston. They had emigrated under the auspices of Peter Robinson, who had a plan to settle them on lands he had secured in the present Peterborough area. But no arrangements had been made for their reception in Kingston or for the continuation of their journey to their new homes. A total of 1,942 immigrants had landed in Kingston by the end of July and there was no word from Peter Robinson.[7]

Sir Peregrine Maitland appointed Colonel Burke to be deputy superintendent in charge of the immigrants in Kingston until

[6] *British Whig*, October 1837.
[7] H. T. Pammett, *The Emigration from Ireland to Upper Canada under Peter Robinson in 1825* (Queen's M.A. thesis, 1934).

Robinson arrived. The Irish were housed in army tents erected on the marshy land near the river. It was an intensely hot summer; the mosquitoes were bad. There were over three hundred cases of malarial fever and thirty-three of the immigrants died. Robinson arrived in Kingston on August 10 and reported that the immigrants were "as comfortable as could reasonably be expected."[8] On August 11 the first lot of five hundred embarked for Cobourg; it was the middle of September before the last of the Robinson group left Kingston.[9]

That health and welfare problem had been handled by government authorities—another advantage available in a garrison town such as Kingston. The town itself had no capability for coping with a problem even one-tenth that size. The magistrates of the Midland District, who administered the town, relinquished their welfare responsibilities in 1819.

NOTICE

The Magistrates having thought proper to discontinue the appropriating any part of the funds of the Midland District for the maintenance of Paupers: It now becomes the duty of each County and Township to make provision for their support. A meeting therefore of the Inhabitants of the County of Frontenac is requested at the Court House in Kingston, on Tuesday, the Fifteenth day of June next, for the purpose of providing the necessary means for their subsistence.

> Kingston, May 28, 1819
> Thomas Markland J.P.
> Peter Smith J.P.
> Lawrence Herchmer J.P.
> William Mitchell J.P.
> G. H. Markland J.P.[10]

The June 15 meeting agreed to collect one farthing on the pound on the rateable property of every individual within the

---

[8] Peter Robinson Papers, quoted in E. Guillet, *Valley of the Trent* (Toronto, 1957).
[9] Pammett, *op. cit.*
[10] *Kingston Chronicle*, June 4, 1819.

townships of Kingston, Pittsburg and Wolfe Island for the maintenance of the poor. They provided, however, that the landowner
might or might not allow his property to be so taxed.[11]

Charity had been dispensed by individuals or through the
churches in Kingston until 1817 when the Kingston Compassionate Society was organized. The stated purpose of this society was
to provide for "the relief of the sick poor in their own homes and
to forward destitute emigrants to their place of destination."[12] The
society supported the 1819 campaign to raise funds for a charity
hospital in Kingston. But that campaign failed when the magistrates discontinued funds for the maintenance of the poor. Para-
graph XII in the Compassionate Society Laws and Regulations
said "In no instance shall this Charity extend to persons who are
entitled to relief from District Funds." But with no district funds
available all donations then had to be used for immediate aid to the
destitute. There were sick poor who could not be cared for in their
own homes and boarding houses were neither cheap nor easily
available. The Compassionate Society received permission to use
one of the empty blockhouses. One room was fitted up as a hospital
"to avoid the expence attending the board of sick persons."[13] It
was intended to be only a temporary expedient. The society
expressed publicly the "inconvenience arising from the want of a
hospital as an asylum for the destitute sick."[14]

In the fall of 1820 the charity work in Kingston was reorganized;
the Compassionate Society split into two groups. To help destitute
immigrants, the men formed a short-lived Emigrant Society. The
ladies organized the Female Benevolent Society to care for the sick
poor. It was a carefully structured Protestant group, mainly Anglican, but the three directresses were an Anglican, a Presbyterian
and a Wesleyan Methodist. The relief work for the sick was thus
concentrated in a more efficient cooperative organization.

The ladies of the Female Benevolent Society operated a hospital

[11] *Kingston Chronicle*, June 18, 1819.
[12] *Kingston Gazette*, December 7, 1817.
[13] *Kingston Chronicle*, November 1819.
[14] *Kingston Chronicle*, February 18, 1820.

—really just a hostel—for the next twenty years. The hospital, first in blockhouses then in an old warehouse, was opened in November and closed in May, providing food and shelter during the winter months. (I have not found an explanation of what happened to the patients still in that hospital when it was closed on May 1). Medical care at no charge was offered by the local directors to the poor both in and out of the hospital.

As the town grew the work of the Female Benevolent Society also grew. Support for their work increased and the ladies were able to fit up a second and a third room in the blockhouse. Then the beginning of the work on the Rideau Canal brought immigrants to Kingston who caused major problems in both health and welfare.

The great bulk of manpower for the clearing, excavation and construction of the canal was provided by Irish immigrants. Peter Robinson brought out two more shiploads of Irish to join the labourers, estimated at two to three thousand, working on the canal.[15] Accidents and especially the swamp fever, a severe type of malaria, forced many of the labourers to leave their work on the canal and go to the nearest community for help. By the end of the first summer (1827) the effect of this influx was felt in Kingston.

> There is scarcely a Hut or log-house here but is filled with sick and needy who are suffering, not only from Disease, but also from Hunger, and from almost every other misery concomitant upon the want of the common necessaries of life. . .
> . . . so much distress . . . and principally occasioned I understand, by the numerous labourers returning from the Rideau Canal, where they have fallen victims of disease.[16]

When the Female Benevolent Society reopened its hospital in November 1827, the ladies had to limit admittance to the sick poor

---

[15] Robert Legget, *Rideau Waterway* (Toronto, 1955), p. 48.
[16] P.A.C., Upper Canada Sundries, R. W. Tunney to Hillier, Kingston, October 24, 1827.

in the town and refuse those from the country. The need for a charity hospital increased each year, as did the need for funds for the society. In 1829, "certain inhabitants of the town of Kingston" applied for a government grant to assist the work of the Female Benevolent Society. A grant of £150 arrived the next May when the hospital closed for the summer.

A year later it was evident that a few rooms in a deserted block-house, with a steward the only attendant, did not meet the need of a charity hospital for Kingston. Furthermore, private charity and volunteer help could not supply the necessary funds or the staff. The care of the sick poor in Kingston could no longer be handled by individual humanitarian efforts, however well they were organized.

But there was a very limited concept of the government's role in health. The authorities were concerned, at first, only in protecting citizens and their property from major disasters. The official attitude was, in effect, "From fire and pestilence, good Lord, deliver us." Positive efforts in prevention and in care of the sick had to be initiated by the citizens themselves. The successful local management of a crisis was often followed by government action to establish health controls or to give assistance to a local organization—after the fact.

The citizens of Kingston met on September 16, 1831, and resolved to set up a fund to build a hospital. They also directed a committee to consider making a request for government assistance.[17] By October 1 nearly £1000 had been subscribed to the fund. With this evidence of local participation and support the committee decided it was the right time to apply for government assistance. On January 28, 1832, the Eleventh Parliament passed an act granting £3000 "in aid of the erection of an Hospital in or near the Town of Kingston." John Macaulay, Dr. James Sampson and Dr. E. W. Armstrong were appointed as "commissioners for superintending and managing the erection and completion of the

---

[17] *Kingston Chronicle*, September 17, 1831.

said hospital, and for purchasing or otherwise obtaining, choosing and determining the site thereof."

Some citizens objected strongly to building a hospital in the town, saying that a hospital was an affliction rather than an object to be desired. The commissioners selected a site near the town, on the lakeshore to the west. They conferred about plans with officials of the Montreal General Hospital, whose building was then just ten years old. No matter how quickly decisions were made there was little chance of having the new building ready for the winter season. Another emigrant season was approaching and the opening of the Rideau Canal was scheduled for May 1832. Even more than the usual number of immigrants could be expected to come to Upper Canada to take up the new land thus opened for settlement.

The government did not yet provide direction and assistance to these immigrants. However, in 1832, Lieutenant-Governor Sir John Colborne did urge citizens throughout the province to form emigrant societies for the purpose of finding work for emigrants labourers and mechanics, and land for new farmers. Kingstonians, on April 25, 1832, organized the Emigrant Society of the Midland District.[18]

But the influx of immigrants into Upper Canada brought a need for more than job placement. The health and welfare problems caused by the normal needs of immigrants could be classed as minor nuisances compared to the disasters caused by the cholera epidemics over the next fifteen years. Out of the tragedies of those early epidemics grew the regulations and controls which form the basis for modern public health legislation.

By early June of 1832 word came that cholera had been discovered in ships arriving at Quebec and Montreal. Soon it would reach Kingston; that was inevitable if any immigrants came up river. On June 14, Kingstonians at a public meeting resolved to adopt measures to prevent the spread of cholera which had already reached Kingston. A committee agreed to clean up the town and

[18] *Kingston Chronicle*, April 17, 1832.

to set up a Board of Health to take certain further measures when necessary.

On June 17 the first death from cholera was reported in the town. The yellow flag was raised on the market place near the harbour. All troops were confined to their barracks and their families were moved to an encampment on Point Henry to institute a close quarantine. The magistrates met in special session. The *Chronicle* reported on June 18 that no boat was to enter the harbour until inspected by the Health Officer. Any master who entered the harbour with a sick or dead person aboard his boat would be fined. The dead were to be buried five miles from the town. All carters were directed to be ready to take, on a doctor's order, persons to the hospital about to be provided.

Three days later the *Chronicle* reported that the Central Board of Health had asked Ordnance for twelve tents to be erected on John Strange's land near the cholera hospital. Dr. Thomas Robison had been appointed Health Officer, and Dr. Evans of the 70th Regiment was in charge of the cholera hospital. On June 23 the *Chronicle* carried a letter from the lieutenant-governor urging citizens of the province to form boards of health and to establish hospitals for the reception of patients. Kingstonians read the item with some satisfaction, being a step ahead of the government. Cholera came with the immigrants to Kingston and ran its course. In October the quarantine was lifted and the cholera hospital was closed.

The lessons learned in that past summer did not go to waste. In February 1833, the third session of the Eleventh Parliament passed "An Act to establish Boards of Health, and to guard against the introduction of Malignant, Contagious and Infectious Diseases in this Province." It provided that the governor might appoint health officers where he deemed it necessary. Those officers were to have the right to enter into and examine the premises of individuals residing within their jurisdiction. They might order the proprietor to clean the premises, or might cause the premises to be cleaned.

The act further provided that the governor-in-council might

make rules concerning the entry and departure of vessels and the landing of passengers "best calculated to preserve the public health." Penalties for disobeying health officers ranged from twenty shillings to twenty pounds. Sir John Colborne appointed John Kirby, a Kingston member of the Legislative Council, as chairman of the Kingston Board of Health. Dr. Thomas Robison was secretary and the members were the politically important men of the town and four doctors. Eight administrative divisions were set up covering the town and immediate area. During the emigrant season the board met each Tuesday at noon.

In 1834 a much more severe epidemic of cholera came to Kingston with the immigrants. Thousands were ill and over three hundred deaths were reported. The *British Whig* said that the deaths reported to the Board of Health were very few in comparison to the actual mortality. The number of deaths among Kingstonians was much higher than in the previous epidemics. And the sad result was the need for more charity to support the great number of widows and orphans among the townspeople as well as among the immigrants.

The hospital building near the town was completed in 1835—or as nearly completed as the funds would allow. The inside had not been painted, no baths or water closets had been installed. There was not one stick of furniture in the building and there were no funds either to maintain it or to operate it as a hospital. In spite of repeated and urgent requests the government had failed to pass an act to endow the hospital because the legislators could not agree on the source of the endowment. The commissioners of the Kingston Hospital appealed once again for a grant of £500 to enable them to finish and furnish this public charity institution.

The Female Benevolent Society continued to operate their wintertime hospital until disaster struck. On December 21, 1835, the old building the society used was destroyed by fire. One patient died and the other ten were placed in private homes. The ladies lost all the material they had accumulated over the years, and the funds of the society were reduced to a mere £6.

The Female Benevolent Society did not elect new officers at the annual meeting in April 1836. According to the editor of the *Chronicle and Gazette*, the ladies expected legislative support for the new town hospital. That would fill the need, so they thought, which the Female Benevolent Society had supplied for so many years. But without legislative support the new hospital did not open, the society was dormant and charity was again left to church organizations and to individuals.

That spring of 1836 came notice of another type of immigrant, mentioned some years earlier by a Select Committee of the House of Commons. "Among the pauper poor it is probable a considerable number would gladly send their children to Canada under the protection of the government, to be provided for, and to relieve themselves of a burthen . . . the parishes in London . . . would very willingly facilitate the emigration of children. . . . Many of these children are orphans and bastards, without any person to look after them. . . ."[19]

This notice appeared in the *Kingston Chronicle and Gazette* on May 7, 1836:

CHILDREN'S FRIEND SOCIETY

The Public are respectfully informed, that 70 Boys and 30 Girls from the above Society are expected to arrive in Montreal by the 20th May current, and a great proportion of them will be conducted to Kingston immediately in charge of the Secretary. Those children have been trained in the Society's Asylums at Home, to habits of industry, and instructed in moral and religious duties. The Girls will be apprenticed as domestic servants to families, and the Boys to mechanics, farmers and others.

Terms—Ten Dollars per annum, Seven of which to be invested in the Savings Bank, for the benefit of the child, and Three Dollars to be remitted to the Society annually. In the event of a Boy deserting his Master's service, without any ill usage on the part of his master, the monies invested in the Savings Bank will revert back to the master.

John Orrok, Secretary for the Canadas

[19] Cattermole, *op. cit.*, p. 137.

> Persons desirous of having these children, are requested
> to apply at the Office of the Chronicle and Gazette. Letters
> to be free of charge.

On June 20 a Branch Committee was established at Kingston for the reception and distribution of children in the Midland District. The men on the committee were mostly Anglican. John Orrok, the Canadian secretary of the Children's Friend Society, informed the public, through the columns of the *Chronicle and Gazette* that he had, to date, received only fifteen children. He expected the remainder, eighty-five boys and girls, to arrive in the course of the season and the applications already received would be attended to. Since the same notice continued to appear for the remainder of the season we can presume that no more children from the society arrived in Kingston.

The government appointed emigrant agents that year, 1836, who would "on application, afford Emigrants information relative to the Crown Lands for sale . . . and the conditions on which they may be obtained." Mr. Anthony Manahan was appointed emigrant agent for the Midland District.[20] The agents were also expected to inform the immigrants how to reach the available lands or where work might be had.

Mr. Manahan's duties as emigrant agent were further widened according to a notice in the July 16, 1836, issue of the *Chronicle and Gazette*.

JOHN CLANCY or DAVID CLANCY

> who emigrated from the County Cork some four years past,
> are informed that the infant children of John Whelan, and
> Ellen Clancy their sister, are now in Kingston under charge
> of Mary Daly, their mother having died on the passage out.
> The children are destitute, and the uncles are requested to
> come speedily to their assistance.
>
> Further information may be had on application to Mr.
> Manahan.
>
> Kingston 16 July 1836

[20] *Kingston Chronicle and Gazette*, June 11, 1836.

Welfare had become a greater problem than health or, at least, of more concern to the government. The boards of health had relieved the government of some responsibility but adequate provision for the destitute was yet to come. Once again local groups initiated welfare plans. The St. Patrick's, St. Andrew's and St. George's Societies offered help to the members of their religious groups. The Female Benevolent Society took up its work once more but this time with a different emphasis—the promotion of industry among the poor.

The ladies solicited from local citizens work which could be done by the widows and orphans. In the case of a mother with small children the society members would deliver the work and arrange for it to be picked up later. The ladies often took the opportunity to deliver also a lecture on the virtues of cleanliness and hard work and the awful evils of intemperance.

Actually the level of employment was high in Kingston over the rebellion years and while Kingston was the capital of the United Provinces. There seemed then no need to put into effect the Provincial Act of March 1837 about Houses of Industry. Under that act the Justices of the Peace—the magistrates—were to provide "suitable Buildings for the reception of the Poor and Indigent, and of the Idle and Dissolute . . . where they shall be kept diligently employed in labour."

It is likely that Kingston's method of welfare provided a little better segregation than did the provisions of the act. Ten years after the act was passed a House of Industry was established in Kingston. By that time the Female Benevolent Society had become the Widows' and Orphans' Friend Society and concentrated its efforts on that particular welfare problem. So although the widows and orphans were kept at the House of Industry with the idle and dissolute, their welfare was of special concern to the ladies of the society.

In 1838, after seven years of petitions, Kingston was incorporated as a town. The town council could then exert a measure of control over their own affairs that had not been possible under the Midland District regime. On August 20, 1838, the Common

Council passed a by-law to establish a Board of Health in the town of Kingston. The board, to be appointed by the council, was to consist of the mayor and four members of the council. Although it was only intermittently effective or even active, the Board of Health justified its existence in crises, such as those caused by cholera epidemics. But welfare problems—not of crisis proportions —continued to be more dependent on the humanitarian impulses of Kingstonians, whether individual or organized, than on the welfare provisions of the council. The emigrant season caused crises in both health and welfare even to the middle 1850s.

Orangeism in
Ontario Politics, 1872-1896

HEREWARD SENIOR

When Oliver Mowat took office in 1872, Orangeism had been established in the province for over two generations. Although the lodges continued to serve first-generation Irish Protestants, they had become a familiar part of the Ontario landscape, and had acquired a large following among native Canadians and Protestant immigrants without Irish background. As the province itself founded colonies in the West and the first signs of industrialization appeared, Canadians of Orange background began leaving rural Ontario for the prairies and the larger cities. Many who left the older centres, such as Perth and Brockville, went West, but some went to Toronto and Hamilton where they might meet cousins recently arrived from Belfast and Londonderry.

These Orangemen were, for the most part, skilled workmen and substantial farmers, with a keen sense of their own respectability. A large number of Orangemen and women belonged to temperance lodges, although there were Orange lodges in which the proposal of numerous toasts frequently provided the pretext for heavy drinking. There was also a rowdy element among Orangemen which delighted in tavern brawls and riots on the Twelfth of July. Within this element were many unskilled labourers, often the employees of more substantial Orangemen. Many of the rowdy Orangemen were also members of the militia, and on St. Patrick's Day in 1863 a serious riot in Toronto only seems to have been prevented by calling out the volunteer militia and keeping them in the armouries.[1]

Although the majority of Orangemen was drawn from the lower classes, this was seldom reflected in their leadership. In the early days of the movement, tavern owners had often been masters of primary lodges, and they continued to play an important role. Yet even in the early days, Orangemen preferred leaders with social prestige and were particularly partial to retired military officers; but by Mowat's time clergymen, lawyers, medical doctors, teachers and small businessmen were more often masters of local lodges and members of the Grand Lodge. Most Orange leaders were also Masons, and the Orange lodges provided an organization, modelled on the Masonic system, which the lower classes could afford to join and which was adjusted to their needs.

For these Orangemen, there was a need for the kind of welfarism which was, in other instances, provided by Catholic Hibernian societies and "sick and death benefit" societies organized by socialists in continental Europe. Orangemen had always been under the obligation to help one another. In some instances, this had meant joining in donnybrooks or helping guilty Orangemen evade justice, but it also meant finding work for a brother Orangeman, caring for indigent Orange families and, above all, providing decent burial for the deceased Orangemen. In small rural communities with a relatively stable population, these services could be provided by a primary lodge, but in large communities some kind of an insurance society was essential.

The need to have the Orange lodges legally incorporated was

---

[1] C. P. Stacey, "A Fenian Interlude: The Story of Michael Murphy," *Canadian Historical Review*, XV (June 1934), pp. 142-45.

becoming increasingly necessary. Without an Act of Incorporation, Orange property and money had to be held in trust by individuals, which, in one case at least, resulted in a loss of $20,000[2] to the Order when this amount was embezzled by the person entrusted with it. Although the bill involved nothing more than ownership of property, it was a difficult bill for a Liberal and, presumably, anti-Orange government to pass. At the same time it was difficult for individual members, conscious of the Orange vote, to reject. In 1873 an Orange incorporation bill was passed, indicating that it had the support of many Liberal members in the Ontario legislature. Mowat, who was reluctant to make an issue of Orangeism, voted for the bill, but all other members of his government voted against it.[3] As a result, the bill was reserved by the lieutenant-governor and the federal government refused to act, on the grounds that ownership of property was a provincial matter. Some indication of the importance which Catholics attached to this bill is given in a letter sent to Sir John A. Macdonald by the Roman Catholic bishop of Hamilton who wrote:

> Unless that incorporation bill is kicked out of the Dominion Parliament, as it should be, you will not have a Catholic supporter of your administration. . . . Toronto, by referring the matter to Ottawa, appears to have been playing a dangerous game. Now is your chance if you wish to annihilate the Grit influence over the Catholics of Ontario. If the Orangemen are incorporated and taken under the patronage of the Government, how can we set our faces against fenian and similar societies?[4]

Subsequent incorporation bills were rejected by the Ontario legislature and opposed by Mowat, who contended that it was now possible for the lodges to be incorporated under a general act

[2] Canada, House of Commons, *Debates*, March 19, 1883, p. 258.
[3] *Annual Proceedings of the Grand Lodge of the Loyal Orange Association of British North America*, 1873, p. 11; see Grand Master Bowell's annual address.
[4] P.A.C., Macdonald Papers, MG 26A, Bishop John Farrell to Macdonald, April 25, 1873.

respecting benevolent societies.[5] These debates on Orange incorporation resulted in vigorous attacks on Orangeism, the most formidable attack being made in 1878 by the chairman of the Board of Works, C. F. Fraser, a Roman Catholic from Brockville. As Brockville was the cradle of Canadian Orangeism and the former residence of Ogle Gowan, Fraser was understandably conscious of the Orange bloc vote. The burden of his argument was that the passage of the incorporation bill would create an Orange ascendancy in Ontario which would have fatal consequences for the Grits and for Catholics, although he admitted that there were "some rare birds . . . some Reformers in the Orange order . . . but they owe their presence there to causes which have now ceased to be operative."[6] These causes he defined as fears of papal aggression which had been shared by Orangemen and Reformers. He suggested that Reformers were not welcome in the lodges and offered evidence that Tory Orangemen were trying to keep them out. At the same time, Fraser attacked those Catholics who supported an alliance of the "Orange and the Green," declaring that the Conservative party was Orange-dominated and its victory would result in the exclusion of Catholics from office.[7]

Fraser's speech was published in pamphlet form and marks the climax of debates on Orange incorporation in the Ontario legislative assembly. Much of what Fraser said about Orange hostility to Reformers could be applied to the Brockville area and to much of eastern Ontario generally, but was hardly applicable in western Ontario. The menace of an Orange conspiracy which he presented was obviously designed to separate Catholics and Conservatives but not likely to impress Conservative Catholics who seldom voted for Orangemen without some kind of compensation.

Mowat's majority continued to defeat Orange incorporation bills until 1882, when Orange leaders shifted their requests for an

[5] C. R. W. Biggar, *Sir Oliver Mowat, A Biographical Sketch*, (Toronto, 1905), I, p. 195.
[6] C. F. Fraser, *Speech delivered in Legislative Assembly of Ontario 25 February 1878 on Orange Incorporation Bill* (Toronto, May 1878).
[7] *Ibid.*

act of incorporation to the federal Parliament, and it was not until 1890 that the Order was incorporated finally by a federal act. This clearly indicates the limitations of the Orange bloc vote in Ontario, and it is significant that in Manitoba an Orange incorporation bill was passed in 1883.

To many Orangemen, the persistent defeat of what appeared to them a necessary and inoffensive measure seemed to suggest that Liberals like Fraser were acting as papal agents, but they found no consolation in the federal Conservative party being tied, as it was, to the *Bleu* interest. To understand the nature of the suspicions this aroused at the time, it is necessary to look beyond Ontario and even beyond Canada.

Mowat took office two years after the Vatican Council of 1870, and his administration coincided with Bismarck's *Kulturkampf* and the re-emergence of militant anti-clericalism in the United States, inspired by the fear of the emigrant bloc vote. Beyond that, there was the question of Western Canada, where the French language and culture had been granted parity in the new province of Manitoba. Yet more immediate in the seventies was the surviving question of the rights of the Protestant population of Quebec, which had led to serious tension in the fifties during the Gavazzi riots and the Corrigan affair. It is important to observe that the redoubtable Father Charles Chiniquy, who had been converted to temperance in the thirties and protestantism in the fifties, became an Orangeman in the seventies.[8] And Protestants who thought themselves or their secularist friends in danger from the Catholic hierarchy were likely to turn towards the Orange movement because it was the largest and most formidable organization of militant Protestants. Anti-clerical editors like Luther Holton in Montreal and George Brown in Toronto exercised wide influence on the reading public and even on the electorate, but they had no network of societies capable of bringing non-intellectuals to the polls or of putting crowds into the street.

While Liberals condemned the Orange lodges as instruments

---

[8] Marcel Trudel, *Chiniquy* (Trois Rivières, 1955), pp. 32, 229, 252; Anon, *Les Orangistes* (Montreal, c. 1878), p. 11.

of toryism, they recognized the existence of an "Orange public opinion" and sought to influence the policies of the lodges. This usually took the form of approving "Orange principles" while accusing Orange leaders of betraying them for political motives. As there were dissident Orangemen willing to present Grit views in most parts of the province, it was possible to turn lodges into forums and to make it difficult and, in some cases, impossible for Conservative Orangemen to deliver an Orange bloc vote.

Orangeism in Mowat's time, then, represented an embryo form of welfarism and a reserve army of militant protestantism, alerted by an international *Kulturkampf*. Yet, it also represented a militant, if somewhat limited, form of Canadian patriotism. The War of 1812 had, perhaps, created the foundation for a national patriotism in Canada,[9] but in the seventies King William was a more impressive figure than Laura Secord, not only because more Canadians had ancestors who had fought at the Boyne than at Lundy's Lane or Beaver Dam, but because the issues of the Boyne were still being contested.

Orangemen had not always been Canadian patriots. At the time of the dismissal of Henry J. Boulton and Christopher Hagerman in 1833, Ogle Gowan, the first Canadian Grand Master, had written, "If our Canadian fellow subjects are disposed to hoist the Canadian flag instead of the British, down with them, say we!"[10] Yet in 1867 Gowan wrote that old issues and party names should be forgotten, that "French and English, Protestant and Catholic, Whig and Tory, Clear Grit and Conservatives" were all merged in the Dominion of Canada. He urged that "hereafter, old distinctions, divisions and parties should be united under the generic and homogeneous name of Canadians. Let this be our future flag."[11]

Although racists and many who were susceptible to racist propaganda could be found in the Orange lodges even in Mowat's time,

[9] Paul Cornell, "The Genesis of Ontario Politics in the Province of Canada 1838-1871," *Profiles of a Province* (Toronto, 1967), p. 62.
[10] *Antidote*, Brockville, January 15, 1833.
[11] P.A.C., T. R. Ferguson Papers, MG 27 I-E 30, Ogle Gowan's address to the electors of Leeds, 1867.

it must be stressed that the lodges consistently repudiated racism. Ogle Gowan, in a lecture called "The Anglo-Saxon,"[12] emphasized the fact that his family was Celtic, and he suggested that had King William instead of King James commanded the Celts at the Battle of the Boyne, the results would have been reversed. Orange lodges have included French Canadians, Germans and Indians in their membership. This lack of racism was acknowledged in an anti-Orange pamphlet published in the seventies which declared, "L'orangisme en Canada est composé d'Anglais, d'Ecossais, d'hommes du nord de l'Irlande descendants d'ancêtres Anglo-hollandais, d'Indiens, de nègres, de renégats français, tels que Chiniquy et Doudiet, et de fait d'hommes de toutes races qui nourrissent de la haîne pour la religion catholique et pour les nations française et irlandaise, parce que ces dernières appartiennent à l'ancienne et véritable croyance."[13]

In the seventies, then, Orangemen thought of Canada as a melting pot, but they insisted on a Protestant and British mold. During his last session in Parliament, Gowan had found that the "force of things" was against the "French language."[14] Yet Gowan and many moderate Orangemen were prepared to let the "force of things" do its work. However, there was a widespread feeling among secularists and militant Protestants that there was a formidable conspiracy against the "force of things" and that the regular clergy and, in particular, the Jesuits, were its prime cause. As the lodges were, in their turn, regarded as a conspiracy by the Roman Catholics, the stage was set for the mutual sabotage of Orange and Catholic welfare work, with Catholics voting against Orange incorporation both in the Ontario and federal parliaments, and Orangemen seeking to prevent incorporation of Catholic charitable societies.

When Mowat became premier of Ontario in 1872, Thomas Scott was dead and Louis Riel was still at large. Many Orangemen felt that the balance of forces was against them and were inclined to

---

[12] Ogle Gowan, *The Anglo-Saxon* (c. 1853), T. R. Ferguson Papers, MG 27 I-E 30.
[13] *Les Orangistes*, p. 1.
[14] *Patriot*, Toronto, April 13, 1859.

blame the federal Conservative government which had evaded taking effective action against Riel. Mowat's predecessor, Edward Blake, had faced the issue by placing a reward of $5,000 on Riel's head, though he was denounced by Ogle Gowan as using this device to win Orange votes.[15] While Ontario Orangemen continued to nurse their resentment over the execution of Scott, the Ottawa-born Thomas Lett Hackett was shot to death in Montreal on his way home from an Orange meeting on July 12, 1877. Protestant indignation in Ontario was expressed without restraint. Some twelve hundred Orangemen from as far away as Kingston and Ottawa attended the funeral in Montreal, marching to Orange tunes played by the militia of the Eastern Townships. As the Grand Master of Kingston put it, "We have come to protect the Orangemen of Montreal on this occasion and woe betide this city if we have to come again."[16] Telegrams of sympathy were sent from most Orange centres in Ontario. A writer to the Catholic *True Witness* of Montreal expressed indignation and alarm because at a meeting in Toronto "a foreigner from Buffalo . . . was not only permitted, but encouraged, to declare that foreign Orangemen would come to Montreal next year to form part of an army of 20,000 men which had been demanded by the Orangemen of Montreal."[17]

What was behind these threats? In appearance, a great deal— perhaps one hundred thousand Ontario Orangemen backed by the moral force of Anglo-American Protestants. In fact, very little. When four hundred Orangemen attempted to parade in Montreal the following year, their procession was banned and they were besieged for several hours until Mayor J. L. Beaudry sent them home in cabs at the city's expense.[18] Telegrams of sympathy arrived from Toronto, but nothing more. The difficulties in sending Orangemen from eastern Ontario to Montreal were formidable,

---

[15] *Sentinel*, Toronto, July 3, 1930.
[16] J. C. Fleming, *Orangemen and the Twelfth of July Riots in Montreal* (Montreal, 1877), p. 41.
[17] *The Orange Question*, (Montreal, 1877), p. 13.
[18] *The True Witness*, Montreal, July 13, 1878.

but the lodges were capable of sending up to five thousand Orange-men to Montreal, if they cared to make the effort. Yet no effort was made. A partial explanation for this can be found in the comment of John White, the representative for Hastings, when speaking in the federal Parliament in 1883 on the Orange in-corporation bill. He declared that during the troubles in Montreal, when he was Grand Master of Ontario, he had prevented all but one lodge under his jurisdiction from proceeding to Montreal, and added: "If we get this Act of Incorporation, no Orangemen from Ontario will go to disturb the peace or hurt the feeling, or injure any party that resides there."[19] Although this statement has to be treated with caution, when considered in combination with the Orange inertia in 1878 it is possible that Orange leaders used their influence to discourage a march on Montreal in 1878.

Although Orangemen were prepared to act in defiance of consti-tuted authority, they disliked doing so. And it was not until the Northwest Rebellion of 1885 that they were able to confront a foe without confronting their own government. The Order claimed that 148 out of 250 men in the Royal Grenadiers were Orangemen, and that this was typical of most Ontario regiments serving in the West.[20] As the suppression of the rebellion was a purely Canadian effort, the character of the Canadian Volunteers could set the tone of the emerging national spirit. All Orangemen were agreed that the West would be Canadian, and that the character of Cana-dianism would be determined by Ontario. Those who accepted the language and values of Ontario were the agents of progress. Among those who held this point of view there was a division between those prepared to let history do its work and those who insisted on the ruthless suppression of anyone who "conspired against progress."

As the defeated enemy of progress, Riel could be forgiven, but Scott's death seemed to be one in a series of incidents, including Hackett's death and the earlier case of Corrigan in the fifties, when Protestants had been killed with impunity. Had Riel been par-

---

[19] Canada, House of Commons, *Debates*, April 16, 1883, pp. 656-57.
[20] L. H. Saunders, *The Story of Orangeism* (Toronto, 1960), p. 38.

doned there can be little doubt that a "Protestant party" would have emerged in Ontario, similar in some respects to the Mercier party which was formed in Quebec after the Riel execution. However, doubts can be raised about the power and permanence of a party based on feelings of indignation which might not survive from one election to the next. The Orange lodges could provide the nucleus for such a party; but, though powerful, they were not as strong as the Catholic Church in Quebec, and were distrusted by Liberal Protestants. The question of a new party did not arise, however, as the Orange grand master could reflect with satisfaction that "we rejoice to know, that, notwithstanding the varied influences brought to bear on the Government of the day, it had the moral courage to carry the just sentence into execution . . . which he [Louis Riel] ought to have met with when he embrued his hands in the blood of Thomas Scott."[21]

While Riel's execution ended the immediate possibility of an Orange revolt against Macdonald conservatism, it led to the emergence of the Mercier government in Quebec which passed the Jesuit Estates Act in the summer of 1888. To Orangemen and many others this was bound to be interpreted as a conspiracy against progress. Among those who accepted this view was the former Regius professor and free trader, Goldwin Smith. Secular and Liberal Protestant anti-clericals, like the Orangemen, distrusted conventional political parties whose leaders thought in terms of elections and majorities. Men like Goldwin Smith had influence and prestige but no effective links with the people. The links could be supplied by the Orange lodges, provided the Liberals were prepared to ignore the tory and imperialist sins of the Orangemen. Goldwin Smith made this sacrifice, and addressed the Toronto Orangemen on July 12, 1888, a fitting occasion for a Regius professor—the two-hundredth anniversary of the Glorious Revolution.[22]

---

[21] *Annual Proceedings of the Grand Lodge of the Loyal Orange Association of British North America*, 1886, p. 24.
[22] Goldwin Smith's address to the Orangemen, July 12, 1888, in Gowan scrapbook (privately held by Colonel T. A. Kidd, Kingston), p. 283.

Smith declared that he used to think that Orangeism had once served a useful purpose but could not do so in the future. He had been mightily mistaken. He protested that, "Orangeism did not want to deprive Roman Catholics of any privileges, honour or advantage . . . they only desired absolute equality. . . . But, unfortunately, Ultramontane Rome wanted domination. . . . The Orange Order must lead the Protestants of Canada in that resistance . . . the Prime Minister of this province is forced to pay homage to this power, and the Dominion Government rests, in no small measure, upon its support . . . the first battlefield will be in the public schools."[23]

Goldwin Smith's presence at the Orange meeting was an indication of the efforts of diverse individuals and groups of anti-clericals to create a pressure group capable of shaking the inertia of politicians. Such a group needed the inspiration of a powerful personality, and the much-needed leader was found in the person of D'Alton McCarthy, the most imposing of the "Noble Thirteen" who had voted for the annulment of the Jesuit Estates Act by the federal Parliament. Although not an Orangeman, McCarthy would draw most of his popular support from the Orange Order.

John A. Macdonald was convinced that the indignation would pass, but, writing on May 19, 1889, he admitted that he would not care to hold an election "just now."[24] The prime minister, who had once considered McCarthy his obvious successor, assumed that his independent stand involved nothing more than a re-emergence of the "independent conservatism" of the fifties which had been led by John Hillyard Cameron and others. Such "independence" had represented little more than an appeasement of the electorate by men as moderate as Macdonald himself. Yet Macdonald had misjudged the man and his times. McCarthy cared more for principle and popularity than for office, and perhaps preferred preaching to the exercise of power. Moreover, it was not, as in the fifties, largely a contest between the roughly equal forces of

---

[23] *Ibid.*
[24] Donald Creighton, *John A. Macdonald*: Vol. 2, *The Old Chieftain* (Toronto, 1955), p. 519.

Ontario and Quebec. Emigration and westward expansion had shifted the balance of power, and the anti-clericals were convinced not only of the righteousness of their cause but of their strength.

Yet the force of inertia was strong, and one powerful element in the inertia of ultra Protestantism was the Orange movement itself. When McCarthy resigned as president of the Liberal-Conservative Union of Ontario and founded the Equal Rights Association, he discovered that it was easier to attract crowds to public meetings than to change the voting pattern. The Grand Master of Ontario West, feeling that more resignations were needed, wrote to Clarke Wallace, Grand Master of the Canadian lodges, inviting him to "unite and organize for a contest at the next election and constitute yourself leader of the United Protestant Equal Rights Party . . . this is a very high hand to play, and it would perhaps ruin your prospects with the present conservative party."[25] Wallace was not yet ready to play a high hand but feeling was strong, and one Ontario lodge insisted that Orange lodges should refuse incorporation at the hands of the Parliament which had voted down the Noble Thirteen, "as it would endanger the success of the present efforts to abolish the French language and separate schools in Manitoba, the North West and Ontario and be most disastrous to British and Protestant civilization in Canada."[26]

Yet the risk of this disaster was accepted by the Grand Lodge when a bill to incorporate the Orange Order was passed in 1890 by the federal Parliament. At the Grand Lodge meeting in August 1890, the skill of Mackenzie Bowell and the political Orangemen was sufficient to smother the militant anti-clericals who undoubtedly expressed the sentiments of the majority of Orangemen. Bowell was able to report to Macdonald that "the malcontents such as Bell, the Equal Righter of Toronto, and John White soon found they had few if any sympathizers."[27] The *Sentinel* might call upon Orangemen "to take no political action unless in con-

---

[25] Public Archives of Ontario, Wallace Papers, W. W. Fitzgerald, Grand Master of Ontario West, to Clarke Wallace, 21 August, 1889.
[26] *Ibid.*, Resolution of Leamington Orange Lodge No. 563, November 7, 1889, to Thomas Keyes, Secretary, Grand Orange Lodge of British North America.
[27] Macdonald Papers, Bowell to Macdonald, August 21, 1890.

nection with a 'United Protestant Party' formed irrespective of political leaning,"[28] but neither Oliver Mowat nor opposition leader William Ralph Meredith, were prepared to provide a party which met this test.

Still, a test of strength could not be avoided. Anti-clerical sentiment was a powerful force, capable of developing at the grass roots if effective leadership could not be found among Conservative politicians or the Orange grand master. It was evident that public meetings inspired by the oratory of such personalities as D'Alton McCarthy could accomplish little, and that patient work was needed to create a pressure group which would either take over or supplant the existing Orange lodges. Nor is it surprising that when such a group was created, it would draw on the experience of American anti-clericals. Orangemen from Canada were active in the American movement and no other inspiration was at hand.

Neither Meredith nor Mowat were prepared to exploit Protestant sentiment in the provincial election of 1890, and John A. Macdonald diverted attention to his National Policy in his final election in 1891. Yet the rising spirit of anti-clericalism was never far below the surface, and if it could not dominate existing organizations, it would create institutions of its own. These were beginning to appear as the Equal Rights Association withered away, but they developed quietly without effective leadership from above.

The Protestant Protective Association, the P.P.A., which first appeared in the Windsor area toward the end of 1891, was modelled on the American Protective Association. The latter had been organized to oppose the Catholic bloc vote which was considered to have undue influence in the Grover Cleveland administration. In spite of its American inspiration, the P.P.A. was organized into local fraternal societies loyal to the British connection.[29] Yet it embodied the spirit of the "Know Nothing" party

---

[28] *Sentinel*, Toronto, February 21, March 17, June 20, 1889.
[29] James Watt, "Anti-Catholicism in Ontario Politics: the Role of the Protestant Protective Association in the 1894 Election," *Ontario History* (June 1967), vol. LIX, no. 2, pp. 58-59.

which was alien to the Orange tradition. Like the "Know Nothings," it stood openly for job discrimination against Catholics, offering the kind of single-minded anti-clericalism which was never able to dominate a movement as old and as complex as Orangeism.

That the P.P.A. would attract more militant Orangemen and many anti-clericals who were outside the Orange tradition was evident. As they were, at first, a small group without well-known leaders, their obvious course was to infiltrate organizations whose membership was susceptible to their views. In this they were amazingly successful, gaining influence not only in the Orange lodges but in the Conservative party and in the popularist Patrons of Industry.[30] Yet their influence was of a local and temporary nature, as they could not capture the Grand Lodge.

The potentialities of the P.P.A. were first noticed when it elected a member to the Ontario legislature in a by-election in 1893 and made substantial gains in the municipal elections of the same year. With the approach of the Ontario election of 1894, P.P.A. members were able to displace, take over, or make an alliance with Conservatives in most constituencies west of Toronto. This created special difficulties for the Orange Grand Master, Clarke Wallace, who was controller of customs in the government of Catholic Sir John Thompson. Wallace served as a link between the Conservative party and the lodges and he undertook the task of restraining primary lodges, which had come under the influence of the Patrons, from making declarations embarrassing to the leaders of the Conservative party. Wallace was soon attacked for having sold "Orange principles," while his salary of $4,000 as controller of customs was referred to as "the price of Orange support."[31] These personal attacks made it easier for Wallace to deal with opposition within the lodges, since the Grand Lodge empowered him to cancel the charter of any primary lodge which took too vigorous a

---

[30] *Ibid.*, pp. 62-64; see also Wallace Papers, R. Tyndhite, Bradford, to Clarke Wallace, November 26, 1894; *Gazette*, Montreal, June 16, 1894.
[31] Wallace Papers, Thomas Wood to Wallace, May 14, 1894, and James Hill, Detroit, to Wallace, September 1893, enclosing a clipping from *The Patriotic American* for September 2, 1893.

stand against Orangemen holding office.[32] This proved to be a formidable weapon, as Orange opponents of the P.P.A. who inspired resolutions condemning political Orangemen could now speak as defenders of Grand Lodge policy. The Grand Master's correspondence reveals the existence of dislike and fear of the P.P.A. among local Orangemen, but a reluctance to quarrel with them openly on the eve of an election.[33] The confusion which this created in the public mind about the exact relationship between the P.P.A. and the Conservatives is illustrated by the comments of an Orangeman who was defeated in a municipal election at Peterborough. He wrote to Clarke Wallace, "The Grits, the P.P.A.'s, and the Catholics voted for the same man. You can imagine how annoyed the latter are over their mistake. . . . These devils the P.P.A.'s will cause great dissension in our Order. . . . I am glad they defeated me. The Catholics now know that the Association is not in complete harmony with the Orange Order."[34]

Mowat's victory in 1894 was a clear indication of the limits of extreme and narrow anti-clericalism. Few felt menaced by the Catholics in the province and, with the loss of the election, the P.P.A. began to follow the Equal Rights Association into oblivion. But the Orange resistance to P.P.A. influence owed much to Clarke Wallace, and it was difficult to convince the electorate that Mowat was unduly partial to Roman Catholic interests. The Manitoba school question was more alarming. Although the federal election of 1896 belongs more to national than to Ontario history, it is important to understand that Wallace, by resigning from the government in 1895 and turning the majority of the Grand Lodge against the Conservatives, unleashed a more powerful if less extreme form of anti-clericalism. Yet even he could not deliver a united Orange vote in Ontario, although he delivered enough of it to ensure a Conservative defeat.

Orangeism in Mowat's Ontario provided for social needs which

[32] *Ibid.*, W. H. Scott to Wallace, August 22, 1893.
[33] *Ibid.*, A. G. Campbell to Wallace, January 5, 1894; R. Lyndhurst to Wallace, June 21, 1893; T. W. Sawyers to Wallace, August 15, 1893; W. R. Wade to Wallace, August 18, 1893; O. F. Wilkins to Wallace, September 7, 1893.
[34] *Ibid.*, T. W. Sawyers, Peterborough, to Wallace, January 2, 1894.

could not be supplied easily by other agencies. The number of Orangemen involved in various Orange social activities and benefits is difficult to estimate. As in the case of most voluntary organizations, the Grand Lodge could not form a precise idea of its total membership. While the number of men and women who had been members of the lodges at some time was perhaps one hundred thousand, the number of regular due-paying members was much less. Since many Orange warrants (that is, the authority to hold a lodge) were dormant, and membership in a single lodge might vary from a handful up to two hundred, the total number of lodges does not give much indication of the total membership. In good years, members may have numbered as many as sixty thousand, and in bad years perhaps half that number. For instance in 1880, the grand secretary admitted that "the progress of the Order has not been as flourishing as in the past,"[35] yet two years later the Grand Master of Ontario West claimed some "600 lodges with an average membership of fifty each, besides twice as many who are out on certificate."[36]

In politics the role of the Orangemen is difficult to explain. Sir Richard Cartwright's estimate that the Orangemen represented a voting strength of one hundred thousand in a voting population of half a million[37] is true only in the sense that this vote could be delivered under ideal conditions. Yet in 1878, on the eve of C. F. Fraser's attack on the menace of political Orangeism, the *Sentinel* lamented that, "Hitherto our strength has been more or less equally divided between the two great political parties . . . from neither of them have we received that even-handed justice which by our numbers and influence we are entitled."[38] Some years earlier, during the debates on the Orange incorporation bill of 1873, Fairbairn, a supporter of Mowat, declared that he did not believe that "the Orange body was a political organization or

[35] *Annual Proceedings of the Grand Lodge of the Loyal Orange Association of British North America*, 1880; see Grand Secretary's report, p. 3.
[36] *Report of the Proceedings of the Imperial Grand Council* (Belfast, 1882); see address of Major James Bennett, Grand Master of Ontario West.
[37] Sir Richard Cartwright, *Reminiscences* (Toronto, 1912), p. 89.
[38] *Sentinel*, Toronto, January 3, 1878.

its members would not be so divided."[39] He commented that formerly Orangemen were nearly all Conservatives but now many looked favourably on the Reform party. The difficulty in delivering the vote is demonstrated further by a speech of the Grand Master of Ontario West who represented South Simcoe in the federal Parliament in the early eighties. He declared, "There are Orangemen all over the Province, and notably in Toronto East, who have so far forgotten their duty to this loyal and Protestant society so as to ally themselves with the Grit-Republican party in the recent election, and in the latter case with a Roman Catholic who, if not a Fenian himself, is at any rate the brother of one who invaded our soil and murdered our brethren at Ridgeway."[40] As these statements indicate, the Grand Lodge could not deliver the entire Orange vote. Yet there was a series of local bloc votes, mostly east of Toronto, which consistently supported the Conservative party. Here, Liberals saw no point in conciliating Orangemen; elsewhere, Liberals might hope for Orange votes.

Oliver Mowat, whose loyalty and Protestantism were never seriously in doubt, did not present a convenient target for Orange Conservatives. Unlike Edward Blake, he made no direct attack upon Orangeism and left the main burden of defeating Orange incorporation to his ministers. To that extent, Mowat himself was a factor in keeping the Orange vote divided. One consequence of this division was that Orange Conservatives enjoyed very little of the patronage at the disposal of the provincial government. But they retained a substantial share of municipal patronage, particularly in Toronto, and could count on the favour of the federal Conservatives.

The part which Orangemen played in party politics was, in theory at least, the means of maintaining their long-term objectives of defending Protestantism against the permanent threat

---

[39] Canada, House of Commons, *Debates*, April 16, 1883, p. 649.
[40] *Ibid.*, March 17, 1884, p. 900.

posed by the existence of the Roman Catholic church and up-holding the crown and British connection in North America. But they never regarded themselves as a purely political organization. The fundamental purpose of the society was to preserve the memories of the "sacrifice" and "heroism" of the Irish tradition arising out of the Protestant community during the campaign of 1690 as a means of inspiring public and private virtue, not only in those born to the Orange tradition, but also among all men of goodwill. In pursuit of this purpose, they preserved a tradition which provided links between Canadian and British history and between Protestants in the various provinces of Canada. In so doing, they made a substantial contribution to a widely held, if somewhat narrow, conception of Canadian nationality.

Something Old, Something New . . . : Aspects of Prohibitionism in Ontario in the 1890s

GRAEME DECARIE

In the 1890s at least forty thousand Ontarians belonged to such organizations as the Sons of Temperance, the Independent Order of Good Templars and the Woman's Christian Temperance Union.[1] They were advocates of the legal prohibition of beverage alcohol and they were officially supported in this advocacy by the Methodist church, the Presbyterian church in Canada, the Congregational church and the Baptist Conference of Ontario and Quebec. They even enjoyed the declared support of many prominent politicians, among them G. F. Marter, leader of the Ontario Conservative party, and G. W. Ross, a member of Premier

---

[1] This is a very conservative estimate, for it excludes a multitude of organizations whose records have disappeared. It also excludes many which counted prohibition as only one of a number of objectives. The major sources for this estimate are: Canada, *Report of the Royal Commission on the Liquor Traffic* (Ottawa, 1895), p. 971; I.O.G.T., Grand Lodge of Canada, *Thirty-eighth Annual Session* (Toronto, 1891), p. 25; *Globe* (Toronto), February 21, 1893; and S. G. E. McKee, *Jubilee History of the Ontario Woman's Christian Temperance Union* (Whitby, n.d.), p. 5.

Mowat's cabinet. Such support was deserved, for the prohibition movement was at the centre of a furious struggle whose outcome would affect the province's political and social development. Curiously, the prohibition movement's position in the struggle was such that it had close ties with both the past and the future.

Some insight into the nature of the prohibition movement is to be found in the results of a plebiscite conducted by the government of Ontario in 1894. The question for the plebiscite was:

Are you in favour of the immediate prohibition by law of the importation, manufacture and sale of intoxicating liquors as a beverage?[2]

Of a male electorate just short of one-half million, over 288,000 cast votes, an impressive turnout for a plebiscite.[3] In addition, almost 13,000 women voted, as the franchise was extended to those women eligible for the municipal franchise. About 63 per cent of the popular vote favoured prohibition, and it is interesting to note that the prohibitionists were in the majority in both city and country, though to varying degrees. The county vote, mostly rural, showed 65 per cent of those voting to be in favour of prohibition. Support in the cities was somewhat less, at 58 per cent. Separated towns, midway between urban and rural status, were likewise midway in support for prohibition, at 61 per cent.

It was popularly held that Ontario Liberals, Methodists, Presbyterians and Baptists tended to be sympathetic to prohibition, but the results of the plebiscite gave support to no such notions. Prescott and Russell, for example, were staunchly Liberal, yet they were far the most hostile ridings to prohibition. Ottawa, in which prohibitionist churches were in the minority, gave 57 per cent of its popular vote to prohibition, a figure just one percentage point less than the average for all Ontario cities. Whatever views were held by the province's political and religious leaders, they

---

[2] R. E. Spence, *Prohibition in Canada* (Toronto, 1919), p. 206.
[3] The results of the plebiscite may be found in Spence, *op. cit.*, pp. 579-80.

do not seem to have been shared by their followers with any consistency.

It is on the map, rather than in tables of statistics, that the voting pattern for the 1894 plebiscite becomes evident. There were two blocs of counties in which the vote for prohibition was substantially higher than the provincial average.[4] In the east-central part of the province was a bloc consisting of Hastings, Northumberland, Durham and Peterborough. The other area began just west of Toronto and penetrated deeply into the Niagara peninsula. It consisted of Brant, Dufferin, Halton, Lambton, Middlesex, Norfolk, Oxford, Peel and Wentworth. Both blocs, except for the northern extensions of Hastings and Peterborough, were in the southern part of the province. Those counties in which the vote for prohibition was substantially lower than average were scattered across the province. In the east were Prescott and Russell, Renfrew and Frontenac. In the west were Waterloo and Essex.

The concentration of strongly prohibitionist counties in southern Ontario is graphically remarkable. All were in the most heavily populated part of the province and all were within easy reach of urban areas. In fact Peel county, which gave prohibition a full 88 per cent of the popular vote, was next to York county, which housed the city of Toronto. There may have been less support for prohibition in the cities than in the countryside, but proximity to urban centres seems to have been a factor in rural interest in prohibition.

The prohibition movement also seems to have reflected a certain tension between the middle class and the working class of Ontario. In the earlier part of the century the use of alcohol had been respectable among all classes, even for consumption by children. A chronicler reported:

> In many families, whiskey was served to each member of
> the houshold in the morning. It was considered to be a

---

[4] For purposes of this analysis, a deviation of 4 per cent from the provincial average was counted as substantial.

precaution against colds and to enable one to do hardy work.[5]

But by the 1890s such attitudes were on the wane. Not only did many churches frown on the drinking member but many fraternal societies such as the Odd Fellows, the Knights of Pythias and the Knights of Columbus closed their membership to those involved in the liquor business.

As respectability fell, so did consumption. The *Globe,* characteristically soft-pedalling the need for prohibition, said in 1890 that consumption had fallen so low it was no longer a matter for concern.[6] Certainly it had fallen greatly. In 1869, annual per capita consumption of spirits throughout Canada was well over one gallon.[7] By 1894, the figure was less than three-quarters of a gallon. For wine, the drop was from .115 gallon in 1869 to .089 gallon in 1894. Only beer rose, from slightly over two and three-quarter gallons to almost three and three-quarter gallons. Nor is it likely that official figures tell the whole story. Ontario was far more a rural province in 1869 than it was in 1894 and "home brew" is more readily made in rural than in urban areas.

These figures reflect another factor in drinking habits, the growth of an urban working class. In 1869, Ontario farmers commonly took their grain to local distilleries and received whisky in part payment. Whisky could not be so cheaply acquired by the urban working man, so beer increased in popularity as the cities grew. It is significant that Ontario, the most urban of Canadian provinces, was also well above average in per capita consumption of beer.[8]

A reading of prohibition literature might suggest that working-class people were sharing in the trend away from alcohol. Union leaders, for example, frequently were referred to as advocates of prohibition. Yet most of the union leaders referred to were

[5] *Napanee Beaver* in Reverend W. W. Peck, *A Short History of the Liquor Traffic* (Canadian Temperance Federation, n.d.), p. 5.

[6] *Globe*, January 16, 1890.

[7] F. S. Spence, *The Campaign Manual* (Toronto, 1902).

[8] F. S. Spence, *The Facts of the Case* (Toronto, 1896), p. 20.

American or British. There was a time when Canadian unions lent some support to the prohibition movement. The 1886 convention of the Canadian Trades and Labor Congress received a delegation from the Dominion Alliance for the Total Suppression of the Liquor Traffic and expressed sympathy with its work.[9] But the congress never committed itself to official support for prohibition and in the 1890s it ceased to express even sympathy.[10] Critics of prohibition were quick to note working-class opposition to the movement and frequently denounced prohibition as class legislation.

By the 1890s, then, if some Ontarians were drinking much less, others, probably the urban working class, were drinking much more. This class distinction in the intimacy of the urban setting seems to have made the working-class drinker a highly visible problem and an irritating challenge to the life style of the urban middle class. Some of this was reflected in the arguments advanced for prohibition.

The basic arguments were still those which had been advanced throughout the century. But the form they took was increasingly oriented to the problem of alcohol in an urban society. Increasingly, too, the arguments took on overtones of social class. The class nature of the question is reflected in one of the basic arguments of the prohibitionists, that liquor was the major cause of poverty. Prohibition literature was full of items like this:

A WRETCHED END

An unfortunate man who has a brother in the House of Commons was frozen to death in a miserable shanty in Winnipeg on Tuesday night while in a state of intoxication.[11]

News items, fiction, verse and cartoons all carried the message of the prosperous labourer brought down to financial ruin by

[9] E. Forsey, "Labour and Liquor, 1892-1898," unpublished mss., pp. 5-6.
[10] *Ibid.*, p. 11.
[11] *The Vanguard* (Toronto, 1893), p. 170.

drink. Drink explained the poverty of the working man and the sufferings of his wife and children. This song, "Father's a Drunkard and Mother is Dead," is typical of hundreds:

> We were so happy till Father drank rum,
> Then all our sorrow and trouble begun;
> Mother grew paler and wept every day,
> Baby and I were too hungry to play.
> Slowly they faded, and one summer's night,
> Found their dear faces all silent and white;
> Then with big tears slowly dropping, I said,
> "Father's a drunkard, and Mother is dead!"[12]

The mode of expression is comically sentimental but it should not obscure the plight of a working-class family of the period when the father failed to provide for its upkeep and at a time when society made little provision for the poor.

Prohibitionist speakers and pamphleteers became very skilful at exploiting the economic aspect of alcohol as an explanation of urban poverty. They even calculated that, on his average income of $410.36 a year, the Ontario working man could live on $364.61, thereby saving $45.75 a year.[13] Result: if he was abstinent, prosperity; if he drank, debt. There was no provision for spending on recreation. In part, this reflected a belief that ample free recreation of the proper moral elevation was to be found in the churches and public libraries. In greater part, it reflected the naïveté of the middle classes when confronted with the difficulties of working-class life.

There was good reason for this concern with poverty. Urban poverty, more visible and often more severe than rural poverty, was rising with the growth of cities. The presence of poverty was an inescapable phenomenon. To a generally temperate and even abstinent middle class, it seemed obvious that the factor keeping the working class below its own level of economic security was

---

[12] *The Sparkling Stream* (New York, 1870). Such collections from the United States were popular among Ontario prohibitionists.
[13] Spence, *The Facts of the Case*, p. 60.

drink. The coincidence of poverty and drink was noted and the conclusion drawn that drink was the cause of poverty. Today such reasoning seems specious, but the consciousness, if not the reality, of urban poverty was then novel to most middle-class Ontarians. The prohibition movement brought them into contact with poverty and conditioned their reaction to it. In time, that contact would add sophistication to their conclusions.

The same sort of reasoning laid most crime at the feet of alcohol. Prohibition journals frequently carried items like the following:

> Drink led astray the son of one of Montreal's best physicians, and on Saturday last the young man was sentenced to five years in the penitentiary.[14]

Both prohibitionists and their opponents made frequent resort to police records to prove their cases. But enforcement of laws was so variable, the record of factors in any given crime so incomplete and the methods of compiling statistics so confused as to render these attempts useless as guides. Prohibitionist concern for the relationship between alcohol and crime can reveal little about the extent of the relationship, but the intensity of that concern reveals something about middle-class fears.

Medical, biblical and economic arguments against alcohol were used throughout the century but do not seem to have undergone any qualitative changes. However, they did experience some change in the frequency with which they were cited.

Medical arguments pointing out the dangers of alcohol gained in importance as the century wore on. Statistics drawn up by life insurance companies assisted, and these and medical findings indicating a relationship between longevity and abstinence were invoked frequently. So strong had the medical case against alcohol become that many life insurance companies offered preferential rates to non-drinkers. This was a reversal of their earlier refusal

[14] *The Vanguard*, p. 170.

to insure non-drinkers on the grounds that abstinence was an unhealthy abnormality.

Religious feeling was strong in the prohibition movement. Devotional periods and Christian ritual had a place in virtually all prohibition societies and many churches were deeply committed to the movement. Yet biblical arguments against alcohol seem to have experienced a decline in popularity. Perhaps it was because the Bible speaks of alcohol in contradictory terms. On one occasion, for example, wine is condemned as a mocker but on another it is that which gladdens man's heart. Faced with the uncertainty of biblical authority, prohibition literature used it primarily in defence against biblical evidence cited by wets rather than as a positive argument in itself. Essentially, prohibitionism was a secular movement. Churches shared in the movement inasmuch as they were a part of the life style of Ontario's middle classes. The extent of that sharing depended, in part, on the existence of favourable conditions emerging from each church's history.

It is an indication of the secular nature of the prohibition movement and of opposition to it that much more attention was paid to economic arguments. Louis Kribs of *The Advocate* (a liquor journal) attacked prohibitionism with an estimate of the economic value of the liquor industry to Ontario.[15] He claimed for the liquor and liquor-related industries of the province an aggregate capital value of over $15 million and 4,300 employees, not counting lesser towns and rural areas.

Prohibitionists showed themselves equally adept at the use of figures, as they challenged this version of economics for the state. F. S. Spence of the Dominion Alliance discounted the investment represented by the liquor industry and the returns to those employed in it on the grounds that both were wasted since they contributed nothing of value.[16] Then he went on to show the cost of the liquor traffic in consumer prices, wasted grain, pauperism, disease, insanity, crime and mortality. By such means it

---

[15] L. P. Kribs, *Report of Louis P. Kribs* (Toronto, 1894), pam.
[16] Spence, *The Facts of the Case*, p. 36.

was possible to charge the liquor industry with a net annual cost to Canada of more than $130 million.

Judging by the space given to economic arguments, one might infer that Ontarians of the 1890s regarded economic prosperity at least as highly as moral well-being and physical health if, indeed, they separated the three at all. It would also seem that the prohibition movement caused them to think more deeply about the social consequences of economic activity.

Both sides could present strong economic cases, but in the quarrel over the enforceability of prohibition, prohibitionists were on the defensive. Usually the examples of unenforceability were drawn from the United States, notably from Maine, Iowa and Kansas. The favourite device of the wets was the anecdote about open drinking and increased drunkenness wherever a prohibition law had been passed.

The almost universal response of prohibitionists was to indict corrupt officials or neighbouring wet communities for making liquor easily available in dry areas. Much of the prohibitionists' defence of the enforceability of prohibition can be found in this extract from *The Vanguard:*

> The difficulties that beset the efforts of those who endeavour to suppress liquor selling by local option, are manifest. Among them are the readiness with which liquor can be procured in adjoining localities under license; the liability to repeal, which is nearly always looked forward to as a possibility, if not a probability, by friends of the traffic, who in this hope persistently make efforts to circumvent a law which has not in it the important element of permanence; the educative influence of contiguous, permitted licensing which prevents the public viewing liquor-selling as they do other violations of the law; and other perplexities and obstacles that will readily suggest themselves.[17]

In this response, it can be seen why local prohibition was regarded as inadequate. It can also be seen why prohibitionists

[17] *The Vanguard*, p. 219.

frequently became involved in attempts to raise the level of honesty in government.

But why prohibition at all? Why not merely a program of education and individual conversion? Or why not an emphasis on what Goldwin Smith called true temperance, that is on the moderate use of alcohol? In taking up their positions, proponents on all sides frequently took up positions sharply at variance with those one commonly attributes to their churches and political parties.

Goldwin Smith, at least, was consistent with his political liberalism in opposing prohibition as an intrusion on individual freedom, including the rights of private property.[18] But it was the Liberal party of Ontario which was most closely identified, however misleadingly, with the enforced conformity of prohibition, and it was the Conservative party which was identified with the doctrines of individual rights and free choice in this matter.

Similarly, among the churches, it was Methodists who issued such statements as the following:

> It is the duty of the Government to extend the aegis of its protection over the people, to shield them from injury or wrong; but, by licensing the liquor traffic, it plies them with temptations to crime, and then punishes them for its commission; it makes a profit out of their unhallowed passion for strong drink, and then inflicts its penalties for the indulgence of that passion.[19]

Another Methodist clergyman was even more explicit about the powers of the state and their relation to individual free choice. He maintained that there was a large class which was unaffected by religious teaching and that this class, through its drinking, produced a disproportionate share of the insane, the sickly and the destitute. Their refusal to listen to reason made them a burden to the community. He concluded:

[18] Goldwin Smith, *Temperance vs. Prohibition* (Toronto, n.d.), pam.
[19] W. W. Withrow, "Legal Prohibition of the Liquor Traffic the Duty of the Hour," *The Canadian Methodist Magazine* (Toronto, 1877), p. 69.

For people of this kind, who will not listen to reason, it is
not undue severity to propose that they be restricted in
their liberty, which they use to such an evil end, and be
compelled to abstain from liquor drinking. Let legal
suasion rule where moral suasion is rejected.[20]

To a degree, Baptists remained true to their belief in individual
salvation by refraining from committing their convention to any
prominent role in the political struggle for prohibition; but even
they offered tacit support by sending delegates to the 1895 Convention of the Dominion Alliance for the Total Suppression of
the Liquor Traffic.[21]

Among the least active churches, officially, in the prohibition
movement were the Anglican and Roman Catholic churches.
Their advocacy of individual rights in this instance would seem
to have been in sharp contrast to their traditional concept of
society as an organic whole and to their traditional willingness to
accept the authority of the state. They were ready to further
moderation and even total abstinence on an individual basis, but
not prohibition by the state.

The reason for these contradictions is that it was not traditional
religious and political beliefs which lay behind the demand for
prohibition so much as it was contemporary social conditions and
social status. In large measure, it was the reaction of a growing
middle class to the poverty that surrounded it. This was exemplified in the attitude of Laetitia Youmans of the W.C.T.U. She
was a former school teacher and the wife of a prosperous farmer.
In her autobiography, she said:

I have narrated these circumstances to show how I became
aroused to active work in the temperance cause; not that
the enemy had entered my own home (its shadows had not

---

[20] Reverend D. Y. Ross, *The Liquor Traffic: Its Evils and Remedies* (Toronto,
1893), pp. 3-4.
[21] *The Canadian Baptist* (Toronto, 1895), p. 1. The Dominion Alliance was a
federation open to all groups in favour of prohibition.

darkened my threshold), but it was desolation all around, and it seemed to me that inaction was criminal.[22]

Such an attitude could only be intensified by the evidences of poverty and vice in the growing cities. England had long preceded Canada in experience of the problems that were to arise from the cities and some Canadian clergy were advocating the response of English churches to these problems. In 1889, a Canadian Methodist, the Rev. Stewart, who had studied the slum missions of London, wrote:

> For Christianity is an eminently practical religion, and where it fails in producing truth, justice, and mercy, it fails altogether. If intemperance and impurity, if avarice and tyranny, if disorder and lawlessness, be allowed to grow up and luxuriate under the very shadow of our churches, then there is not only an impediment to the progress of the gospel of a most alarming character, but a discredit is entailed upon its Divine claims.[23]

He went on to quote an English mission preacher: "I have held up Christ as the author of social as well as individual salvation."

By the 1890s the problem was as evident in Toronto and other Ontario cities as it had been in London, and the *Globe* echoed the warning that had been sounded in England:

> All who have reflected seriously on the pressing problems of our civilizations know that the question before the churches is not so much the reconstruction of creeds as the application of the eternally true principles of Christianity to suffering, diseased, despairing nineteenth-century life.[24]

[22] L. Youmans, *Campaign Echoes: The Autobiography of Laetitia Youmans* (Toronto, 1893), p. 91.
[23] Reverend Professor Stewart, "Home and Foreign Missions," *The Canadian Methodist Quarterly* (Toronto, 1889), p. 142.
[24] *Globe*, January 11, 1890.

This mundane application of the principles of Christianity was a part of what was to be known as the "social gospel." Prohibition was closely associated with that message; it preceded the social gospel and broadened to embrace it.

One reason for the association between prohibition and the social gospel was the identification of alcohol with poverty and vice. The association had long been an obvious one to most of rural Ontario and the extremes of poverty and wealth, of vice and morality were greater or, at least, more evident in the cities than they had been in the country. It was natural that there should be a heightened concern for the eradication of poverty and vice and that the prohibition of alcohol should be seen as the means. It was equally natural that the evangelical churches should be in the van of this movement. Revivalism had conditioned them to a reforming and regenerative role and their old hostility to alcohol had conditioned them to see it as the greatest obstacle to reform.

There was another factor which made Methodists, Presbyterians and Baptists concerned about drinking habits in society. Those habits constituted an affront to their life style. Risen to middle-class prosperity and affluence through habits of abstinence and hard work, they were threatened by the growth of an urban working class which combined intemperance (and its supposedly attendant vices) with poverty. It is in this light that one should re-read the statement of the Rev. Stewart which I have quoted.

The churches had played a part in forming the life style of the middle classes, and the churches, in their standards and their physical existence, had become a part of that life style. Now, both standards and physical existence of the churches were being threatened in the cities. In 1882, a survey indicated that almost 45 per cent of the population of Toronto attended church at least once each Sunday.[25] This survey and others have been used as evidence of the "goodness" of Toronto, particularly, it has been argued, since the survey was conducted in winter when church

[25] *Globe*, February 7, 1882.

attendance might be expected to be low.[26] In fact, church attendance is usually high in winter, and one could as well draw a
negative conclusion from the statistics, that well over one-half
of Toronto's population did not attend church at least once each
Sunday. Moreover, while rural churches usually served regions
which mixed all economic levels, the nature of urban settlement
was such that each church tended to be much more homogeneous
in the economic level of its membership. This made it impossible
to ignore the differences in church support among the various
economic districts of the city.

So serious was the threat to the Sabbath that, in 1889, the Presbyterian General Assembly authorized a conference of churches
to deal with it. The outcome was the Lord's Day Alliance, formed
to preserve Sunday against encroachments in the name of profit
and of worldly recreation. Many churches saw that they could
no longer concern themselves solely with salvation of the individual. They were caught up in the effort to preserve the life style
of which they were a part against the assaults of urban and
industrial influences.

Prohibition was a part of this struggle and, for the same reasons
that voluntary, individual salvation was not enough for some
churches, voluntary, individual salvation was no longer enough
for prohibitionists. They were not seeking merely to reconstruct
individuals but to reconstruct a whole society. The movement had
not begun with such an intention; it was the problem of the
individual drinker which had started the drive for temperance.
But the challenge of alien elements in society and the threat that
they might come to dominate spurred the movement to a more
ambitious goal. By 1894, prohibitionists were advocating the regulation of a business in the interests of the community while
the wets were arguing for the rights of the individual. It was
a fundamental cleavage which had wider implications than the
drinking of alcohol.

It would be too much to say that the nature of this cleavage was

---

[26] D. C. Masters, *The Rise of Toronto: 1850-1890* (Toronto, 1947), p. 193.

very widely understood in the 1890s. This lack of understanding may explain why the two sides failed to make any intellectual impact on each other; they were arguing within different frames of reference. Even within the movements for temperance and prohibition, some of the cleavage was evident. Some were concerned solely about the problem of alcohol; others, like the W.C.T.U., were consciously treating prohibition as one aspect of the general rehabilitation of society. While individualism still survived and was to survive in the prohibition movement, there was also evident a tendency to an organic view of society. Evidence of this tendency was to increase as the challenge of a changing society became more evident and as prohibitionists became more familiar with the nature of the urban problem.

The scope of the problem was nowhere more evident than in the activities of the W.C.T.U. At the Ontario W.C.T.U. convention of 1896, for example, though alcohol held a central place in discussion, other interests had developed from it. Tobacco and opium were condemned; there was concern expressed for the morals of children, the secularization of the Sabbath and the moral and physical safety of female workers in the cities. Moreover, the tenor of the resolutions makes it clear that the W.C.T.U. was seeking to use the power of the state to assist in the maintenance of its ideal of society.

In all of this, it was implicitly recognized that many of the concepts of liberal individualism were becoming obsolete. The influences of the law, of the home, of the church and of that part of the community represented by social betterment societies were being summoned to combat vaguer influences which seemed to be shaping society. The crusade against alcohol owed part of its strength to the ease with which the forces of alcohol could be isolated and identified. They were often referred to as the alcohol "interests," meaning hotelkeepers, brewers, distillers and corrupt politicians. Within a few years, the adjective "alcohol" was dropped, as more interests came to be identified as hostile to an ideal of society.

The reference to corrupt politicians is an important one. The belief in the existence of this corruption was a major factor in a growing disillusionment with the old parties, and one day it would lead some prohibitionist leaders to flirt with strange new political affiliations. In the 1890s, however, the main casualty of this disillusionment was the status of the male. Since few women could vote, there began a broad condemnation of the male voter. In a typical prohibitionist stance, J. W. Bengough charged both parties with being controlled by the liquor interests and he accused church-going men of perpetuating the hold of liquor by continuing to support the old parties.[27] A similar point is made in a prohibition verse of the time:

> We women pray for better times,
> And work right hard to make 'em;
> You men vote liquor with its crimes,
> And we just have to take 'em.[28]

In such verses lay a challenge to one of the fundamental values of nineteenth-century Ontario. It was an attack on the male as the leader of the family and the bulwark of middle-class respectability.

It had begun, perhaps, with the farm wife who had to wait at home for her husband to come home drunk and abusive from his night at the hotel, resenting, as much as his behaviour, his means of escape from the home that had to be so much of her world. But this cannot be the whole story for the attack on men. Even a casual reading of the records of women's temperance societies indicates that many, perhaps most, of the women active in the movement were those whose husbands did not drink, women who had little direct experience of the effect of alcohol on family life. Why, then, did they join in the attack?

The answer to that question would constitute a study in itself. Part of it may be found in the frustrations of a life still confined to home and family. There must have been resentment of the husband's ability to have interests away from home even in the

---

[27] J. W. Bengough, *The Gin Mill Primer* (Toronto, 1898).
[28] Reverend D. Rogers, *The Gatling* (Toronto, 1894).

course of work. All of this must have been intensified as mothers watched their children grow away from them and as they became fearful of their capacity to continue to attract their husbands. These feelings gave rise to intense self-pity, very evident in this verse about a mother:

> She was so weary; but we never guessed
> How weary, till she smiled at set of sun
> And whispered, as she drifted into rest—
> "My loving now is done."[29]

This self-pity was a staple of women's literature in the prohibition movement.

The resentment against men is most clearly shown in those stories which placed the innocence of childhood on the side of mother against the drinking husband. In one such story, the drunkard's young children go to the polls during a local option vote and explain to the (brutish) men at the poll why they want to vote:

> "I want to vote for my pa."
> "Shimmie's doing to vote for our pa," repeated Mamie, in a prompt, clear voice, "so 'e won't do to s'loon!"
> The merriment was over. An almost painful awe crept over that assembly of men, as if in the voice of helpless childhood they had heard the voice of God.[30]

The repetitions of this theme are too frequent to be ignored. They are found in most of the range of temperance literature, but they are most frequent in that literature intended for women. The standard plot, with a thousand slight variations, features the saintly mother, made miserable by the weak or even brutish husband who is redeemed through the innocence of the children, who take mother's side. There was more than this to the interest

---

[29] *Canadian White Ribbon Tidings* (Toronto, 1907), p. 799.
[30] *Ibid.*, p. 800.

of women in prohibition, but the attack on men was an important part of it.

The belief in masculine weakness and feminine purity was a factor in the agitation for woman suffrage; and a demand for the vote was included in the resolutions of the Ontario W.C.T.U. convention of 1896. In this context, it was more than a demand for the rights of women; it was a condemnation of the evil and weakness inherent in the male condition. It was not a demand for equality. Rather, it was an assault on male domination of society in the expectation that the purity which was the common denominator of womankind would achieve domination over the multiple weaknesses of men.

Throughout the 1890s the prohibitionists of Ontario were battling to preserve what they understood to be traditional values concerning thrift, work and morality. The battle had begun in a rural context with alcohol the sole and easily identifiable enemy. But by the 1890s Ontario was changing and the prohibition movement was changing with it. Against an urban backdrop, there were added such complications as class tensions and the more visible problems of human need. Alcohol seemed to provide a thread of continuity between the old problems and the new, so that prohibitionists could be among the first to react to these complexities. There were many prohibitionists who confronted the new urban problems without recognizing any need for change, but others were driven to question values as traditional as those they were defending. In seeking to preserve elements of a life style rooted in Ontario's past, they were driven to attack concepts of individualism and masculinism with roots fully as deep. This amalgam within one movement made it a link between Ontario's past and its future.

Part Three

The Protective Impulse: An Approach to the Social History of Oliver Mowat's Ontario

MICHAEL BLISS

Small businessmen in the towns and cities of Oliver Mowat's Ontario were bedevilled by the problem of long working hours. An elementary fact of business life was that any merchant who stayed open while others closed gained a significant competitive advantage. Therefore all Ontario merchants in the 1870s and 1880s tended to stay open until there was no more business for anyone to do. Because of the working class's habit of evening shopping this resulted in retail stores staying open until nine or ten o'clock every night of the week, the Sabbath excepted. Few merchants and fewer of their clerks enjoyed this situation. To remedy it, to protect themselves from this debilitating effect of unrestrained competition, they turned to collective action.

"Early Closing" movements became a regular feature of municipal business life in the 1880s and 1890s. They usually consisted of draft agreements circulated among local merchants for their signatures, each pledging to restrict his hours as long as everyone else did. These failed with monotonous regularity because there was always some individualist who would not sign or would break his agreement after he had signed. If local businessmen were ever to enjoy reasonable working hours some form of compulsion was necessary to stop these renegade competitors. The only effective instrument of compulsion was the power of government. Accordingly, the ever-compliant Mowat government in 1888 amended the Municipal Act to permit municipalities to pass early closing by-laws at the request of a certain percentage of merchants in a given trade.[1]

The problem was not at all solved, for it proved difficult both to get by-laws passed and to enforce those that were passed. But it is the principle involved in this legislation that should interest us. By this simple action the Mowat government had given legal sanction to merchants' collective attempts to limit competition in the hours of business. Using the force of law to restrict a man's right to keep store the hours he saw fit was a direct attack on the idea of free trade, on the principles of an open, individualistic, free-market economy.

The early closing movement with its accompanying legislation was far from an isolated phenomenon in Oliver Mowat's Ontario. It was one example of a general movement to stem the effects of competition on significant economic groups in the province in the late nineteenth century. In key areas of economic life doctrines of individualism and open competition had given way or were about to give way to collectivism and regulated competition, symptomatic of what can be called the protective impulse in economic life. This paper describes a number of the manifestations of this protective impulse, explores in a tentative and oversimplified way some of the broader implications of the movement, and suggests that it might be considered as an explanatory theme in our future studies of the social history of late nineteenth-century Ontario—or, for that matter, of Victorian Canada as a whole.

[1] *Monetary Times*, June 1, 1888, p. 1482; Winnipeg *Commercial*, June 18, 1888, p. 996.

State-enforced discrimination against foreign competition became Canada's National Policy in 1879. The protective tariff was
the most spectacular and controversial example of the protective
impulse at work in nineteenth-century Canada. But this was only
the tip of the iceberg, the highly visible foreign policy, as it were,
of the protective movement amongst central Canadian businessmen. In the depression year of 1883, for example, cotton manufacturers, fire insurance companies, and wholesale grocers—all
centred in Ontario and Quebec—each initiated price-fixing combinations to eliminate major areas of competition from their
industries.[2] In that same year the Grand Trunk and Great Western merger effectively eliminated railway competition throughout
much of Ontario, something the two companies had been trying
to achieve for more than a generation. Later in the decade the
Grand Trunk and C.P.R., although publicly at loggerheads, would
privately negotiate common tariff schedules and agreements to
limit services on their passenger trains, all in the interests of what
Van Horne called "reform in traffic matters."[3] By 1888, when a
Select Committee of the House of Commons investigated business
combinations, these earlier conspirators against the free market
had been joined by biscuit and confectionery manufacturers,
wholesale jewellers, oatmeal millers, cordage and barbed wire
manufacturers, coal merchants in Toronto, London, and Ottawa,
egg buyers (it was remarked that even eggs had fallen under the
"yolk" of the trusts), and undertakers. Stove manufacturers and
iron founders in the province had had a price-fixing trade association in continuous existence since 1865.[4] Salt combines had existed
on and off in the province since at least 1871; the salt ring was
temporarily moribund during the investigations of 1888, but reformed itself in 1889—just at the time when the first anti-combines
legislation was before the House of Commons—and raised the

[2] *Monetary Times*, October 12, 1883, p. 403; September 7, 1883, p. 260; *Report of
the Select Committee . . . to Investigate and Report upon Alleged Combinations
in Manufactures, Trade and Insurance in Canada* (Ottawa, 1888), p. 10.
[3] P.A.C., C. P. R. Papers, Van Horne Letterbooks, #5, #10; Van Horne Letter-
book #14, Van Horne to G. M. Bosworth, December 8, 1885.
[4] *Select Committee to Investigate Combinations*, pp. 5-10.

price of salt to the Ontario consumer by 90 per cent in a single day.[5] The first association of bankers in Canada had been formed in Toronto in 1887. It became the Canadian Bankers' Association in 1891 and immediately began to attempt to fix the maximum interest rate on savings deposits and make other special agreements regarding the handling of forms, bills, and special deposits.[6] By the early 1890s there had been, as Clarke Wallace put it, attempts to burden the people with combines "from the cradle to the grave . . . from Nestle's food in infancy to the coffin in which they were carried to the grave."[7]

And these were still only the most visible businessmen's combinations in restraint of trade. Competition was sharpest in the late nineteenth century among the overcrowded ranks of small businessmen, notably retailers; and it was in this sector of the economy that attempts to limit competition were the most frantic and varied. In addition to the ubiquitous early closing movements, collective action was taken by local retailers' associations to fix prices, end the expensive tradition of giving Christmas presents to customers, buy up the stocks of bankrupt traders to avoid cut-price sales, and compile black lists of bad credit risks. Fierce and perpetual running battles were carried on against manufacturers and wholesalers trying to sell at retail, against the price-cutting department stores run by Timothy Eaton and Robert Simpson, and the "guerilla trade" of farmers, pedlars, and other transient traders.[8] The aim of all of this activity was to close off the free market in goods and services in order to give the small businessman a measure of economic security.

Business rhetoric about competition echoed business practice. It is not true that businessmen in Ontario—or anywhere else in North America—were apostles of a highly individualistic, competitive, free enterprise business system. On the contrary, it is

---

[5] House of Commons, *Debates*, April 8, 1889, p. 1112.
[6] *Journal of the Canadian Bankers' Association*, vol. III, no. 1, October 1895, p. 20; vol. VII, no. 2, January 1900, pp. 97, 98, 110.
[7] *Canadian Grocer*, November 7, 1890.
[8] *Canadian Grocer*, 1888-1893, *passim; The Retail Merchants' Journal of Canada*, 1903-1907, *passim*.

virtually impossible to find an Ontario businessman in the 1880s and 1890s who had a good word to say for the idea of free competition in his own trade. They always spoke of "cutthroat" competition, "demoralizing" competition, "unfair" competition, and reversed an old maxim to proclaim that competition was likely to be the death of trade. Social Darwinist phrases like "the survival of the fittest" were used, but only to describe the competitive situation as it existed, not as businessmen hoped it might be. Social Darwinism was explicitly condemned in the *Canadian Grocer* as a mere "biological theory" which seemed akin to the middle ages' practice of testing morality by the ordeal of combat.[9] If the *Canadian Grocer*—Canada's most influential specialized trade journal—could have had its way, a system of "limited" (i.e. fixed) prices would have been extended to every article in trade. Other businessmen hoped to see a system of licensing set up to limit the number of traders in any given line, or entrance qualifications to limit competition by weeding out most would-be businessmen.[10] As the *Monetary Times* and other business journals noted, the thrust of the business collectivism of the 1880s and 1890s was ultimately directed at a return to the old guild system under which closed corporate bodies had totally eliminated competition in most lines of trade.[11]

The restrictive or protective practices of businessmen came under heavy public criticism in the late 1880s as being conspiracies against the consumer. Businessmen vigorously denied this, mobilizing a battery of arguments ranging from the need to fix prices in the interest of paying high wages through claims that unregulated competition destroyed business morality and led to adulteration of the quality of goods. Therefore, combinations in restraint of trade were really in the public interest. Above all, businessmen commonly proclaimed their right to combine to achieve what they

---

[9] *Canadian Grocer*, October 2, 1891.
[10] *Canadian Grocer*, April 18, 1890; *Monetary Times*, May 10, 1889, p. 1901; August 29, 1898, p. 145.
[11] *Monetary Times*, August 23, 1889, p. 223; *Le Prix Courant*, December 17, 1889; *Journal of Commerce* (Montreal), November 25, 1887, p. 1001; June 26, 1891, p. 1222.

called a "living profit," in other words, a fair return on their labour
and investment. That too, they thought, was or should be in the
public interest.[12]

The most revealing arguments used in defence of business protectionism emphasized how other groups in society were being
permitted to get away with the same thing. On the one hand
there were unions of workingmen trying to close off the free
market in labour, and using exactly the same methods of organization and coercion that business associations wanted to use. On the
other hand there were the professional groups such as doctors,
lawyers, and druggists who were given legal authority to limit
entrance to their professions, discipline their members for such
"unethical" (read "competitive") practices as advertising, and fix
their fees for service. "Nearly every calling has some standard as a
basis for protection to itself and guarantee to the public," argued
the secretary of the Toronto Board of Trade in the midst of the
combines uproar. "Capital, like everything else, has, by universal
consent, an undoubted right to protection when in danger, and to
refuse it would be oppression in its worst form."[13]

This business rhetoric must be taken seriously. To write off the
combination movement in business as just the predictable behaviour of greedy capitalists is to misunderstand what was happening in Ontario life at the end of the nineteenth century.
Business apologists were accurate in claiming that they wanted to
protect themselves in the same ways that unions and professional
organizations were trying to protect their members. There was no
difference, for example, between the methods of associations of
businessmen trying to close off the free market in goods and those
of trade unions trying to close off the free market in wages.

[12] The debate on combination versus competition was carried on in all of the trade
journals in the last two decades of the century, but particularly in the years 1888-
1892.
[13] P.A.C., Sir John A. Macdonald Papers, p. 150845, "Report of Committee on
Combines to the Council of the Board of Trade of the City of Toronto," February
26, 1889; also *Journal of Commerce*, August 20, 1886, p. 529; *Canadian Manufacturer*, March 15, 1889, p. 178; Winnipeg *Commercial*, November 22, 1897,
pp. 267-75.

Businessmen conspired to fix prices; workingmen conspired to fix wages. Business associations discriminated against traders who would not join and abide by their rules; unions did the same to the non-unionized worker. The business equivalent of "scab" labour was the "price-cutter" who broke a combine (which explains, among other things, why Timothy Eaton was the most hated and feared businessman of his generation. He was the Honest Ed writ large of nineteenth-century retailing.). Trade unions managed to limit entrance to their trades, thus restricting competition, by manipulating apprenticeship practices and by obtaining legislation restricting the labour of women and children. Business associations would dearly have loved to do the same (and in part did so, for the early closing legislation of 1887 had certain effects analogous to those of the Ontario Factory Act of 1884). On the other hand unions envied businessmen their tariff protection, supported the tariff insofar as it protected their jobs, and lobbied for the same kind of protection against imported workers. Workingmen claimed their right to a "living wage"; businessmen claimed their rights to a "living profit." Organization for self-protection from the chaotic effects of a free market was the central aim of both the union movement and the combination movement in business. That is why in 1889 Dominion legislators would have such difficulty drafting a combines law to strike at business combinations while not restricting the operations of trade unions.

Professional associations were also organizations that concerned themselves with the self-protection of their members. The privileges of professional self-government, deriving in most cases in Ontario from legislation passed by Mowat's administrations, gave skilled tradesmen such as doctors, lawyers, dentists and pharmacists effective control over entrance to their profession as well as the legal power to weed out people their associations considered to be behaving "unprofessionally." On their part businessmen thought the price-cutter was unprofessional, workingmen thought the scab was a traitor to his class. Both groups would have leaped at the chance to exercise powers of self-government that could drive an offensive person out of their midst. Similarly the establishment of standard fees for service was a common aim of professional organizations and was no different from the attempts of workingmen to fix wages or businessmen to fix prices. "If banking is worthy of the name of a profession," ran an argument in the *Journal of the Canadian Bankers' Association*, "there should be certain things universally considered unprofessional within our ranks. Giving service without profit or at an actual loss should be unprofessional. Solicitation of business by offering to work more cheaply should be as unworthy a banker as we consider it unworthy a doctor."[14] Businessmen were correct in believing that society allowed the professional man to play by a different set of rules from those it expected of the man in business. In a society that truly respected the idea of the free market anyone who wanted to should have been able to call himself a doctor, lawyer, or dentist, and charge any fee he cared to for his services. The invisible hand of the marketplace would have sorted out the competent from the quacks, just as it did in most lines of trade and labour.

The protective impulse, then, was a common basis of the activities of business, labour, and professional organizations in Mowat's Ontario. In very real ways they were all collectivist conspiracies against the idea of a free market. This should not be surprising in view of the fact that a highly competitive social and economic order naturally had the same effects on all of its members. How could any citizen of Mowat's Ontario guarantee that he would make a "living" wage, professional fee, or profit? How could he prevent competition with other people in his line of work from driving the return on their joint efforts to zero? How could he protect himself from the competition of incompetent people or simply too many other competent people all offering to perform his function at less than a living return? How could he escape from the need for endless effort to hold his own in the competitive scramble and begin to enjoy a quiet life? How could he become his own master rather than the slave of the invisible forces of the

---

[14] David R. Forgan, "Banking as a Profession," *Journal of the Canadian Banking Association*, vol. VI, no. 1, October 1898, p. 52.

marketplace? The common aim of citizens as economic producers, then, was self-protection. Their common means were organization, regulation and, where possible, legislation.

This interpretation of an important aspect of the social history of Mowat's Ontario, emphasizing the fact of competition and the various collective attacks on it, opens up a number of possible lines of inquiry, several of which I would like to explore briefly.

The realization that the competitiveness of life in nineteenth-century Ontario was in itself a major cause of social tension might open up a discussion of patterns of living that can extend far beyond analyses of union, business, and professional organizations. Recent sociological studies of working and middle-class family life, for example, stress that the primary economic and social function of the family has been to protect its members against the insecurities of highly competitive social orders. Can some of these insights be tested empirically for the nineteenth-century Ontario setting in the way that Richard Sennett, for example, has recently examined them in the context of urban life in Chicago of the 1880s?[15] To take another example, the educational system of the province of Ontario was coming under criticism by the end of the Mowat regime for putting undue competitive pressure on students.[16] Did it? If so, why? Was there some relation between the idea of competition in educational philosophy and the fact of competition in economic life? Alternatively, to what extent were the critics of competition in the schools acting on some broad variation of the same protective impulse that stirred labour, business and professional reformers? In another area what degree of truth was there in the frequent complaints by doctors that the rush of modern society, the competitive scramble for affluence and

[15] Richard Sennett, *Families Against the City* (Cambridge, Mass., 1970); Herbert Gans, *The Urban Villagers* (New York, 1962).
[16] "The Education of Our Girls," *Canadian Health Journal*, vol. II, no. 12, December 1876, pp. 333-35; "The Over-Working of Boys and Girls," *ibid.*, vol. II, no. 7, July 1890, p. 121; "Overstudy in Young Girls," *Dominion Medical Monthly*, vol. VIII, no. 8, August 1897, p. 698; "School Examinations Condemned," *Journal of Commerce*, April 22, 1898, p. 574.

advancement, put intolerable strains on the human physique, leading too often to mental and physical collapse?[17] Was this critique
of modern society by medical men also a part of the rejection of a
competitive society in the late nineteenth century? How did it,
as well as all of the other complaints against competition, relate
to and reinforce agrarian resentment at the rush and tumult of
the developing urban life of Mowat's Ontario? Finally, to swing
farther afield, may it not be that the middle-class sexual ethics of
the late nineteenth century, stressing the need for the repression
of sexual energy and its sublimation into work-oriented activities,
was in part a response to a competitive social order in which
success and security could only be gained at the price of incredible
self-denial?[18]

A less fanciful, more precise kind of investigation might centre
on the means by which interest groups tried to legitimize their
claims on society for a measure of self-protection. We know, for example, that unions successfully played on the humanitarianism of
the people of Ontario to permit them to drive young women and
children out of the labour force, and eventually won broad social
acceptance of their right to a living wage (though not necessarily
to use the means they proposed to attain it). On the other hand,
most forms of business protectionism never attained the same
degree of legitimacy, for consumer opinion (often including other
businessmen in their roles as consumers) tended to believe that a
living profit was likely to involve gouging the public in ways that
a living wage was not. Still, it is important to note that Canada's
first combines legislation was so weak precisely because legislators
accepted in large part the idea that business combination was

[17] Dr. Stephen Lett, "The Health of Businessmen," *Monetary Times*, December 23,
1887, p. 790; G. Rauzier, "Neurasthenia," *Canada Lancet*, March 1894, pp. 199-
201; John Duffy, "Mental Strain and 'Overpressure' in the Schools: A Nineteenth-
Century Viewpoint," *Journal of the History of Medicine and Allied Sciences*, vol.
XXIII, no. 1, June 1968, pp. 63-79.
[18] See Michael Bliss, " 'Pure Books on Avoided Subjects': Pre-Freudian Sexual
Ideas in Canada," Canadian Historical Association, *Historical Papers 1970*, pp.
89-108.

sometimes permissible, thus beginning the long Canadian tradition of distinguishing between good and bad combines. Further, the protective subsidies given manufacturers and others under the National Policy tariff were legitimized because they could be wrapped in the seamless cloak of Canadian nationalism. Manufacturers' foreign policy was accepted as legitimate; their domestic policy, on the whole, was not.

The struggles of professional organizations for legislative favours are perhaps the most interesting examples of the legitimization of the protective impulse, and yet we know little about them. What would the histories of the medical and legal professions of Ontario show about the motives of professional leaders who demanded restrictive privileges from the legislature? D. W. Gullett's *History of Dentistry in Canada* certainly suggests mixed motives at the base of arguments for legislative protection by one group of advancing professionals. Their case for tighter professional control was always presented in terms of the need to protect the public from frauds and to raise standards of service. But it is clear that the most urgent problem of nineteenth-century dentists was to be able to make a living at their profession, and there was thought to be a symbiotic relationship between the dentist's income and the quality of service he could render his patients. Even the sympathetic Dr. Gullett admits a continuous tendency on the part of his subjects "to think that the answer to all problems lay in seeking legislative amendments granting more powers to the profession."[19] But this was not particularly surprising in the Ontario context where dentistry had become a recognized profession for the first time (in 1868) and enjoyed unique privileges to run its own affairs. Curiously, dental protectionism won a legitimacy in Oliver Mowat's Ontario it had not yet achieved anywhere else in the world. I suspect that the legislative history of professional regulation in Ontario would reveal a fascinating series of Byzantine struggles between proponents of corporate protectionism and believers in professional "free trade," both

[19] D. W. Gullett, *A History of Dentistry in Canada* (Toronto, 1971), p. 56.

groups always arguing in the name of protecting the public interest.[20]

The apparently built-in ambiguity of motives and effects has to be one of the central themes of any study of the protective impulse. A protective tariff may have built the Canadian nation; it also involved legislatures giving businessmen opportunities to make money that were denied to others. Labour unions almost certainly had beneficial effects on the lives of their members. But these were not accomplished without social costs in terms of the problems restrictions on the market created for unorganized workers, immigrants, small employers and others, as well as in the potential for irresponsible behaviour that was inherent in the growth of powerful workers' bodies. The eventual crushing out of quack doctors, lawyers, dentists and druggists may have improved standards of professional service in the province. It also raised their cost, may have denied useful semi-professional services to the poor (did the farmer with a toothache find the unlicensed "tramp" dentist better or worse than no dentist at all?), and it personally enriched those who could find admission to the corporate bodies of law, medicine, dentistry and pharmacy. The code of ethics of the Ontario Undertakers' Association guaranteed that the local funeral director would don properly sombre dress and mien; the association's very tight restrictionist practices meant he could smile all the way to the bank.[21] In general, for every benefit to the public weal created in the granting of special privileges to organized interest groups there was created an equal danger that special privileges would be used for selfish interests.

[20] Gullett does not explain the power of the profession in Ontario. Its formal legislative achievements may be somewhat misleading, for there were many instances of individuals who could not obtain a licence from the Royal College of Dental Surgeons, being granted one by special decrees of the legislature. Nor was dental advertising significantly blocked by the profession until the twentieth century.

A not untypical example of legislative manipulation by professionals was the 1893 attempt by a front group for the Ontario College of Pharmacy to have the sale of patent medicines made a legal monopoly of druggists by having their ingredients classed as poisons. It was a brazen attempt to use the legislature to increase druggists' incomes, and failed.

[21] *Select Committee to Investigate Combinations*, pp. 706-10.

Another merit of the theme of protectionism is the possibility of extending the analysis backward and forward in time. There was nothing radically new about the protective impulse as such in the late nineteenth century. No one ever liked competition in practice; as Adam Smith realized, wherever two or three businessmen gathered together there was likely to be a conspiracy in restraint of trade. What was new was the predominance of economic theories stressing that competition and laissez faire were social goods—indeed, in the language of classical economics, moral goods. At the same time people found themselves in increasingly integrated economies rocked by technological change and the roller-coaster effects of the business cycle. New outbreaks and forms of competition required new collectivist responses, though it was a very ancient protective impulse at work. Now, as well, the process of erecting restraints against the operations of the market seemed both novel and slightly shady because for the first time in human history there was a dominant body of thought celebrating competition and condemning attempts to regulate it.[22]

The protective impulse naturally varied in a more or less direct relationship to the degree of competition in any given sector of economic life. It reached its climax in Canada, for example, in the depression of the 1930s, when competition for economic survival reached fever pitch and all organized groups lobbied fiercely for state intervention to protect them from the consequences of competition in an overcrowded marketplace. (R. B. Bennett's "New Deal" is best understood as the closest Canadians came in peacetime to a general abandonment of the free market in the hope of protecting all interest groups. Bennett's and H. H. Stevens' denunciations of laissez-faire capitalism were not as extraordinary as historians have thought, but were soundly rooted in a long tradition of business resistance to the free market. Stevens' Royal Commission on Price Spreads and his Reconstruction Party were the independent retailers' last stand in the battle against depart-

---

[22] There is a fine realization of this process at work by a noted economist responding to the Canadian combines agitation in W. J. Ashley, "The Canadian Sugar Combine," *University Quarterly Review*, vol. I, no. 1, February 1890, pp. 24-39.

mental and chain stores that had begun in the 1890s.)[23] It is probable that a combination of the protective legislation that was achieved in the depression, the social programs of the welfare state, the new Keynesian techniques of economic management, and seemingly endless economic expansion, has muted the protective impulse since the Second World War. Yet in the Ontario of the 1970s such disparate issues as the strength of construction unions, teachers' demands for professional self-government, the marketing of dentures, taxicab drivers' complaints against airport monopolies, the problem of early closing, student resentment at faculty tenure, and intellectuals' demands for a cultural tariff against American competition all continue to raise basic issues of the extent to which the public interest is served by acceding to the protective impulse. Light can be shed on many of these issues, I believe, by analysing them in historical perspective.

Finally, what was happening in Ontario life in the late nineteenth century was only a microcosm of events in the larger western community. In *The Great Transformation* Karl Polanyi argues convincingly that belief in the virtues of a free-market economy operating on principles of open competition, was an unnatural and short-lived phenomenon in the history of western man. As soon as societies realized that this system of "crude fictions" had the result of reducing human beings to economic ciphers—mere puppets dancing to the strings held by the invisible hand—there was a spontaneous and massive counter-movement to etsablish barriers against the destructive forces of the competitive marketplace. Human values of status, security and order reasserted themselves against the classical economists' goal of maximum economic performance. The result was the growth in western society of collectivist movements that supported every imaginable kind of regulatory and legislative device to subvert the workings of competition. The protective impulse represented the yearnings of nineteenth-century men to bring order out of the

---

[23] See the Introduction to L. M. Grayson and Michael Bliss, eds., *The Wretched of Canada: Letters to R. B. Bennett, 1930-1935* (Toronto, 1971).

chaos of their society.[24] Perhaps if we can understand these yearnings in all of their ramifications it will help us inject some order into the chaos of our writing about the social history of Oliver Mowat's not-so-unique Ontario.

[24] Karl Polanyi, *The Great Transformation* (Boston, 1944); see also Robert H. Wiebe, *The Search for Order* (New York, 1967), and Samuel H. Beer, *British Politics in the Collectivist Age* (New York, 1966).

Empire Ontario: The Problems of Resource Development

H. V. NELLES

Professor Bliss, in his contribution to this volume, has invited us to consider the protectionist impulse as an organizing concept in the study of business conduct on both sides of the bargaining table in Oliver Mowat's Ontario. He suggested that we look inward from the tariff to the numerous "miniature replica" protectionist policies that restrained commercial intercourse within the domestic economy. In what follows I will examine a variant of the protectionist impulse that existed among Ontario businessmen working within the continental resource economy, a sector which had just begun to assume some importance at the end of the last century.

In this sector the instrument analogous to the tariff and the combine was called the "manufacturing condition." It was both a policy, expressed in statutes and regulations, and a frame of mind, another protectionist way of thinking about economic questions. Bluntly put, the manufacturing condition demanded that Ontario's natural resources be manufactured into finished products within the boundaries of the province. This idea was formulated by certain organized interest groups, popularized by the financial, trade and daily press, and eventually adopted as policy by the provincial government. Their intention was to stop the free export of raw materials in the expectation that the American industries dependent upon Ontario sources of supply would be compelled to relocate within the province. The manufacturing condition constituted a barrier, much like an export tariff, between Ontario and the United States through which such products as sawlogs, pulpwood and nickel ore could no longer pass. Businessmen and politicians sought through this policy to profit from processing as well as extraction in the resource industries. In simple terms this meant more jobs, more sophisticated jobs, and increased export values—a development strategy referred to by economic historians as forward linkage.

Just like the tariff, the trade restrictions Professor Bliss calls to our attention, such as combines and trade associations, were mainly defensive or protective in their nature. The manufacturing condition, on the other hand (though it contained some defensive elements), was manifestly a policy of aggression, a demand that resource-using industries locate their manufacturing processes within the province of Ontario where they obtained their raw materials. If the archetypal National Policy tariff, upon which business groups in the domestic retailing and manufacturing sectors patterned their behaviour to protect themselves against competition, was a defensive development strategy, then the provincial equivalent must be regarded as offensive; the manufacturing condition was a policy of insistence.

Ontario's manufacturing condition advanced on three fronts through three separate pieces of provincial legislation: an 1898 amendment to the Crown Timber Act forbidding the export in unmanufactured form of logs cut on crown lands; an order-in-council approved in 1900 extending this prohibition under the Crown Timber Act to pulpwood as well; and in the same year an amendment to the Mines Act which imposed a prohibitive tax on the extraction of copper-nickel ores, to be rebated if those ores were worked into fine metal in Ontario. These three measures taken together constituted the concrete results of the manufacturing condition agitation. The policy rested in law upon the provincial government's retention of some proprietary right in the crown lands and therefore its absolute control over the lumbermen licensees, and upon the plenitude of provincial jurisdiction in the mining field under the British North America Act. And perhaps more important than the legal sanction was that the manufacturing condition also commanded the support of the Ontario Lumberman's Association, pulpmill proprietors and promotors, and those influential Ontarians who wanted to break a near monopoly in the nickel-refining business. These groups, though they did not always act in concert, composed the tight power nexus that provided the force to convert the idea into a policy; civil servants and journalists broadcast the propaganda that created the appearance of public sanction of the policy.

Within this framework the questions I would like to ask about the manufacturing condition are these: Where did the policy come from? How was it that the provincial government assumed the initiative in this aspect of controlling trade in the interests of economic development rather than the federal government? What were the practical limitations of such a policy of insistence within the new continental economy?[1]

The threat posed by the Dingley Tariff, passed in the United States in 1897, provided the stimulus that grouped the Ontario businessmen in the resource sector together into a protective, retaliatory configuration. Out of the campaign against this tariff came the manufacturing condition. For the three years preceding 1897 Ontario lumbermen had experienced the supposed Victorian nirvana of free trade. This proved to be but a transitory phase in commercial relations between Ottawa and Washington. Unhap-

---

[1] Of necessity in a brief paper such as this complex matters must receive superficial treatment. For detail, readers are referred to my dissertation, "The Politics of Development: Forests, Mines and Hydro-Electric Power in Ontario, 1890-1939," unpublished Ph.D. thesis, University of Toronto, 1970.

pily for the lumbermen of Ontario it just happened to coincide with the depression of the early nineties, which resulted in a drastic cutback in consumption, falling prices and a glut in the American market from American sources. This left little room for Canadian imports, and what Canadian lumber did make its way to market succeeded primarily in antagonizing American competitors even further. As a result continental free trade in lumber products failed to bestow any great blessings upon the sawmilling industry in Ontario. Not surprisingly, the Dingley Tariff represented a return to normalcy in the lumber trade: tariff war. But the new tariff went beyond merely reinstating the old $2 per thousand board feet duty on Canadian sawn lumber. Anticipating a reimposition of Canadian export duties on sawlogs bound for the United States, the draftsmen of the Dingley Tariff cleverly provided that the sum of any retaliatory Canadian duties would automatically be added onto the tariff against incoming Canadian lumber. This would have the effect of setting the Canadian loggers against the sawmill owners and thereby thwart any firm Canadian counter-measures. For their part the Ontario lumbermen correctly interpreted the new tariff as a "grab" on the part of American sawmill owners who would remain comfortably ensconced behind a tariff wall on the southern shore of the Great Lakes, commanding the Ontario forest to come to them. To say the least, self-respect demanded a response. But what retaliation could be taken in view of the retributive extraterritoriality of the Dingley Tariff?

The Canadian pulp and paper industry, then only in its infancy, faced a similar dilemma. Under the McKinley and Wilson-Gorman tariffs Canadian pulp and paper had to surmount a 15 per cent *ad valorem* duty on entry to the United States, whereas raw pulpwood bound for American mills entered free. The Dingley Tariff replaced the *ad valorem* rate with a schedule of specific duties on Canadian paper, retained pulpwood on the free list and repeated the anti-retaliation clause for this class of wood as well. Here the tariff balanced the American newspapermen's lobby for cheap paper (by continuing the free listing of Canadian pulpwood) against the papermakers' demands for protection against

Canadian competition. However, Canadian observers tended to regard the tariff as yet another indefinite postponement of the promised beginnings of a Canadian pulp and paper industry.[2]

The threat from the United States to Canadian lumber and pulp and paper industries was similarly being felt by the Canadian nickel-mining companies. In the 1890s nickel was an astonishing new non-corrosive metal of great strategic importance. When alloyed with steel it produced ideal armour plate and, in the cruel dialectic of war, projectiles that pierced armour plate. Ontario possessed the world's largest known deposits of nickel-copper ore. With resources of such richness and abundance publicists and politicians like Sir Charles Tupper confidently predicted that Canada would shortly control "the character and efficiency of the guns and navies of the world."[3] But in this case Canada's imperial ambitions and industrial designs were doubly confounded by the bias of the American tariff against refined metals and the monopolistic structure of the nickel-refining industry. North American production of the metal was controlled by the Orford Copper Company of New Jersey, which owned a secret process for refining the refractory ore, and, just as important, an exclusive supply contract for the American navy. A subsidiary with minority Canadian ownership, the Canadian Copper Company mined the ore and roasted it into a more concentrated form for shipment from Sudbury. Ludwig Mond's refinery at Swansea, Wales, which imported some of its raw materials from Canada, supplied the British market. The Rothschilds' syndicate, Le Nickel, with mines in the French penal colony of New Caledonia in the South Pacific, had the European market to itself. Like Gaul, the industrial world was divided into three parts. In fact, it was this rigid control exercised by private corporations that hindered the development of an integrated Canadian nickel industry. The Dingley Tariff

[2] For further detail on the lumber duties see: R. C. Brown, *Canada's National Policy* (Princeton, 1964), pp. 193-95; A. R. M. Lower, *The North American Assault on the Canadian Forest* (Toronto, 1938), pp. 156 ff. On pulp and paper see: J. A. Guthrie, *The Newsprint Paper Industry* (Cambridge, Mass., 1941), p. 40; L. E. Ellis, *The Print Paper Pendulum* (New Brunswick, 1960 ed.), pp. 16 ff.
[3] Quoted in T. W. Gibson, *Mining in Ontario* (Toronto, 1937), p. 83.

merely reinforced in law the character of the marketplace; it was the political arm of monopoly capital. A prohibitive 15 cent per pound duty on refined nickel effectively guarded against the unlikely event of Canadian, British or French competition arising within the American preserve. Of course, nickel ore and its smelted concentrate called matte, like other raw material requirements of American industry, were admitted free. Canada might have the world's largest and richest deposits of ore, but the tariff against nickel, like that against lumber and newsprint, seemed to ensure that the United States would retain for itself the industry based on them.[4]

Ontario businessmen with ambitions in the natural resource field confronted the organized power of a much more mature industrial system in full control of a tariff policy which it manipulated in such a way as to compel the subservience of adjacent, resource-rich regions. Moreover, American businessmen possessed experience, an established position in the market, technological mastery and, of course, the capital required to develop the resources of their hinterland to their full. The industrialization of the provincial resource base would most certainly open up profitable new opportunities for Canadian businessmen, but orthodox thinking on this subject invariably linked this kind of industrial expansion with the wholesale migration of American capital and entrepreneurship into Canada. Collective business reaction to the American tariff structure did not take the form of a nationalist assault against the American industrial system, but rather of a complaint against its immobility. If American entrepreneurs failed to respond to polite invitations to develop Canadian resources, Canadians would take steps to force their attention.

Canadian businessmen were not entirely defenceless—nor lacking in allies within the United States. In the first place, Canadian resources were so rich, so well serviced and so ideally situated in

---

[4] On the nickel tariff see: O. W. Main, *The Canadian Nickel Industry* (Toronto, 1955), pp. 51-53; J. F. Thompson and N. Beasley, *For the Years to Come: A Story of International Nickel of Canada* (Toronto, 1960), p. 116; A. P. Coleman, "The Sudbury Nickel Region," Ontario Bureau of Mines, *Annual Report, 1905*, Part III, pp. 168-83.

relation to the American market that the United States was to a certain extent already dependent, and would inevitably become increasingly reliant, upon them. That offered some leverage. By contrast with Canada the accessible resource endowments of the American north-eastern and north-central regions showed unmistakable signs of depletion. American profligacy guaranteed that in the near future Canada must become the major source of lumber and paper consumed within that country. Industrialization and urban expansion had exhausted the forests of the Great Lakes basin. Now mass circulation newspapers, bulging with display advertising, exerted yet another demand upon the dwindling American forest. Only the forests of Canada seemed immense enough to satisfy these requirements. On top of this, Canada held a monopoly on what seemed certain to become an essential metal. In view of Canada's apparently strategic market position Canadian promoters were justifiably confident about the long-run trend. However, the tariff of 1897 revealed the stubbornness of American industrialists and how far off the future might be.

Resource developers, angered by the Dingley Tariff, addressed their complaints to the federal government which had, up to that time, been responsible for trade in these commodities. In previous tariff battles Ottawa had shouldered the burden. Now, after the free trade interlude, these businessmen expected the federal government to pick up where it had left off. Indeed, the new Laurier administration took immediate action on the complaints. W. S. Fielding, the minister of finance, introduced legislation giving cabinet the authority to reimpose export duties on sawlogs, pulpwood, nickel, silver and lead ores if and when it saw fit. Sir Charles Tupper, speaking for the opposition, concurred in the action. "While it is not desirable to adopt any policy that might be considered a policy of retaliation," he said, "the time has arrived when it is absolutely necessary that the Government and Parliament of Canada should look solely to Canadian interests in regard to these matters."[5] Nevertheless, the federal government remained

---

[5] 60 Vict., ch. 17; for the debate see Canada, House of Commons, *Debates*, 1897, Vol. II, Fielding, p. 3872, and Tupper, p. 3873.

hamstrung by the extraterritorial provisions of the American tariff. Whatever export duties it might levy on outgoing Canadian raw materials would automatically be added onto outgoing semi-manufactured goods at the American border. The cabinet possessed the authority to retaliate but feared the consequences, with the result that the export duties were not proclaimed. Instead, Ottawa hoped to renegotiate more favourable tariffs on a much wider list of goods—the pilgrimages to Washington had not yet ended. But grand commercial strategies hardly satisfied the immediate needs of the nickel interests, lumbermen and pulpmill promoters.

The Ontario lumbermen, whose livelihood depended upon access to the American market, were the first to see a way around the vindictive clauses of the Dingley Tariff. After failing to press the federal government into action it suddenly dawned upon them (possibly it was suggested by federal officials) that the tariff responded only to federal retaliation but said nothing of provincial regulations. Two prominent lumbermen, John Bertram and E. W. Rathbun, revived the long-dormant Ontario Lumberman's Association to bring pressure to bear upon the Ontario government. Bertram, a well-known Liberal party financier, worked privately upon members of cabinet, while Rathbun publicized the idea of a provincial ban on sawlog exports through pamphlets and letters to the editor. "It would be far better," Rathbun argued, "that the American mills should stand closed, their workmen remain idle and the trailways be lessened, than that corresponding interests in Canada should so suffer because of their unfair discrimination." Strangely, out of this negative blue funk of the lumbermen emerged a new, aggressive philosophy of resource development.

In the curious process of the expansion of a private interest into the public interest, retribution became a positive development strategy, and a protective contraction laid the foundations for a new form of economic nationalism. In the public forum, emphasis on the proposed sawlog export ban shifted from the protection it would afford existing vested interests toward its merits as a means of industrializing Ontario's natural resources. Rathbun, the public spokesman for the organized lumbermen, appealed to nationalism and conservation sentiment in making his case for protection. American sawmill owners who owned limits and cut their timber in Ontario, he argued, had no special interest in promoting the Ontario economy or protecting its forests:

> The American lumberman whose mills are across the border and who is a Canadian limit holder, simply because his own country has been stripped of this raw material, is here largely as an exploiter. He seeks the resources that are essential to his business, giving the very minimum of cost and labour at which they can possibly be secured. He is hardly likely to be more conservative in his methods, more interested in the welfare of the foreign country from which he draws his wealth than he has been in that of his own.

The Canadian mill owner on the other hand was a study in contrasts:

> He does not look at matters solely from the standpoint of the immediate profit to be realized by the cutting of so many logs. Usually he is a man of varied interests and extended business relations outside of his principal vocation, which depend upon and are interwoven with our national life. He is a stockholder in Canadian banks and loan companies. He owns land, farms and factories. He has an interest in insurance, railway and joint stock enterprises of all kinds and in the well-being of his fellow citizens of the working class. His home is here, his family and connections are here. In every way his fortunes are bound up with those of the country in which his lot is cast, so that he can be successfully appealed to co-operate with the Government in carrying out any policy having in view the public interest.[6]

What did gentlemen such as these want? Simply a countervailing Canadian response to the American tariff, which, Rathbun

---

[6] E. W. Rathbun, *Shall We Place an Export Duty on Sawlogs and Pulpwoods?* (Deseronto, 1897), pp. 7-8; *The Conference and the Lumber Question from a Canadian Standpoint* (Deseronto, 1898), pp. 2-7.

argued, would not perpetuate at public expense an uneconomic industry but rather promote the rapid growth of an industry that by right belonged to Canada. "A sound and sensible policy of protection, whether by tariff or otherwise," he insisted, "seeks not to encourage the introduction of industries which are pursued here at a relative disadvantage, but to develop what may be termed natural, as distinguished from exotic, manufactures." Sawmills and wood-using factories were surely such natural industries given the abundance of Canada's forest resources. Rathbun and the lumbermen called upon the provincial government to adopt "a forward policy of encouraging a great industry throughout its higher and more profitable forms of fine and finished manufacture, making Canada as she should and might be the wood-working nation of the world. . . ."

The Ontario Lumberman's Association, at a convention in October of 1897, called on the province to halt the export of un-manufactured pine. Following public hearings during which the views of Canadian and American lumbermen were amply aired, Premier Hardy announced his intention to bring in a bill such as the Canadian lumbermen requested, leaving the Americans sufficient time to liquidate their holdings fairly.[7] In the Assembly, Hardy argued that adverse trade conditions necessitated such a drastic step if Canadian workmen and industries were to be protected against "American aggression."[8] The opposition agreed in principle. But a certain degree of anxiety prevailed on both sides of the House. The new regulations were to come into effect two months after the general election that had been called for March 1, 1898. In that campaign the manufacturing condition was a low profile issue, the only serious matter of dispute over it between

[7] See the *Canada Lumberman*, November 1897, for a verbatim report of the convention held in Toronto on October 16, 1897. Resolutions called for export duties on sawlogs (unanimous), an imposition of the manufacturing condition (42-4 votes) and import duties on incoming American lumber. See also Crown Lands Department, *Annual Report, 1899*, p. xi, and a circular letter to lumbermen from Aubrey White (deputy minister) to Mossom Boyd October 9, 1897, informing him of the terms of the legislation. Public Archives of Canada, Mossom Boyd Papers, Box 132.

[8] See the *Globe* for reports of the debate, December 3, 10, and 16, 1897.

the two parties being its Liberal or Conservative paternity. Uncertainty reigned as both lumbermen and politicians marked time, waiting to see just what would happen. For the time being at least there was nothing to boast about and a greal deal to fear.[9]

First, the attack on the policy by the aggrieved parties had to be turned back. The American lumbermen complained to their Secretary of State of the "practical confiscation" by Ontario of property rightly belonging to American citizens. Then the victimized lumbermen petitioned the federal government to disallow this act which clearly trenched upon its jurisdiction over trade and commerce. Finally, one of their number sought redress in the courts. Laurier, though pressed by influential friends, refused to intervene. The Ontario Court of Appeal affirmed that under the constitution the province could demand whatever terms it saw fit in the regulation of its property. Further, the court ruled that the amendment in question only incidentally affected trade and commerce as any legislation touching on property or civil rights might.[10] The manufacturing condition had withstood its first test in the courts, but the question remained: would it work?

The caution that had characterized the implementation of the manufacturing condition melted away during its first full year of operation. "1899 will be remembered as one of the most eventful in the history of the trade," John Bertram reported to a convention of Ontario lumbermen early in 1900. The year had opened with low prices and moderate demand but miraculously closed "with

---

[9] On this point see the Liberal literature, *Ontario General Elections, 1898*, "The Export of Sawlogs," p. 1. See also the editorial in the February 1898 issue of the *Canada Lumberman*: ". . . it remains to be seen what the immediate future of the lumber trade will be. The action taken . . . was one which could not well have been avoided; it would have been an acknowledgement of utter helplessness to have permitted Americans to come here, cut down our forests, raft the logs to their mills in the United States free of export duty, while our own mills were closed down, our workmen idle, and the demand lost for all the subsidiary work and supplies required in running a sawmill."

[10] See P.A.C., Laurier Papers, undated letter of lumbermen to Secretary of State Lyman J. Gage; J. M. Gibson to David Mills, December 20, 1900, in *Provincial Legislation, 1896-1920*, Vol. II (Ottawa, 1922), p. 22; Laurier Papers, Bertram to Laurier, January 15, 1897. For opposition to the policy see *ibid.*, Senator Edwards to Laurier, November 15, 1898.

higher prices for common timber than had ever been obtained
either in Canada or the United States."[11] These and other remarkable occurrences were generally attributed to the new government
policy. Both Bertram and officials of the Crown Lands Department
pointed proudly to the manufacturing condition's accomplishments, and all along the Georgian Bay shoreline new sawmills
were either in production or under construction. The *Canada
Lumberman* calculated that these mills added 265 million board
feet annually to Canadian sawmilling capacity. A department
memorandum credited the policy with the creation of a thousand
new jobs paying wages of $1.50 per day.[12] The promoters and
pamphleteers had been right, for when the supply of Ontario
timber was shut off the American sawmills had had to move across
the lakes into Canada. Onlookers quickly assumed that similar
embargoes on the export of other natural resources would produce
similar results, and the prototype sawlog manufacturing condition
suddenly became a general resource development strategy.

The lumbermen had added, almost as an afterthought, that the
paper industry would benefit from a manufacturing condition as
well. "All I can say of pine," Rathbun noted in one of his
polemics, "applies to spruce, in fact more so."[13] Canada's pulp
and paper manufacturers agreed. In September 1898 seven of their
number convened in Ottawa to ask the federal government to levy
an export duty on outgoing raw pulpwood until such time as the
Americans removed their duties on incoming Canadian paper.[14]
The Laurier government turned them down, as it had so often
before, but in the province of Ontario the manufacturing condition
spirit was abroad. J. R. Stratton, in a widely praised speech on
the industrial potential of northern Ontario, urged a pulpwood

[11] Public Archives of Ontario, Ontario Lumberman's Association, *Minute Book*,
February 21, 1900.
[12] *Canada Lumberman*, March 1902; Ontario Department of Lands and Forests,
Woods and Forests Report Book No. 3, "Memorandum on the Benefits of Sawing
Logs in the Province," pp. 407-8, and also Crown Lands Department, *Annual
Report, 1900*, p. v.
[13] *Shall We Place an Export Duty on Sawlogs and Pulpwood?*, p. 6.
[14] *Monetary Times*, September 16, 1898; see also Laurier Papers, William Van
Horne (part owner of Laurentide Paper Mills) to Laurier, November 28, 1898.

manufacturing condition during the session of 1899: "We should decide to sell them [the Americans] our paper, but not one stick of spruce." With appropriate assistance from the legislature, he argued, Ontario industry could go into the markets of the world and beat the Americans with paper, just as it had done with cheese.[15] Officials in the Crown Lands Department, in reporting the success of the pine sawlog export prohibition, drew attention to the struggling pulp and paper enterprises then under contruction in what was now called "New Ontario." The juxtaposition was clear: the pulp and paper industry would be as well served by a manufacturing condition as the sawmilling industry had been.[16] Meanwhile politicians began to receive indications from the press and their correspondents that the policy of protection was extremely popular in the constituencies.[17] Even the free trade *Globe* and the leading financial paper, the *Monetary Times*, supported the extension of the manufacturing condition concept.[18] In 1900 the Ross government, by order-in-council, applied the restrictions prevailing on sawlog exports to pulpwood as well. Thereafter, all spruce cordwood taken from crown lands (though not of course fee simple, private lands) had to be manufactured into mechanical or chemical pulp in Canada.

The nickel problem was somewhat more complex. There the American mining company owned its mineral properties at Sudbury outright. The provincial government had no proprietary claim upon the mines as it had upon pine timber and spruce cut under timber licences. Secondly, the demand for a nickel manufacturing condition was bound up in an attempt by a group of Hamilton industrialists to break the monopoly of the Canadian Copper–Orford Copper axis. It was further complicated by the vengeance of Samuel J. Ritchie, the promoter of Canadian Copper, who had been frozen out by the more cautious American board of

[15] *Monetary Times*, March 10, 1899.
[16] Crown Lands Department, *Annual Report, 1899*, p. xiii.
[17] P.A.O., Whitney Papers, J. S. Macdonald to J. P. Whitney, undated, enclosing a clipping from the *News* dated December 17, 1899.
[18] *Globe*, April 30, 1900; *Monetary Times*, April 2, 1897.

directors and had now allied himself with the Hamilton interests to bring his enemies to their knees. These intricate coils, though interesting and enlightening in themselves, cannot detain us here.[19] It need only be said that the Ritchie group had acquired a patent for a new electrolytic nickel-refining process and was interested in establishing an integrated nickel-steel industry in the vicinity of the existing Hamilton iron smelting complex. To that end they had launched three separate companies: a mining company, a refining company and a nickel-steel manufacturing company. Parenthetically it should be noted here that the government of Ontario, inspired by an awareness of the metal's strategic importance in naval construction, had itself tried unsuccessfully to break the American monopoly on nickel in 1891. In fact, Oliver Mowat had attempted to interest the British Admiralty in a joint public venture in the nickel-steel field, but the Admiralty after some study turned this patriotic gesture down.[20] In 1898 Ritchie, on behalf of his new Canadian associates, began lobbying for greater protection for the nickel-refining industry. A mere 10 cents per pound export duty on nickel ore and matte, he pleaded in numerous letters to the Prime Minister of Canada, would revive the dormant iron mining industry and create a viable nickel-steel industry:

> The issue is therefore clearly made and joined between the Government and Parliament of Canada representing the people of Canada, on the one side, and the officials of the Canadian Copper Company representing nobody but themselves on the other side, as to whether the great natural resources of the country shall be made to serve the interests of two or three Americans who are alternatively persuasive and coercive in the policy and methods adopted

[19] For details see among others O. W. Main, *The Canadian Nickel Industry*, pp. 39-60.

[20] Alexander Campbell to Secretary of State, April 6, 1891; order-in-council, April 7, 1891; and report of A. S. Hardy, pp. 4-6, in *Papers, Orders-in-Council and Correspondence on the Mining and Treatment of Nickel and Copper Ore in the Province of Ontario* (Toronto, 1899).

before the Government and Parliament, to use the resources of the country for their personal gain. . . .[21]

John Patterson, the Liberal president of the Nickel Steel Company, and J. M. Gibson, the company's solicitor and the provincial
attorney general, prevailed upon the prime minister. But to no
avail. The Canadian Copper Company replied to Ritchie with
ad hominem letters and pamphlets of its own. Robert M. Thompson, president of Orford Copper, privately informed the prime
minister that his company owned properties in New Caledonia
(to underscore the point that Canada had no monopoly on nickel
ore) and argued strenuously that nickel refining could only be
economically performed in New Jersey given the readily available
supplies of coke, iron, coal and chemicals. If Laurier brought down
an export tariff, Thompson warned coldly, Canadian Copper
would simply close down its Sudbury mine. "I must tell you in all
sincerity," Laurier replied to Gibson, "that the Government is not
prepared, at this moment, to impose such a duty. The matter must
be very carefully looked into before such a conclusion is arrived
at."[22]

Rebuffed by Ottawa, the Hamilton group turned to the provincial government, where it already possessed enormous influence
in the person of Gibson. Here the request for protection received
an understanding hearing. In a memorandum dated November
23, 1899, the director of the Bureau of Mines argued the case for a
manufacturing condition on nickel ore. Now, he pointed out, even
the Admiralty recognized the critical importance of nickel-steel as
a factor in sea power. Secondly, financial considerations alone
recommended a policy of home manufacture. Between 1892 and

---

[21] *The Question of Export Duties on Nickel and Copper Mattes: The Anonymous
Circular Answered*, Ottawa, 1898, pp. 2, 8; Laurier Papers, Ritchie to Laurier,
December 22, 1897, Jan. 29, 1898, Feb. 18, 1898 and June 18, 1898.
[22] *Ibid.*, John Patterson to Laurier, July 19, 1898, and petition July 23, 1898, June
28, 1899; Gibson to Laurier, personal, June 27, 1898. See also Laurier to Gibson,
June 28, 1898. For the Canadian Copper side of the case see the pamphlets *The
Nickel Question* and *The Practical Side of the Export Duty Question*, both 1898,
and Laurier Papers, Stevenson Burke to Laurier, February 22, 1898, and R. M.
Thompson to Laurier, May 5 and November 2, 1899.

1898, he calculated, Ontario had exported over $4 million worth of nickel matte. Had this been refined in Canada and sold at market prices it would have returned over $14 million and Ontario would have received the benefit of that additional $10 million which had been divided between the workmen, coal and chemical companies, railroads and financial houses of the United States. On the basis of this memo the cabinet decided the next day to reopen talks with Admiralty officials and to impose the equivalent of an export duty on nickel ore and matte.[23] Since the government felt it had no authority to levy an export duty on minerals taken from private property, it chose instead a licence fee to be paid by each mining company at the rate of $60 a ton. If, however, the ore raised was refined in Canada the whole licence fee would be refunded. In this way the government amendment to the Mines Act brought down in 1900 penalized the American companies while promoting the interests of the Hamilton group.[24]

Thus by the end of the session in 1900 the manufacturing condition applied to sawlogs, pulpwood and nickel. It was expected that its application to the latter two resources would produce results similar to those achieved with the first. Needless to say, it did not. By 1904 the two major pulp and paper concerns that had been under construction as this debate unfolded collapsed into receivership. The same year the nickel-steel works at Sault Ste Marie were declared bankrupt, and the Hamilton nickel-refining group never progressed beyond the prospectus stage of development. The sawmilling industry had prospered, it was true, but extension of the manufacturing condition to pulpwood had had no measurable effect on stimulating pulp and paper production in Ontario. And, as we shall see, the manufacturing condition could not be applied to nickel. The varied response to and uneven application of the manufacturing condition, therefore, invite speculation

[23] Memorandum for the Commissioner of Crown Lands, November 23, 1899, and order in council, November 24, 1899, in *Papers, Orders-in-Council and Correspondence* . . . , pp. 13-15.
[24] T. Gibson, *Mining in Ontario*, p. 20; Royal Ontario Nickel Commission, *Report*, Toronto, 1917, p. 13; Main, *The Canadian Nickel Industry*, pp. 55-59. The relevant statute was 63 Vict., ch. 13.

on the conditions under which it was effective and the factors which inhibited its application.

Six major factors determined the effectiveness of Ontario's manufacturing policy. Not surprisingly, orthodox market conditions demand first consideration. Protective policies could do nothing to lower factor costs. People tended to associate the expansion of sawmilling completely with the manufacturing condition, but rising prices and stronger demand were plainly independent phenomena and every bit as important as government action in the location of the new sawmills. Ontario possessed a comparative advantage in the production of lumber in 1899 and that was what made the manufacturing condition work for the sawmilling industry.[25] Such was not yet the case in the nickel-steel or paper industries. Given the particular refining technique used by the Orford Copper Company, its argument that Canadian production would have been uneconomic was technically correct. When that technique changed from a heat process, in which the United States had an advantage, to an electrolytic process, in which Ontario with abundant, cheap hydroelectricity held a comparative advantage, then Ontario would become the seat of the nickel-refining industry. Coercive legislation would not be effective until this technological shift occurred. In 1900 the United States still possessed unexhausted stands of pulpwood close to market. Until scarcity drove prices up and until all available outside supplies of pulpwood were shut off, the established American industry was under no strong economic compulsion to move despite the Ontario prohibition. Thus market factors remained necessary conditions for industrial location but were not, it must be noted, sufficient in themselves.

The second limitation ironically arose from the very success of the protective lobbyists. After being turned down by Ottawa, they eventually convinced the Ontario government to act on their behalf. That represented an initial victory, but it also created another

---

[25] For lumber price indices, see M. C. Urquhart and K. A. H. Buckley, *Historical Statistics of Canada* (Toronto, 1965), p. 292, col. 26; for newsprint, see J. A. Guthrie, *The Newsprint Paper Industry*, pp. 40 ff.

problem. Henceforth, if the protective impulse in the resource sector were to be expressed as a national policy, all of the provinces would have to act in concert. In the case of pulpwood export prohibitions, for example, that proved to be a very difficult result to obtain. Quebec declined to join with Ontario, which left a gaping hole in the barrier raised between Canadian resources and American consumers. Quebec, being somewhat closer than Ontario to the wood-using industries of the American north-east, had already developed an extensive export business in sawlogs and pulpwood associated with both commercial operations and a northern settlement program. Ontario could make sweeping policy statements without conflicting too seriously with firmly established business patterns. But in Quebec, where vested interests and the church confounded attempts to extend the manufacturing condition on sawlogs and pulpwood across the inter-provincial boundary for another decade, that was not the case.[26] Coordination of provincial policies was now, in this sector, the only method of establishing coherent national resource policies.

A third qualification on the effectiveness of the manufacturing policy arose from the complexity of technology and the relative intensity of capital embodied in the desired industry. Capital-intensive, technologically complex industries resisted pressures toward mobility. It was easy enough to move a sawmill, but a pulpmill or a nickel refinery was another matter. Paper-making technology had stabilized by the turn of the century but it was still complex, and still best understood by the Americans who had perfected it. Canadians could see readily enough the applicability of that technology, but they had not mastered the technique themselves to any great extent, nor had a sufficiently large body of capitalists come forward to underwrite such enterprises. Nickel-refining technology had not yet stabilized by 1900. Moreover, the Sudbury ores proved to be extraordinarily complex and the only two processes then known capable of solving the problem remained the secrets of their owners, Ludwig Mond in England

---

[26] The relationship between church and export policies is first suggested by A. R. M. Lower in *Settlement of the Forest Frontier in Eastern Canada* (Toronto, 1936), pp. 76-93.

and R. M. Thompson of the Orford Copper Company. To break into the nickel business one first had to discover a suitable refining technique, and no Canadian had yet accomplished that. The Hamilton group had purchased an untried but promising process; everything depended upon its success. Financing research was as risky a proposition and as expensive as tackling an American corporate giant.

Fourthly, the relative legal access the provincial government possessed to the resource developer also seemed to set limits on the effectiveness of policy. Loggers did not own their timber limits; they rented them from the government on certain expressed conditions. It was a simple matter for the landlord (the government) to insert regulatory clauses into the tenant's (the lumbermen's) lease. That was the mechanism through which the sawlog and pulpwood restrictions worked. And the courts, as we have seen, upheld this as a legitimate use of the provincial proprietary right. But action on nickel followed a much more circuitous route because that resource had been converted into private property. Mining lands were sold in fee simple; therefore, the minerals raised were the private property of the miner. Here it appeared that the government's freedom of movement was limited. For example, there was a good deal of doubt whether, in the case of the $60 per ton licence fee, the government of Ontario was within its rights.[27] Its jurisdictional right was of a much lower power than the proprietary right exercised in the other two cases.

[27] Attorneys for the company and associated complainants argued that the $60 licence fee was a plain attempt to regulate trade and commerce and as such was (a) confiscatory, and (b) unconstitutional. W. R. P. Parker to Governor General in Council, September 13, 1900; J. M. Clark, Memorandum as to Disallowance of 63 Vict., ch. 13, March 1901, both in *Provincial Legislation*, Vol. II, pp. 9-12, 20-22. See also Laurier Papers, Parker to Laurier, March 19, 1901, and R. V. Sinclair to Laurier, April 22, 1901. For its part the province denied any intention to interfere with trade, arguing that the licence fee was but an attempt to raise revenue, a right in which the federal government had no power to "hamper, impair or interfere." See the Report of the Attorney General of Ontario, December 20, 1900, *Provincial Legislation*, Vol. II, pp. 20-22. The Minister of Justice in reply noted that the nickel ore was not taken from crown lands; that therefore the manufacturing condition argument of the sawlog case did not apply and that the licence system was in substance an attempt to regulate trade, a matter clearly beyond the competence of the provincial authority; see *ibid.*, Mills to Ross, May 7, 1901, pp. 37-39.

Next, if Canadian businessmen seriously hoped to move capital-intensive, technologically sophisticated industries they had surely to form a united front to do it. Cracks in the façade could be exploited; internal divisions and factions made a determined policy in the face of strong resistance almost impossible. Such a degree of uniformity did not exist within the Canadian business community then or now. Only minor internal opposition arose to the sawlog and pulpwood actions, but the nickel export restrictions raised a storm of protest. Not all of this came from interested quarters nor, given the fact that Canada was a capital-importing country, could all of the protests be lightly dismissed. And the resource developers themselves were not unanimous. John Bertram, one of the foremost advocates of the sawlog policy, appealed to Laurier to disallow the nickel counterpart because it was "detrimental to further investment." Respected bankers and financiers agreed. E. S. Clouston, the general manager of the Bank of Montreal, warned Laurier of a flight of capital:

> The inevitable result, if it is permitted to remain on the Statute Book will be, the closing of the doors to the flow of English capital. Dr. Mond is a very prominent man not only in the scientific but also in the manufacturing world, and if it is known in the London markets that after investing very largely in this country his property was practically confiscated by the Ontario Legislature, it will have a very serious affect on future English enterprise here.[28]

Petitions and letters poured in on the prime minister from all sorts of respected sources.[29] The very fact that so many enterprises depended upon capital imports made it extraordinarily dangerous

---

[28] Laurier Papers, Bertram to Laurier, April 11, 1901, and May 15, 1901 (confidential); E. S. Clouston to Laurier, May 6, 1901. For Laurier's replies indicating his eagerness to press on see Laurier Papers, Laurier to Bertram, May 16, 1901, and Laurier to Clouston, private, May 7, 1901.

[29] In the public debate the Ontario Conservative party, the *Globe*, the *World*, the *Mail and Empire,* the *Canadian Engineer* and the *Canadian Manufacturer* all supported the Ontario government's policy. The *Canadian Mining Review* and the Ontario Mining Protective Association fought for disallowance.

to embark upon a policy of coercing capital by restrictive legislation. In the unorganized, decentralized sawmilling industry this question did not arise. Nor did it come up over the pulpwood prohibition because the most important province, Quebec, took no action. Nickel, in which Ontario held a monopoly, was another matter entirely.

The last point to be considered is simply the power of the opposition and its skill in using the means at its disposal to counter the moves of the political authority. Orford Copper, the forerunner of International Nickel, provides an excellent illustration of the skilful use of concentrated economic power. Its opinions, resting as they did upon its financial strength, its mastery of a strategic technology, its contracts with the navy and major steel producers, and its informal agreements with its international quasi-competitors, carried enormous weight. If its directors made up their minds to refine Canadian ore in New Jersey, they were not easily moved by criticism, even coercion. They knew how to defend themselves, and they could afford a good defence. A well-advertised purchase of a New Caledonian orebody, no matter how inferior, gave them a second supply of natural resources with which to silence Canadian critics. Should Canadians insist on their foolish designs everything would be moved to New Caledonia. This threat proved decisive in public and private counsels.[30] It was especially useful in inflaming opinion in and around Sudbury and among the Canadian mining fraternity whose Ontario section depended to a large extent upon the nickel mines. Orford had strength and knew how to use it. Through an informal arrangement with Mond, the American company brought a re-

---

[30] For the pressure of the Orford interests upon the federal government see, *inter alia*, Laurier Papers, Stevenson Burke to Richard Cartwright, January 20 and February 8, 1900. On January 12, 1900, the miners at Sudbury called an open meeting to denounce the licence fee; see Whitney Papers, J. A. Orr to Whitney, April 12, 1900. An organization called the Ontario Mining Protective Association was quickly got up to fight the amendment. For a full transcript of its convention see the pamphlet, *The Ontario Mines Act*, Ottawa, 1900. This group arranged several deputations to Ottawa.

spected British ally into battle on its behalf, even though Mond's company was expressly exempted from the Ontario regulation.[31]

Moreover, the Orford officials knew how to work the Dominion-provincial machinery and successfully mobilized the senior level of government against the junior. Laurier permitted himself to become convinced that the Ontario legislation was "absolutely prohibitory," that it "could not be defended on general principles," and announced his intention to have it disallowed. He persisted even after the Liberal premier of Ontario warned him: "This disallowance would lead to a rupture between the two governments that might lead to disastrous results. We could not, you easily see, acquiesce in disallowance now any more than we did when the 'Rivers & Streams' Bill was disallowed by Sir John. . . ."[32] Nevertheless, Laurier stood his ground and the provincial government had to back down. It had no confidence in the legality of its case and, as time passed, no desire to test the Orford bluff. Laurier did not have to disallow the legislation for the simple reason that the Ontario government never proclaimed it. The provincial government and the Hamilton interests behind it had simply been outmanoeuvred by a much stronger, smarter opponent. It would take great cunning and confidence to erect a more durable policy in the face of such corporate determination. As Professor Armstrong reminds us in his contribution to this volume, the resource developers did not invent the Dominion-provincial game but they did advance it to its highest form.

---

[31] See that in the case of Clouston it was Dr. Mond's intervention on the side of Orford Copper that convinced him that a stoppage of capital would result if the act were left to stand; see above, note 28. Professor Main, in *The Canadian Nickel Industry*, suggests collusion between the two major refiners in mutual self-defence. It happened in 1900; it would happen again later. The circumstantial evidence here is very strong indeed. The Mond group only broke the united front with International Nickel once, and that was at the outbreak of the First World War and it was done on the advice of Byron Walker.

[32] Laurier Papers, Ross to Laurier, private, April 27, 1901. He goes on to say that the history of that case "tells all that need be known" of the political implications of such a rift. Here the correspondence is too extensive to list in its entirety; see the Laurier Papers for April and May, 1901.

Social Change and Political Crisis in Rural Ontario: The Patrons of Industry, 1889-1896

S. E. D. SHORTT

In 1889 an assemblage of Ontario Farmers formed the Grand Association of the Patrons of Industry. Beginning as a secret rural society, the organization rapidly became a political movement and, in the process, issued a comprehensive critique of Canadian economic and political life. The Patron crusade illustrated the dilemma of the farmer in a society in transition. The accelerated shift from a predominantly agricultural economy towards an industrial urban society produced a vocal response from the small-propertied interests of rural Ontario. These farmers were caught in what contemporary observers referred to as the "Social Crisis," or in what the American historian, Robert Wiebe, terms "The Search for Order."[1] Professor Michael Bliss has dealt with the response of business and labour to the social disorder of the 1890s in his discussion of the "protective impulse." But, unlike urban

[1] R. H. Wiebe, *The Search for Order, 1877-1920* (New York, 1967).

dwellers, Ontario farmers were unable to abandon classical economic liberalism in favour of collectivist action. Awed by the growth of monopoly capitalism, big government, and organized labour, the farmers, through the Patron organization, stood committed to a traditional "anti-protective impulse." Marshalling both laissez faire economic arguments and the rhetoric of democratic politics, their protests represented the dying cries of old Ontario agriculture. After a brief flirtation with independent political action, a final attempt to defend anachronistic rural values, the farmers of Ontario conceded the struggle. They returned to traditional party alliances, diversified their crops, and accepted the changes which accompanied the prosperity of the Laurier era. Yet the brief career of the Patrons of Industry was not without significance. They exemplified the problems encountered by agrarian politics in a heterogeneous society and also illustrated the difficulty in reconciling traditional values to an evolving social order.

I

The Patrons of Industry were founded in 1887 at Port Huron, Michigan, as a secret rural lodge.[2] Before the order's American demise in 1892, a branch was established near Sarnia. By 1891 all ties with the parent organization had been severed, and two years later the association claimed 100,000 members in Ontario, orga-

---

[2] For a study of the American Patrons see Sidney Glazer, "The Patrons of Industry in Michigan," *Mississippi Valley Historical Review*, Vol. 24, No. 2, 1937. While an off-shoot of an American organization, the Patrons were not greatly influenced by American farm politics. As Paul Sharp suggests of western Canada, Canadian farmers simply responded to similar economic circumstances in the same fashion as their counterparts in the United States. See P. F. Sharp, *Agrarian Revolt in Western Canada* (Minneapolis, 1948), p. 58. It is interesting to note the prominence of former Canadians in Kansas Populism, described by Walter Nugent in *The Tolerant Populists*, (Chicago, 1963), pp. 135, 202, 223. For an account of the Patrons in Manitoba, see Brian McCutcheon, "The Patrons of Industry in Manitoba," in Donald Swainson, ed., *Historical Essays on the Prairie Provinces* (Toronto, 1970).

nized in two thousand local clubs.[3] This rapid growth was a reflection of the precarious state of Ontario agriculture in the early 1890s. Farmers were in the process of shifting from grain-raising to dairy and livestock production, while at the same time they bore the burdens of steadily declining prices and rural depopulation. The price levels for grain, livestock, and cheese reveal this dilemma. Prices fell rapidly during the early 1890s, rose briefly in the middle of the decade and declined steadily until the late 1890s.[4] By 1896 the *Farmer's Advocate*, often unduly optimistic, described the preceeding summer as "one of the most trying seasons [to which] Ontario agriculture has ever been subjected." Patron Grand President C. A. Mallory evidenced a similar concern when he stated, "Our aim has been to discover as far as possible the causes of the depression in the agricultural interests of this country."[5] While the Patrons were by no means concerned solely with economic matters, their initial growth was largely due to prolonged agriculture depression in a period of crop transition and rural depopulation.

The Patrons rapidly established a formal organization in Ontario and undertook a number of economic ventures: retail agreements with local merchants, the successful leasing of a salt mine at Kincardine, and the establishment of cooperative enterprises such as the Patron Cordage and Implement Company at Brantford. Of more significance, however, was the acquisition of a newspaper. The *Weekly Sun* had begun publication in London under the editorship of George Wrigley in 1892. It became the official Patron journal, changed its name to the *Canada Farmers'*

[3] Fred Landon, *Western Ontario and the American Frontier* (New Haven, 1941; reprinted in the Carleton Library, No. 34, 1967), p. 257; L. A. Wood, *A History of Farmer's Movements in Canada* (Toronto, 1924), p. 118; *Farmers' Sun*, February 21, 1893.

[4] C. C. James, "The Development of Agriculture in Ontario," *Appendix To the Report of the Ontario Bureau of Industries for 1896* (Toronto, 1897); *Ontario Agriculture Commission*, Vol. 2, Appendix B (Toronto, 1881); *Farmer's Advocate*, Vol. 25, 1890, p. 2; *Farmers' Sun*, February 13, 1895; Canada, Department of Agriculture, *Federal Census*, 1931, Vol. 1, pp. 366-67.

[5] *Farmer's Advocate*, Vol. 31, 1896, p. 2; *Farmers' Sun*, February 21, 1893.

Sun, and moved to Toronto. According to Liberal party organizer
Alex Smith, by 1894 Liberal journals had been abandoned in
rural areas in favour of the *Sun*. Two years later, however, after
the political demise of the Patrons, the *Farmers' Sun* faced financial ruin. It was acquired by Dr. Goldwin Smith, and managed by
the Sun Printing Company under Caleb Mallory and Walter D.
Gregory. Renamed the *Weekly Sun*, the journal's circulation of
twelve thousand was soon cut in half due to "The Bystander's"
opposition to the Boer War. Nevertheless, Smith's dying words in
1910 were reported as "Forward the Toronto *Sun*." The paper did
continue, and in 1918 became the official organ of the United
Farmers of Ontario.[6]

With a weekly newspaper at their disposal, the Patrons began
to publicize their critique of the Canadian economy and politics
in 1892. The focus of their criticisms was the National Policy,
through which the Conservative party had unsuccessfully attempted to revive the languishing Canadian economy for a dozen
years. Ironically, even if the National Policy had succeeded, the
results would have been of little benefit to rural Ontario. It was
hardly in the interest of the central Canadian farmer that settlers
should fill the West, that expensive railways should span the
continent or that a protected steel industry should develop to
monopolize the farm implement market. Economic policy, the
farmers reasoned, was a function of political power. The origins
of the National Policy obviously rested with a group whose
interests were opposed to those of agriculture. The *Farmers' Sun*
described the "capitalist" architects of this policy when it lamented
that in Canada one found

> the greatest aggregation of plunderers that ever sought . . .
> to rob, debauch, or tyrannize any people . . . they represent
> almost every industry on which the nation must depend . . .

---

[6] P.A.C., Laurier Papers, Smith to Laurier, December 7, 1893; M. H. Staples, *The
Challenge of Agriculture: The Story of the United Farmers of Ontario* (Toronto,
1921), pp. 105-110; R. C. Brown, "Goldwin Smith and Anti-Imperialism,"
Canadian Historical Review (C.H.R.), XLIII, 2, 1963, p. 196.

they possess a power and wield it with a defiance of public interest.[7]

In the minds of the Patrons, economic discontent had fused with political frustration to produce a vehement condemnation of the National Policy. Their initial discontent centred on tariffs, artificial monopolies, extravagant railway construction, and expensive immigration schemes. Searching for an explanation of these maleficent policies, the Patrons isolated two major factors: disproportionate urban political influence, and a generally corrupt system of party politics. For each of these abuses the farmers offered a remedy; the result was a program of reform which questioned the economic and political basis of the National Policy.

The protective tariff provided a convenient point of departure for the Patron critique of public policy. The London platform of 1891 called for a revenue tariff falling exclusively on luxuries, world reciprocal trade, and the maintenance of the British connection. By 1896 the Patron platform no longer mentioned the British connection, and the *Sun* openly opposed an imperial zollverein, advocating instead a scheme of continental union.[8] This apparent shift towards continentalism, however, was largely due to the influence of Goldwin Smith, who financed the *Farmers' Sun* after 1896. While historians have often held that rural western Ontario, the heart of Patron strength, was the centre of annexationist sentiment,[9] the attitude of the Patrons would seem to qualify this judgment for the 1890s. President C. A. Mallory concisely stated the Patron position in answer to an inquiry from T. M. White, secretary of the Continental Union Association. He wrote:

. . . so far as I have been able to learn there is no general feeling of favour to Political Union existing among the

[7] *Farmers' Sun*, November 8, 1892.

[8] *Ibid.*, May 15, 1892; February 27, 1895; September 30, 1896.

[9] Goldwin Smith, *Canada and the Canadian Question* (Toronto, 1891), p. 282; D. F. Warner, *The Idea of Continental Union* (Lexington, 1960), pp. 183, 190; R. C. Brown, *Canada's National Policies, 1883-1900* (Princeton, 1964), p. 135.

> Patrons of Industry. We favour more strongly free trade
> with Great Britain rather than the United States feeling
> that the Americans could not maintain a high tariff against
> us in that event.[10]

Nevertheless, while disavowing continental union, the Patrons remained adamantly opposed to the protective tariff.

A particularly malignant side effect of protection, the Patrons felt, was the growth of monopolies. The farmers did not oppose the process of industrialism, but they emphasized that "just wealth" could result only from actual labour. "One of the greatest evils society has had to contend with," wrote the *Farmers' Sun*, "has been a faulty and unequal system of distribution, by which the actual producer whether of the city or country, has been despoiled to enrich the non-producing class—capitalists, traders, professional men and middlemen." To control the growth of despoiling combines the Patrons suggested a number of reforms— anti-trust legislation; higher taxation on profits from mortgages, stocks and debentures; and finally, increased consumer credit through the monetization of silver. One form of monopoly which the Patrons singled out for special criticism was the railway company. According to the *Sun*, "Cheap railway rates are a necessity if the majority of our people are not to become mere hewers of wood and drawers of water to the bondholders of Canadian railways." The journal advocated the use of American Atlantic ports, condemned "the all-red line" as a tax on farmers to send manufactured goods to the Australasian part of the Empire, considered the C.P.R. land grant system to be corrupt, and demanded an end to federal rail subsidies.[11] Combines in general, and railways in particular, were condemned by the Patrons.

The farmers were scarcely more favourable towards government sponsored immigration. According to the *Sun,* immigration schemes had cost the Dominion $3.75 million between 1879 and

[10] Queen's University Archives, Walter Dymond Gregory Papers, Mallory to White, October 31, 1892.
[11] *Farmers' Sun*, February 6, 1893; February 21, 1893; December 27, 1892; May 15, 1894; June 12, 1895; September 30, 1896; October 21, 1896; February 27, 1895.

1893. The expenditure, the journal felt, was excessive and, except by providing extra labour for harvest, in no way aided the farmer. In fact, by opening the West for agriculture, immigration had actually harmed rural Ontario. Wrote the *Sun*: "Profit in grain raising in older Canada ceased when we taxed ourselves to develop the great grain producing prairies of the North-West." "Trumping up immigration," continued the journal, "out of the dissatisfied and n'er-do-well class in any country is a business for which the people cannot afford to pay."[12] Federal immigration schemes were clearly an anathema to the Ontario farmers.

When the Patrons turned from their pragmatic criticism of the National Policy and searched for the cause of their discomfiture, disproportionate urban political influence was labelled as a primary factor. Farmers, according to the *Sun*, held little influence in determining public policy. "A nation of farmers with a cabinet of lawyers!", the journal exclaimed. "Is it any wonder we howl about hard times?" This urban domination was exacerbated by the city dwellers' image of the farmer. Wrote the *Sun*: "The prevailing idea in the cities is that as a class farmers are a close-fisted miserable lot of people. . . ."[13] As a consequence, urban politicians exploited the farmer's franchise by soliciting his vote yet ignored his demands. To improve the political influence of rural areas the Patrons offered two policies: the organization of agrarian interests, and the decentralization of the governmental process.

In the preamble to the Patron constitution it was stressed that "commerce, manufacturing and all other enterprises of importance" had organized for their own benefit. To compete with these urban groups the farmers formed the Patron movement and excluded from membership "all persons of proved immoral character, and lawyers, Doctors, Merchants, Liquor Dealers, Manufacturers, Party Politicians, and those whose interests conflict with those of Farmers and labourers."[14] Through rural solidarity the

---

[12] *Ibid.*, October 3, 1894; February 13, 1895; June 26, 1895.
[13] *Ibid.*, November 28, 1893; May 10, 1892.
[14] P.A.C., *Constitution and Rules of the Patrons of Industry* (Strathroy, 1892), pp. 3 and 4.

Patrons hoped to counterbalance the political influence of urban groups, but they also advocated extensive reforms designed to allow increased measures of local political autonomy. It was suggested that electoral districts should be drawn to preclude gerrymandering and, at the same time, conform closely to established municipal boundaries in order to preserve the existing "unity of interests." These boundaries would be designated, not by Toronto politicians, but by prominent and impartial local men who would also prepare the district electoral lists. The judicial system of the province, according to the Patrons, should also be decentralized. They recommended that the Superior Courts be localized and the jurisdiction of Division Courts be extended. Finally, the Patrons suggested that all local officials, with the exception of judges, should be appointed by the counties rather than the province.[15] By decentralizing the functions of everyday government and organizing the farmers to manipulate these new units of administration, the Patrons hoped to destroy urban political domination.

Yet certain functions of government by necessity would remain with the authorities at Toronto and Ottawa. This situation raised the second major political abuse criticized by the Patrons: a corrupt and unprincipled system of party politics. "We believe party politics is the anvil on which our chains are being forged," the *Farmers' Sun* lamented, "partisan politics is the anesthetic given while it is being done." The men associated with this partisanship the *Sun* described as a great "aggregation of plunderers" representing selfish industrial concerns. These men dominated both the Liberal and Conservative parties which were said to employ extensive political machines and corrupt electoral practices. Under such conditions party principle disappeared and public issues were resolved solely on the basis of graft and patronage. This system placed inept persons in the public service, conferred titles on Canadians who possessed political influence, issued railway passes to members of Parliament, maintained extravagant offices at the farmers' expense, and granted special privileges to the medical

[15] *Farmers' Sun*, May 10, 1892; May 16, 1894; December 27, 1892; April 18, 1893.

and legal professions.[16] Each of these abuses the farmers noted and sought to eliminate in their platforms.

The solution to the problem of partyism and corruption, according to the Patrons, was the popularization of government. Wrote the *Farmers' Sun*: "There never was and there never will be for any length of time a government for the people until there first comes a government by the people." To this end the Patrons advocated the use of the initiative and referendum. Not only would these procedures diminish corruption, but the voters would also receive a political education and more "social legislation" would be placed under serious consideration. In the selection of municipal councils the Patrons recommended the adoption of proportional representation to ensure seats for farmers and all "others interested in social reform." The Patrons also demanded that women be enfranchised and a more adequate system of revision for voters' lists be devised. The Senate was dismissed as "of no practical value" and its abolition urged. Civil service reform was suggested through appointment on merit and promotion according to seniority. Locally, a system of continuous inspection was recommended to destroy corruption in county offices.[17] Generally, the guiding principle of the Patron program for political reform emerged as an attempt to popularize the selection and operation of government.

"The *Farmers' Sun*," wrote the *Hamilton Herald*, "is the Richard Cartwright of Canadian journalism . . . it devotes its energies to finding fault with the politicians of both camps and sowing seeds of discontent."[18] Yet the Patrons and their journal were more than congenital dissidents. Ultimately, their critique of the economic and political implications of the National Policy was directed at the restoration of a system of liberal democracy which they felt had been subverted by monopolists, professionals and

[16] *Ibid.*, June 6, 1893; November 8, 1893; July 4, 1894; September 5, 1894; May 31, 1892; February 20, 1894; September 26, 1893; September 19, 1894.
[17] *Ibid.*, November 8, 1892; July 5, 1892; January 17, 1893; October 10, 1894; July 24, 1898; February 27, 1895; September 5, 1894.
[18] *Ibid.*, July 3, 1895.

politicians. They hoped to return to the farmer the right to compete in an uninhibited market and to exercise his vote in equal effect with other citizens of the province. Such aspirations, the farmers eventually realized, could not be effected through protest alone—only through political action as a class could the farmers hope to reform Canadian public life and policy. The *Farmers' Sun* issued the call for action:

> The farmers of Canada represent the greater part of the national wealth. They pay the major part of the taxes and if we look way off in the future we may easily forecast the continued increase of our burdens unless we revolt under the yoke of our modern Rehoboams—Messrs. Foster and Company. . . .[19]

II

The initial stage in the political evolution of the Patrons was the transformation of the order from a quasi-secret rural society to an active political party. In August of 1892, Grand President Mallory indicated that Patrons were far from uninterested in public affairs. While the movement was non-partisan, he declared, the Patrons were "intensely political" in their commitment to rural betterment. When farmers responded to Mallory's call for rural solidarity at a London rally in September, they were informed by Grand Trustee T. O. Currie that extreme partyism and a lack of principle characterized Canadian politics. Currie told his audience that the Patrons could best deal with the situation by carefully casting their vote for honest men. If there remained any doubt that the Patrons were rapidly approaching political organization, these doubts were dispelled the following spring. The Perth County Patrons nominated a candidate for the provincial legislature and the reaction of the *Farmers' Sun* was indicative of the approaching transformation. "Let Patrons in

[19] *Ibid.*, June 6, 1893.

other counties go and do likewise," the journal advised; "the day of judgment is coming."[20] Upon the motion of George Wrigley, publisher of the *Sun,* the Patron Grand Association in Toronto resolved to contest all forthcoming elections.[21] "Lines of political history are being written every day," was the *Sun*'s jubilant comment, "and the Patron order is wielding an important influence in guiding the inscribing pen." Despite the reservations of individual members,[22] with this apocalyptic outburst the Patrons of Industry became a political party.

The second stage in the political career of the Patrons opened with their active entry into provincial politics. Their platform was an amorphous creation, often concerned with issues outside provincial jurisdiction, but emphasizing economic and honest administration. According to President Mallory, the movement hoped only to secure the balance of power in the provincial assembly. This view was also expressed by Grand Trustee J. L. Wilson, who told the Toronto *Globe* that his organization would not join Meredith and the Conservatives to defeat the Liberals, provided Premier Mowat responded to the Patron policy of "give and take."[23] Principal George Grant of Queen's University applauded this non-partisan approach to politics:

> A new factor promises to exert an important influence on both Dominion and Provincial politics. The Patrons of Industry represent the most numerous, the most healthy and the most reliable element in the country. . . . If the leaders of the new organization are unselfish men, they may exert a vast influence for good in breaking up party lines that represent dead issues, as well as obtaining for us simple and economical government, lessening the amount of patronage or bribery . . . and taking the shackles off trade, commerce and industry.[24]

[20] *Ibid.,* August 30, 1892; September 27, 1892; May 16, 1893.
[21] Toronto Public Library (T.P.L.), *Minutes of the Second Annual Meeting of the Grand Association of Patrons of Industry* (Toronto, 1893), p. 23.
[22] *Farmers' Sun,* July 11 and July 18, 1893.
[23] *Ibid.,* May 15, 1894; January 9, 1894; December 12, 1893.
[24] "Current Events," *Queen's Quarterly,* I, 3, 1894, p. 252.

Premier Oliver Mowat's reaction to the Patron order was understandably less enthusiastic. He stated that his government had already implemented many programs for the farmers and concluded:

> Not one article . . . in [their] platform affects farmers specifically or otherwise than in common with all the other classes. Of articles affecting provincial matters, one only is not in accordance with the policy and practice hitherto pursued by the Ontario Reform Government, and that one is respecting patronage.[25]

Despite Mowat's attempt to minimize the differences between the Patrons and the Liberal party, the results of the 1894 provincial election indicated that many voters felt a need for independent representation. The Patrons entered 56 candidates in the election, of whom 17 were successful. However, in twenty constituencies an average shift of 3 per cent of the voters would have resulted in Patron victories. In these areas, two-thirds of the seats were narrow Liberal victories. Had the Patrons actually taken them, the legislature composed of 50 Liberals, 23 Conservatives, 17 Patrons, and 4 Independents, would have been radically altered. The Patrons would have held 37 seats, the Liberals 36, the Conservatives 17, and Independents 4. Indeed, a Patron government might well have anticipated the United Farmers of Ontario electoral victory in 1919 by a quarter-century.[26]

The main area of Patron electoral strength lay west of a line drawn from Midland to Guelph and then to Niagara Falls. The farmers were also strong in ridings from Prince Edward County to the Quebec border. Approximately half the victories were in established Liberal areas, while the other half were traditionally Conservative. At least half the ridings which elected Patrons

[25] Cited in C. R. W. Biggar, *Sir Oliver Mowat* (Toronto, 1905), pp. 500-501.
[26] *Farmers' Sun*, April 17, May 8, June 27, 1894; Wood, *op. cit.*, pp. 139-140; *Sessional Papers of the Province of Ontario*, XXVII, Part I, 1895; *Canadian Parliamentary Companion*, 1897 (Ottawa, 1897). In 1919 half the ridings which had elected Patrons returned U.F.O. members.

returned to old alliances in subsequent elections. In the constituencies in which the farmers were successful, major religious groups (Church of England, Roman Catholic, Presbyterian, Methodist, and Baptist) were usually balanced in such a fashion as to give no single group clear numerical superiority. In areas where Patrons were clearly defeated there tended to occur large single religious groups, often Methodists but in two cases Roman Catholic. In ridings which came very close to electing Patrons, religious distribution varied between balanced and large groups of Methodists. No discernible differences existed on an ethnic basis among constituencies in which Patrons were elected, almost elected, or defeated. All three types showed approximately the same proportion (20 per cent) of foreign-born citizens. In areas of Patron strength there seemed a very slight tendency towards larger groups with Irish or Scottish ancestry, while in defeated areas the trend was slightly towards English.[27] No pattern emerges from the electoral results, then, on the basis of traditional voting behaviour, religion, or ethnic origins. The pattern most clearly discernible is geographic: the best agricultural areas in the province tended to show Patron strength.

The unprecedented Patron success in two-party Ontario paved the way for the third and final stage in the Patron political career, the entry into national politics. The federal ambitions of the Patron party did not pass without notice, least of all by Sir Richard Cartwright. The veteran Liberal campaigner anticipated a growing Patron influence and sought to fuse the farmers with his own party. "I am . . . on every account," he wrote, "strongly in sympathy with the Patrons of Industry as far as Dominion politics are concerned." Cartwright pledged his support for a low tariff, and the Liberal platform of 1896 emphasized not only freer trade, but also honest, economical administration and decentralization of government—all primary Patron demands.[28]

[27] *Canadian Parliamentary Companion*, for 1881, 1885, 1887, 1891, 1897, 1901 and 1905; *Federal Census*, 1931, Vol. 3, pp. 252-288 and 339-351.
[28] *Farmers' Sun*, October 24, 1896; January 23, 1895; also Cartwright's *Reminiscences* (Toronto, 1912), p. 337, and Laurier Papers, Cartwright to Laurier, October 22, 1894.

Across the Dominion, individual Liberals spoke directly to the farmers. "I denounce the policy of protection as bondage—yea, bondage," proclaimed Wilfrid Laurier, "and I refer to bondage in the same manner in which the American slavery was bondage." The rhetoric was indistinguishable from that of any farm radical. Clifford Sifton made a similar appeal when he explained Liberal tariff policy to a rural audience: "Free coal oil, free clothing, and free implements you shall have if the Liberal Party are returned to power."[29] Despite these Liberal attempts to win farm support, it appeared that the Patrons rejected any electoral coalition. Sir Richard Cartwright was condemned as an "industrialist" and the *Sun* declared that farmers were justified in voting for a Liberal only in constituencies which no Patron candidate contested.[30]

While Cartwright sought Patron support on one side, D'Alton McCarthy and his disaffected Conservatives approached from the opposite direction. McCarthy's campaign was characterized by opposition to a high tariff and a vehement anti-Catholicism. The Patrons were free-traders and doubtless individual members were Equal Righters or connected with the Protestant Protective Association. With this somewhat similar outlook, a form of electoral alliance might have been expected. Yet the Patrons rejected a formal coalition. To the farmers, McCarthy was a lawyer and consequently excluded from joining, much less leading, the Patron party. The Patrons had no desire to be associated with McCarthy's militant Protestantism, and charged that his followers merely detracted voting strength from the Patron campaign. McCarthy himself lamented his lack of farm support. In 1895 he wrote to the *Farmers' Sun*:

> I have never had any quarrel with the Patron movement. I do not admire class legislation . . . but while I say that of the Patrons, and I have a regard for them, I find they have

[29] Cited in V. C. Fowke, *Canadian Agricultural Policy* (Toronto, 1946), p. 262. Note the low opinion of the Patrons held by J. D. Edgar, Laurier Papers, Edgar to Laurier, December 23, 1893, and by J. S. Willison, *ibid.*, Willison to Laurier, November 29, 1894.
[30] *Farmers' Sun*, November 14, 1894.

no regard for me . . . I think it would have done no harm
for us to go along together as far as we could agree.[31]

Not only did the Patrons recoil from McCarthyite overtures,
but they also took pains to deny charges of intolerance by emphasizing that their organization was rigidly non-sectarian. At a
Liberal rally in North Bruce Premier Mowat charged the Patrons
with supporting a P.P.A. candidate in the Lambton by-election.
The *Queen's Quarterly,* usually sympathetic to the farmers,
warned:

> It is no mark of real independence in the Patrons to regard
> the C.P.A. [Canadian Protective Association, successor to
> the P.P.A.] as having the same right to exist politically as
> any inoffensive Roman Catholic; nor is it any mark of real
> independence that a Patron may be a member of the C.P.A.
> though he must not be either a Liberal or a Conservative.

Innuendo of this type forced the Patrons to appoint a Committee to investigate the order's relations with the P.P.A. Reporting to the third annual meeting in Toronto in 1894, the committee
stated that the Patrons were strictly non-sectarian; that individual
Patrons were Roman Catholics or members of the P.P.A. according to choice; and finally, that allegations of Patron religious
bigotry were a device employed by the partisan press to discredit
the farmers.[32]

It would appear that the Patrons were not greatly influenced
by currents of anti-Catholic nativism. While the strength of both
the Patrons and the P.P.A. lay in western Ontario, the latter
found a large portion of its strength in towns. There was definitely
political support lent to the Patrons from P.P.A. groups and
individuals in certain rural ridings. In North Bruce and Simcoe
Centre P.P.A. members ran as Patron candidates, while in North

[31] *Ibid.*, March 18, 1894; December 12, 1893; July 8, 1896; January 3, 1895.
[32] *Constitution and Rules* . . . , pp. 4, 14; *Farmers' Sun*, November 28, 1893; "Current Events," *Queen's Quarterly*, I, 4, 1894, p. 334; T.P.L., *Minutes of the Third Annual Meeting* . . . (Toronto, 1894), pp. 25-26.

Middlesex and North Oxford support was withdrawn from nom-
inees when P.P.A. connections were revealed. Of the 17 Patrons
elected to the legislature, only 2 had P.P.A. ties; at least 8
Conservatives had such connections. Two constituencies which
elected Patrons, Glengarry and Stormont, had large proportions
of Roman Catholic voters, while in Prescott and Russell constituencies, both largely Catholic, the Patrons were soundly
defeated. Roman Catholic voters apparently felt no discernible
affinity or hostility towards the Patrons. Such neutrality supports
the Patron claim that they had no anti-Catholic views. In one
of its rare facetious moments the *Farmers' Sun* actually poked
fun at the charges of bigotry. "The P.P.A. will live in history,"
it wrote. "It is the Patron-Prohibition Alliance."[33]

While at pains to avoid entanglements with both Liberals and
McCarthyites, the Patrons seemed to welcome the support of
organized labour. In the 1880s, a similar concept of social reform
underlay the rhetoric of both labour and farm organizations. The
Knights of Labor condemned the aggregation of wealth by unscrupulous "capitalists" and argued that the benefits of labour
correctly accrued to the labourer alone. To promote such a belief
they came together as a class, excluding from their ranks professionals, businessmen, and "purveyors of intoxicants." Many of
their social assumptions were shared by the Grange and their
political demands were often similar—establishment of cooperative
enterprises, an end to land speculation, the abolition of partyism,
and public ownership of communications. In view of this similarity
in outlook, in 1886, the Trades and Labor Congress of Canada
attempted to interest the Grange in "securing closer relations . . .
on all matters looking to the elevation of the working classes
and adequate representation of their interests in our legislatures."
But "the little clique of antiquated barnacles who at present

[33] J. T. Watt, "Anti-Catholic Nativism in Canada: The Protestant Protective Association," *C.H.R.* XLVIII, 1, 1967, p. 50, and "Anti-Catholic Nativism in Ontario
Politics: The Role of the Protestant Protective Association in the Ontario Election
of 1894," *Ontario History*, LIX, 3, 1967, pp. 62-64; *Federal Census*, 1891, Vol. III,
pp. 252-288; *Farmers' Sun*, June 26, 1895. Nugent reaches similar conclusions
concerning the American Populists.

constitute the ruling power of the Granges," in the *Labour Palladium*'s phrase, rejected manhood suffrage in favour of an education qualification, preferred an income rather than land tax, favoured assisted immigration, and condemned the eight-hour day.[34] As a result, no alliance was concluded between organized labour and farmers.

As the depression deepened in the 1890s, the farmers became more militant and attempts were made to link the Patrons of Industry and the Trades and Labor Congress. According to the Patron constitution, "farmers and employees upon whose labours depend the prospects of the nation are almost entirely unorganized." Consequently, the Patrons would be "an organization of farmers and others, whose interests are identical with those of the farmers . . . to advance the moral, intellectual, social, political, and financial conditions of the said classes in this country, and to generally develop a higher character of that great industrial class that performs so important a part in providing for the subsistence and advancing the prosperity of all nations." The spirit of producing-class solidarity was emphasized again in March of 1893. At the second Annual Convention of the Patrons, President Mallory stated, "All are anxiously looking forward to the time when the toilers of the Dominion will be able to declare, through a united brotherhood, that 'industrial moral worth, not wealth shall be the standard of individual and national greatness.'" At a later session, addressing both farmers and labour representatives, Toronto Trades and Labor Council President T. W. Banton concluded by declaring that "all classes were uniting in one great democratic movement towards a common goal, which must eventually elevate the industrial classes to their proper place in society."[35]

Though less impressive than sweeping declarations of solidarity, the published platforms of both farmers and workers evidenced

[34] Martin Robin, *Radical Politics and Canadian Labour, 1880-1930* (Kingston, 1968), pp. 20-26; Wood, *op. cit.*, p. 104.
[35] *Constitution and Rules* . . . , pp. 3-4, *Minutes of the Second Annual Meeting* . . . , p. 2; *Farmers' Sun*, March 7, 1893.

a solid basis for political cooperation. Both groups called for the abolition of the Senate, female suffrage, an end to assisted immigration, the establishment of technical and agricultural schools, restrictions on usury, and the prohibition of government aid to railways. Further, certain individuals seemed to maintain personal contact with both farm and labour groups. W. C. Good, later prominent in the United Farmers of Ontario, recalls in his autobiography attending meetings of the Canadian Socialist League. More significant is the case of George Wrigley, who not only founded and edited the *Sun,* but also founded the Canadian Socialist League and its journal *Citizen and Country.*[36]

Concurring in the labour theory of value and in hostility to "middleman rake-off," agreeing on numerous political demands, and united by specific personalities, the farmers and workers naturally attempted formal organization. In early 1893 the Trades and Labor Congress and the Patrons established a continuing committee on cooperation. The labour group subsequently agreed to submit civil service reform to its members for ratification, while the Patrons were asked to consider the initiative and referendum as well as proportional representation. In September 1893, the Dominion Trades and Labor Congress debated whether a Patron could join the Knights of Labor, and at the Tenth Annual Session of the T.L.C. the Patrons were admitted to full membership. In return, the Patrons invited labour representatives to their 1894 convention and considered establishing urban branches of the Patrons to attract working-class membership. In 1895, however, the T.L.C. barred the Patrons from their organization, and no formal alliance was ever concluded. Nevertheless, cordial relations continued between farmers and labour. The *Industrial Banner,* for example, praised the Patron delegation in the legislature for its continuing fight against undue privilege.[37] Friend-

---

[36] H. A. Logan, *Trade Unions in Canada* (Toronto, 1948), pp. 62-70; W. C. Good, *Farmer Citizen* (Toronto, 1958), p. 45; Paul Fox, "Early Socialism in Canada," in J. H. Aitchinson, *The Political Process in Canada* (Toronto, 1963), p. 88.

[37] *Farmers' Sun,* March 7, April 25, September 12, 1893; Robin, *op. cit.,* p. 32; Wood, *op. cit.,* p. 121; *Farmers' Sun,* August 29, 1894; October 27, 1895; April 26, 1896.

ship rather than formality characterized the relationship between the Patrons and organized labour.

Despite similarities in outlook, labour and farmers held basically incompatible attitudes towards society. The Patrons expressed an almost classical liberal economic doctrine, which revealed their own small-propertied interests. Reflecting entrepreneurial ambitions, the farmers diagnosed the economic plight of Canada as one of corrupt public intervention rather than one of lethargic government. The farmers opposed, as a result, subsidies to farm products, legislation awarding employer accident compensation to farm labour, and the use of the strike or boycott in labour disputes. Only the passage of anti-trust legislation was favoured, for it would advance the liberal end of free competition. This type of economic attitude was not unlike that expressed by the Knights of Labor, who sought a return to a small artisan economy and deplored the "wage-slave" system. As long as labour expressed such views, some cooperation with farmers was possible. But in the later 1880s, Canadian labour adopted "business unionism" in preference to the utopian reformism of the Knights.[38] This change indicated an acceptance of very large-scale industrialism, agitation for shorter hours, the occasional use of strikes and boycotts, demands for welfare legislation—in short, recognition of the existence of a permanent urban working class with interests entirely peculiar to itself. These interests, by necessity, required a retreat from a laissez-faire economy and limited government. As a result, the business unionism of labour proved incompatible with the farmers' liberal economic attitudes. Not until 1919, when the United Farmers of Ontario received the backing of the Independent Labour Party, would farmers and labour unite effectively for political action.

[38] *Farmers' Sun*, January 17, April 18, March 7, February 21, 1893; Gerald Grob, *Workers and Conflict: A Study of Ideological Conflict in the American Labor Movement, 1865-1900* (Evanston, 1961); Norman Pollack, *The Populist Response to Industrial America* (New York, 1966); Bernard Ostry, "Conservatives, Liberals and Labour in the 1880's," *Canadian Journal of Economics and Political Science*, XXVII, 2, 1961, pp. 158-161.

III

Reflecting on the farmers' foray into politics, Goldwin Smith recalled, "The Patrons with their political inexperience, and their simple-minded openness to intrigue, were between the two regular parties as a flock of sheep between two packs of wolves, and the result was a collapse." In his terse fashion Smith had summarized the electoral disaster which befell the Patrons in 1896. On June 6, some two weeks before the federal election, a story of political intrigue was revealed by the London *Free Press* and reprinted by the Toronto *Daily Mail and Empire*. Grand Secretary L. A. Welch, disillusioned by the actions of former Grits within the Patron order, released a private letter in which President Mallory outlined an electoral alliance between the farmers and a combination of Liberals and McCarthyites. Mr. Edward Farrer had acted as the Grit emissary and it was agreed, on April 8, that the Liberals would not contest thirteen Ontario ridings in return for Patron support elsewhere. According to Mallory's letter, "McCarthy will do all in his power quietly to help us, and there will be no conflict between us." The Patron executive agreed to the arrangement and received financial aid to publish the *Farmers' Sun* during the campaign. The damage done to the Patron cause by these revelations must have been considerable. Much of the movement's appeal was based on its non-partisan approach to politics and its emphasis on morality in public affairs. When the electoral returns were complete the Patrons had elected only three of their twenty-five candidates. The *Farmers' Sun* was suddenly less critical of the Liberal party:

> A modern Babylon has fallen and great is the rejoicing thereat. . . . As never before the people of Canada have appreciated the responsibility resting upon them, and they have burst the shackles of partisanship . . . realizing their power to increase the opportunity to earn a livelihood and to create . . . a high degree of brotherhood . . . throughout the nation. Patrons have not been as successful as they hoped to have been in this contest, but at least they stimu-

lated others to think and to act as they have never done before.[39]

Despite this optimistic view of Patron political influence, with the defeat in 1896 the organization's political career was at an end.

In 1894 the Patrons of Industry had been in existence for less than half a decade, yet captured almost one-fifth of the provincial legislature. Two years later only three Patrons were elected to Parliament. While economic motivation in large part explains the formation of the Patron organization, changing economic conditions do not appear to account for the Patron demise. The year of the largest agrarian electoral success, 1894, was a year of extremely low farm prices. Likewise, the rural economy was depressed in 1896 and 1897, yet in these years the Patron support rapidly disappeared. Factors other than economic conditions must account for the Patron decline after 1896.

A number of elements doubtless contributed to the destruction of the Patrons. By 1896 the high-tariff policy and incipient imperialism of the Americans had detracted from whatever appeal was offered by continental union. Yet the Patron journal, under Goldwin Smith's influence, encouraged closer ties with the United States. The stigma of association with the Protestant Protective Association discouraged Roman Catholics and intellectuals from supporting the Patron cause. The attempts by the Liberal party to solicit farm support and the resulting electoral scandal doubtless contributed to the immediate collapse of the party. Yet these external factors were less detrimental to the Patrons of Industry than were their own inherent weaknesses. The Patron platform was largely negative and somewhat narrow in its expression. It stressed criticism of existing conditions, decentralization and economy of government rather than offering imaginative or innovating reforms and policies. Despite several attempts to win the support of organized labour, the Patrons failed to conclude

[39] Goldwin Smith, *Reminiscences* (New York, 1911), p. 448; Toronto *Daily Mail and Empire*, June 8, 1896; Wood, *op. cit.*, pp. 144-45; *Farmers' Sun*, June 24, 1896.

any political alliance with the urban working class. Finally, having attained a significant position in the Ontario legislature, the results of this position—possibly due to a lack of experienced leadership—proved largely inconsequential.[40] The Patron movement was the rural victim of a heterogeneous and politically sophisticated society. By advocating in place of the National Policy what appeared to be archaic agrarian reforms, and by failing to appreciate the implications and methods of political organization and action, the Patrons of Industry ultimately accounted for their own demise.

In large measure this dissolution was a function of the social composition of the Patron order and its accompanying value structure. The Patrons represented an attempt by independent farmers of Ontario to preserve their place in society in the face of urbanization and the attendant organization of both labour and capital. The emerging urban society seemed oblivious to the interests of the farmers despite the contention of the *Farmers' Sun* that "a more honourable lot of men can be found nowhere." Worse still, it ignored the basic economic belief of rural dwellers expressed by President Mallory when he stated "Agriculture is the basis and source of all permanent national wealth."[41] It was this physiocratic doctrine which underlay most Patron thought. As long as this belief corresponded to the realities of Ontario society, the farmers participated in normal party politics. But as urban areas and new forms of economic activity assumed a growing importance, the farmers felt threatened in both their economic status and social convictions. The result of this challenge was the rapid rise of the Patron order designed to preserve traditional economic and social relationships.

A sample of Patron membership seems to confirm the assertion that the order represented not indigent agrarians on the verge of ruin, but small, reasonably affluent farmers fighting to continue a traditionally acceptable social structure. The farmers elected to

---

[40] W. L. Smith, "When the Patrons Swept Ontario," *The Grain Growers Guide,* XIX, 29, 1926, p. 6; Smith, *Reminiscences,* p. 448.
[41] *Farmers' Sun*, May 10, 1892; March 7, 1893.

the Ontario legislature and several members of the Patron hierarchy form a sample of twenty men. The selection is dictated by
the available information and is distorted in favour of the more
prominent and prosperous examples. Yet the rank and file Patrons
presumably selected men of their own social type to represent
them in their association and legislature. Certainly, their frequent
complaint that lawyers and merchants failed to express properly
the farmers' point of view substantiates this assumption. Again,
the men described here had experience in local government which
indicates approval by their social peers. Finally, the areas of
greatest Patron strength were, under normal economic conditions,
areas inhabited by reasonably prosperous farmers.[42] Without,
then, drawing exaggerated conclusions concerning the nature of
the Patrons in general, what social characteristics emerge from the
selected sample?

Three-quarters of the men had been born in Canada, largely
Ontario, while the remainder had come, at an early age, from
the British Isles. Ages ranged from early 30's to late 60's, with
over half the group in the 40 to 60 category. Few had been
educated beyond the elementary school level while all appeared
to have been Protestants. Without exception they were by occu-
pation farmers, but here an interesting qualification must be
noted. At least one-quarter of the sample had other occupations,
which mark them as men of some material stature. Thomas Pardo,
M.L.A. from West Kent, engaged in grist and saw milling and
at one time had held almost one thousand acres of land in Raleigh
Township. David Macpherson from Glengarry riding owned a
model farm near Bainsville. He operated several cheese factories,
known locally as the "Allan Grove Combination," and his supporting cheese-box factories had expanded to produce wood
fixtures and door frames. Finally, Patron Grand Secretary J. L.
Wilson of Alexandria was not only one of the province's largest
exhibitors of pedigree cattle, but also a director of the Canadian
National Exhibition, and managing director of Farmers' and

[42] *Annual Report of the Bureau of Industries for the Province of Ontario*, 1907,
Part I (Toronto, 1908).

Traders' Assurance Company. If these men were in any fashion typical of their fellow Patrons, the basic source of their discontent was less the immediate effects of the depression than the long-run fear for the security of their independent economic and social position.

The single most consistent characteristic of the men in the sample was extensive experience in local government. Grand President Caleb Mallory had been a township reeve for sixteen years and warden of Northumberland and Durham as well. John Macdonald, who had settled in Huron Township in 1855 "with no more of this world's possession than the ordinary settler," had served as councillor, treasurer, and reeve before election to the legislature. Thomas Gamey from South Grey, a former militia captain, was a Justice of the Peace and had filled the post of county reeve for thirty-three years.[43] Clearly these men were considered representative by their fellow rural residents and were closely tied to traditional forms of local government. It was natural that they should feel their interests threatened by a centralized provincial government increasingly attuned to urban problems. This attitude may explain why few prominent Patrons participated in the government subsidized Farmers' Institutes. In much the fashion that E. C. Drury or Melville Staples later viewed the Farmers' Clubs of Ontario, the Patrons may have seen the Institutes as an attempt by Queen's Park to channel and quell rural discontent.[44] In general, the political background of the men in the sample clearly confirms the local and traditional nature of Patronism. This localism, in turn, explains the rapid demise of the Patron order by 1896.

Despite their localism, their unsophisticated economic theories

[43] Biographical data was obtained from the *Canadian Parliamentary Handbook*; H. J. Morgan, *Canadian Men and Women of the Time* (Toronto, 1912); Victor Lauristan, *Romantic Kent, 1626-1952* (Chatham, 1952); J. C. Harkness, *Stormont, Dundas and Glengarry: A History* (Oshawa, 1946); Norman Robertson, *The History of the County of Bruce* (Toronto, 1906).
[44] *Ontario Sessional Papers*, 1893, Vol. 25, and 1895, Vol. 27; E. C. Drury, *Farmer Premier* (Toronto, 1967), p. 68; M. H. Staples, *The Challenge of Agriculture: The Story of the United Farmers of Ontario* (Toronto, 1921), p. 40.

and class analysis, and their irrational fear of bigness and change, the Patrons were not without significance. They vividly illustrated the dilemma of the farmer in an age of transition. In so doing, the Patrons revealed many parallels with the American Populist movement. The order's venture into politics provides a type of paradigm for farm politics in Canada. Many of the problems encountered by the Patrons—the response to economic dislocation, the decision to enter politics, the failure to ally with labour, the need to "broaden out" electoral appeal—were later faced by both the United Farmers of Ontario and the Progressive Party. Finally, the Patrons represented a healthy spirit of dissent, a departure from the stifling consensus of unprincipled party politics. Despite their many obvious weaknesses, this, surely, was a major contribution to the Canadian political tradition.